Praise for Stephanie Saldaña's

The *Bread* of *Angels*

"Brace yourself for an intense inner and outer journey. *The Bread of Angels* is a many-layered personal story, ricocheting from Damascus to Texas to the desert fathers to scruffy Cambridge. A passionate young scholar confronts war, love, the mysteries of language, and God. Stephanie Saldaña is up to the task. A brilliant debut."

—Frances Mayes, author of *Under the Tuscan Sun*

"A fascinating, back-alley travelogue of contemporary Damascus, as well as a journey to the core of the Quran. Most of all . . . , an inspiring document of battle-tested faith."

—*San Antonio Express-News*

"What sets Saldaña's book apart from so many others is the very convincing way in which she writes about prayer—and the difficulty of praying."

—*Newsweek*

"A remarkable, wise, and lovely book from a truly gifted new writer, *The Bread of Angels* brims with originality and insight. There is poetry here— the language and the depth of attention recall the young Annie Dillard. But this is, above all, a love story, and a compelling one. Not many people can write transcendent, mystical prose and also create a page-turner that keeps you up nights. Stephanie Saldaña's achievement is extraordinary."

—Geraldine Brooks, Pulitzer Prize–winning author of *March*

"Saldaña vividly evokes life in [Damascus], where Arab and Armenian Christians have lived for centuries. . . . Her perceptive comments on life in Syria, her account of teaching in a Muslim school, and her friendship with a female Islamic scholar who taught her about the Koran and the Muslim Jesus further enrich an already superior work. . . . Luminously rendered."

—*Richmond Times-Dispatch*

Stephanie Saldaña

The *Bread* of *Angels*

Stephanie Saldaña grew up in Texas and received a B.A. from Middlebury College and a master's degree from Harvard Divinity School. She was a Watson and Fulbright scholar and has won several awards for her poetry. She lives in Jerusalem and teaches at the Honors College for Liberal Arts and Sciences, a partnership of Bard College and Al-Quds University.

The Bread of Angels

A JOURNEY TO LOVE AND FAITH

Stephanie Saldaña

Anchor Books

A DIVISION OF RANDOM HOUSE, INC.

NEW YORK

FIRST ANCHOR BOOKS EDITION, FEBRUARY 2011

The Library of Congress has cataloged the
Doubleday edition as follows:
Saldaña, Stephanie.
The bread of angels : a journey to love and faith /
Stephanie Saldaña.—1st ed.
p. cm.
1. Saldaña, Stephanie. 2. Damascus (Syria)—Description and travel.
3. Damascus (Syria)—Social life and customs.
4. Damascus (Syria)—Religious life and customs.
5. Christianity and other religions—Islam.
6. Islam—Religious—Christianity.
7. Americans—Syria—Damascus—Biography.
8. Christians—Syria—Damascus—Biography.
9. Young women—Syria—Damascus—Biography.
10. Damascus (Syria)—Biography. I. Title.
DS99.D3S25 2009
956.91'4—dc22 [B] 2009016852

Anchor ISBN: 978-0-307-28046-6

Book design by Pei Koay

www.anchorbooks.com

Printed in the United States of America
10 9 8 7 6 5 4 3 2 1

Author's Note

This memoir tells the actual story of a year I spent in Syria between September 2004 and September 2005. All of the characters are real people. I have chosen to change many of the names of the individuals I met in order to preserve their privacy. I have also removed characters from scenes and occasionally altered the order of events in order to organize the flow of ideas. But I have always remained faithful to life as I lived it in Syria, a year of such impossible richness that it needed no embellishment.

ELIJAH WAS AFRAID AND RAN FOR HIS LIFE. When he came to Beersheba in Judah, he left his servant there, while he himself went a day's journey into the desert. He came to a broom tree, sat down under it and prayed that he might die.

"I have had enough, Lord," he said. "Take my life. I am no better than my ancestors." Then he lay down under the tree and fell asleep.

All at once, an angel touched him and said: "Get up and eat." He looked around, and there by his head was a cake of bread baked over hot coals, and a jar of water. He ate and drank and then lay down again.

The angel of the Lord came back a second time and touched him and said, "Get up and eat, for the journey is too much for you." So he got up and ate and drank. Strengthened by that food, he traveled forty days and forty nights until he reached Horeb, the mountain of God.

—I KINGS 19:3–8

Contents

Part One THE FALLEN WORLD

Unfortunately, it was paradise.

—MAHMOUD DARWĪSH

1.

I'VE FINALLY FOUND a house in Damascus.

By house, I mean a room in a house—in this case my very own corner of a majestic, three-story Ottoman giant I stumbled upon early last week, when I was knocking on doors in the Christian Quarter of the Old City, searching for a place to live. My house was so thoroughly hidden behind high external walls that I was lucky to have noticed it at all. But from my room inside of those walls I can hear the entire world outside: church bells ringing and the call to prayer drifting through the air from distant mosques, the woman next door gossiping with her husband and the nearby vendors shouting out the prices of their wares. Every morning my neighbors scrub their laundry by hand in our single marble fountain, and in the afternoon I watch from my window as the courtyard fills up with their shirts hung out to dry, some of the arms pinned up in the air, others with their sleeves wide open, embracing the light.

When I arrived in Damascus from Boston ten days ago, I had little more to my name than two black wheeled suitcases, an outdated Syrian guidebook, and a modest supply of textbook classical Arabic. I didn't have a single friend in the city, a place to live, or even a concrete plan for what I was going to do with the next twelve months of my life. I also had no idea how to navigate the local real estate market, which is how I ended up doing the only thing that I could think of under the circumstances and knocking door to door in the neighborhood of Bab Touma, asking total strangers if they had any interest in giving shelter to this young, lost American girl for a year.

It was the beginning of September, and the summer heat was still beating down on the cobbled streets and infusing them with a blinding, almost white quality. I walked close to the alley walls, where external balconies and opposing walls would every now and then cast a thin sliver of shade that I could find respite in as I made my way from house to house. I ended up in a neighborhood just off Straight Street, the famous road where St. Paul took shelter after falling and being blinded by a flash of light on his way to Damascus. Two thousand years later, it looked more like Istanbul than ancient Rome, a labyrinth of tiny alleyways and sprawling old houses pressed up so closely to one another that the roofs overlapped into layers of red tiles. Only the very tops of the houses were visible behind the alley walls, and though every now and then a set of windows peeked out into the street, it was impossible to know if behind any given door was a tiny apartment or a palace.

I had been searching all day, but by late afternoon I still hadn't found anything. Several old women had rejected me outright, which is perhaps understandable when an American goes knocking door to door in Syria during the height of the Iraq war, asking for favors. Two other women who offered to show me their homes led me into ancient Ottoman houses that looked as if they hadn't been renovated in a hundred years. One small, windowless room had clearly been a broom closet in its previous incarnation and had been emptied out to make just enough space for a poor and desperate student. In the second house a single toilet was being shared by all of the house's inhabitants, who by my count numbered at least ten.

By the time I trudged down a nondescript alley back toward the main road, I was so deflated that I was ready to retire to my grimy hotel and give up for the rest of the afternoon. I might not have knocked on the door in front of me at all, had it not been marked mysteriously by a white license plate imprinted with the English words *10 Downing Street*. The rest of the house was completely concealed except for a pair of badly painted brown double doors, an iron lantern, a cluster of doorbells with their wires exposed and labeled with illegible Arabic names, and this single, enticing sign marked with the address of the British prime minister.

So I knocked.

A few seconds later, an old man peeked his head out of the door and, seeing me, smiled broadly as though he had been waiting all afternoon for my arrival. I liked the look of him. A thin layer of white hair had been carefully combed across his head, and he had a bristly mustache without a beard, rosy cheeks, and an oversized belly held up by polyester brown pants and a belt cinched too tightly across the waist. In fact he looked remarkably like the Wizard from *The Wizard of Oz*.

"*Ahlan wa sahlan!*" he announced. "Welcome! Welcome!"

"Do you have any rooms to rent?" I asked him in my fumbling Arabic.

I waited for him to shake his head and close the door in my face, but instead he beamed, swinging the front doors open with great theatricality and gesturing inside.

"*Ahlan wa sahlan!* Welcome! Welcome!" he announced again.

I could only hope that this meant yes.

I FOLLOWED THE WIZARD through a narrow corridor and into the central courtyard, where a sprawling house unfolded before my eyes. It was a miracle of a house, completely enclosed and concealed from the outside world, the entire rectangular complex facing toward itself, with all of the rooms looking in on a marble fountain at the center of the tiled open-air courtyard. Behind wooden shutters, glass windows at all angles peered down from at least a dozen rooms. A series of outdoor staircases began in the courtyard and wound their way up to the second and third floors and the roof, making each level of the house wholly independent and yet part of the single, unwieldy whole—less a house than a miniature village. It was roughly the size of four normal houses, and my guess was that at one time an entire family of aunts, cousins, brothers, sisters, and in-laws had shared this single complex, the architecture granting them privacy from the outside world.

The Wizard removed a heavy, ancient key hanging from a nail on the wall, the kind I had seen only in films when heroes are presented the keys to entire cities, and unlocked two wooden doors opening into a room on the ground floor. It was a generous room, containing little except for two beds, old spearmint-painted wooden beams crossing the high ceiling, and spare furniture painted with gold baroque outlines inspired by Louis XIV and left over from the French Mandate. In the front of the room, two large arched windows looked out into the courtyard to face the fountain, and I could imagine myself sitting there and writing in the mornings with the sun coming in. I knew from the instant that I saw it that this room would be mine. That it was already mine.

The man pointed to the crumbling walls. "What could you possibly want more than this?" he asked me in Arabic so heavy with dialect that I could barely understand him. "You won't find a better room anywhere in Damascus. This is the most beautiful room in all of Bab Touma!"

The room *was* beautiful, but in that particular way that ruins are beautiful, or certain old women whose faces take on a peculiar serenity just before they die. Dust-stained curtains sagged over the windows, and large patches of white plaster were disintegrating from the walls. The courtyard doors had eroded at the bottom, and the rose and gray marble floor tiles were faded in color. Yet the room also wore a thin, almost translucent dress of light, and from the front windows I could see the branches of a citrus tree growing from the courtyard floor and extending to the highest level of the three-story house.

The most beautiful room in Bab Touma—along with a separate kitchen with pipes held together by electrical tape, a nonflush toilet in a tiny closet near the refrigerator, and a room connected to the opposite side of the kitchen with a metal basin to wash—would cost me one hundred and forty dollars a month, including utilities. I had no idea if I was paying too much, but it was one-fourth of what I had paid for a much smaller room in a house in Boston. I shook the man's hand to confirm our arrangement.

"My name is Juanez," he told me. "You know, the name from Brazil, Juanez? I lived many years in Brazil."

"My name is Stephanie."

"Stephanie? Stefanito!" He mimicked an Italian accent, raising his eyebrows suggestively and talking in the air with his hands. "*Ciao* Stefanito! Stephanissimo!" He abruptly changed accents and began speaking in a deep, suave voice. "*Bonjour*, Stefanito. *Tu parles Francese?*"

"No."

He shrugged. "Too bad. *Ju parle Francese.* Do you speak Portuguese? *Italiano? Turki?* Armenian?" He chuckled. "I speak all of these languages *très bien*. Do you understand me? *Très bien*. If you need anything here you come to me, do you hear me? You don't go to anyone else. I can take care of everything.

"Ahhh, Stefanito," he continued. "Are you studying Arabic here? What is this Arabic you speak? Where did you learn that? Don't you know that no one speaks like that? You must learn to speak Arabic the way we speak it. I'm Armenian and I can speak Arabic just like the Arabs. Where are you from?"

Just trying to understand his sentences was exhausting me. "America," I told him.

He snorted. "America? Do you know George Bush? Ha, ha."

I turned to shut the door to my new room, but then I felt his hand on my shoulder. He leaned in close to my face. "Stefanito, it really is the best room in Bab Touma," he assured me. "It isn't noisy like other places. Here people will leave you alone."

THE NEXT DAY I WAS AWAKENED at seven in the morning by church bells chiming from the direction of the Roman Catholic church down the street, faintly, but still in long and rapid succession. A few minutes later a set of louder, more insistent bells joined from the opposite direction of the Greek Catholic church across the road. Soon, bells from what must have been the Greek Orthodox church started ringing from the west, and finally what I guessed were the Armenians from the east, until I resigned myself to the cacophony that clearly would awaken me each day.

After fifteen minutes the bells quieted down, and I managed to slowly coax myself back to sleep. But, just as I was drifting off, the sound of men yelling and the violent clapping of horse hooves against stone jolted me awake.

Maharim! Maharim! Maharim! Maharim!

Gaz! Gaz! Gaz! Gaz!

Watermelons, twenty lire! Watermelons, twenty lire! I have peaches! Peaches! Peaches!

I crawled out of bed, and, mindful of my modesty even in my half-awakened state, I threw on a pair of jeans and a long-sleeved T-shirt. Then I walked across the courtyard, ducking beneath the clothes hung out the night before, which were now dry and gleaming under the early morning sun. On the other side of the clotheslines I found my way through the corridor and to the front door and peered cautiously outside. Somehow, in the previous five minutes, the alley in front of my house had morphed into a one-ring circus. Just in front of me, a tissue-paper vendor was pacing back and forth, steering a cart piled high with mountains of Kleenex wrapped in plastic bags and shouting at the top of his lungs:

Maharim! Maharim! Maharim! Maharim!

Ahead of him, a gas vendor with a cap perched on his head was bouncing up and down on a wagon drawn by a black horse festooned with ostrich feathers, beating a metal wrench against the tin gas canisters like he was playing brass cymbals in a marching band.

Gaz! Gaz! Gaz! Gaz!

Cantaloupe and banana carts wove back and forth, taxis honked, and neighbors greeted one another by yelling above the traffic.

Sabah-al kheir! How's your health? How's your family? My God, it's hot today, isn't it?

I closed the door, snapped the latch back into place, and made my way through the laundry again and back to my bedroom. It was only my third morning in Damascus, I was still jet-lagged and exhausted from my marathon house search, and I was determined to get at least a few hours' more sleep. But the street vendors had set in motion a series of events that I could not undo. Five minutes later, I heard a knocking on the window, and when I got up to pull the dusty curtains aside, the grinning, whiskered face of the Wizard was staring back at me.

"*Yalla*, Stefanito!" he shouted. "It's time for coffee!" And so my first day in the house off Straight Street began, to a strong glass of muddy Arabic coffee, in the most beautiful house in Bab Touma, where everyone will leave you alone.

I HAD COME TO DAMASCUS on a Fulbright fellowship to study the prophet Jesus in Damascus, the Muslim prophet who many locals believed would one day descend from heaven and alight upon the eastern minaret at the Umayyad Mosque just a few minutes from my new house to announce the coming of the end of time. It was perhaps not the most obvious research topic for a Catholic from Texas, but then little had seemed obvious in my life for a long time. I had spent much of my twenties working and studying in the Middle East, and what I had discovered about Islam had surprised me. In Egypt and in Lebanon, in Jordan and in the West Bank, I had often heard Muslims speaking of Jesus and Mary with reverence, calling Jesus by his Islamic name—*The prophet `Issa, peace be upon him*—and even quoting to me the stories of his life. More than once, I came upon Muslim women in their headscarves visiting Christian shrines to the Virgin Mary, or Maryam, paying homage to the woman in the Quran who is known for her piety.

My fellowship was specifically to study Islam for a year in Syria, the American government's modest attempt to foster greater American understanding in a post–September 11 world. But I was just as eager to learn about Christians living and practicing their faith in an Islamic country, which was why I was excited about finding a house in the ancient Christian neighborhood of Bab Touma. Growing up in Catholic schools, I had always been taught that Christianity was a "Western religion" and Islam an "Eastern religion," but my journeys in the previous years had turned all of that on its head. I had visited nearly-two-thousand-year-old Christian communities in Egypt and talked to Arabic-speaking Christians living in Palestinian cities who dated their origins back to the time of Jesus. I had stared at ancient Christian maps on church floors in Jordan and walked through villages of Arab Christians still speaking the language of Jesus. I traveled through the cities in Turkey where St. Paul had spread the gospel. In time I learned that Christianity had come of age largely in countries we now see as Eastern and Muslim. None of those countries fascinated me more than Syria, where the famous Umayyad Mosque was once a cathedral holding the relics of St. John the Baptist and where over a million Arabic-speaking Christians still live in one of the most vibrant Islamic countries in the world.

For the past two years I had been preparing myself for this journey, studying Arabic, Eastern Christianity, and Islam at divinity school, reading as much as I could about the history of Islam in Syria, where Muslims and Christians had been living side by side for more than a thousand years, ever since St. John of Damascus had served under the Umayyad government in the eighth century and had famously mistaken Islam for just another Christian heresy. My plan was to study enough

Arabic in Damascus so that I could finally read the Quran in the original language and have a chance to speak to Muslims about the role of Jesus and Mary in their faith.

That is, at least, what I told myself as I settled into my room in Damascus. The truth was, I was running away from a broken heart.

2.

I SPENT MY FIRST FEW DAYS trying to make a home of my new room, which despite its initial charm revealed itself to be much too big for a single person, its high ceilings and open spaces endowing it with a lonely quality. I lined up my books on the shelves built into a white alcove in the far wall: the Quran, the Bible, *The Sayings of the Desert Fathers*, two Arabic dictionaries, some monastic texts, a collection of the sayings of the prophet Jesus, and a beginner's guide to the Arabic language. They'd barely fit in my suitcase, but now they took up only one small shelf. I unpacked the second suitcase, taking out long, flowing pants and conservative shirts with buttons all the way up to the neck, my brand-new Syrian wardrobe, and I hung them side by side in the gold-lined baroque armoire. They, too, filled up just a corner, so that the rest of the wardrobe and most of the drawers were left vacant. Last of all, I removed the single thin, floral dress I'd brought with me, even though I knew it would be much too short to wear in the streets of the city. I hung it in the back of the wardrobe away from my other clothes and watched it sway like a talisman, all light cotton and pastel flowers, a reminder of the braver, happier person I had been just a few short weeks before.

Every few hours or so, the Wizard knocked on the window and interrupted me with his gleeful refrain: "It's time for coffee!" I dutifully abandoned my unpacking to join him in his tiny bedroom, where we sat in front of his television and watched montage after montage of flashing images of the war in Iraq, shampoo advertisements, and Mexican *telenovelas* translated into Arabic. If we were lucky we'd catch a historical television series set in Damascus in which the characters all wore long Arab robes and had complicated family feuds, sometimes resulting in sword fights. The Wizard couldn't get enough of it.

"Do you want me to get you a television, Stefanito?" he asked me a few days after I moved in.

"No thanks, Juanez."

"What are you going to do all year if you don't have a television?"

"I guess I'll study."

"Study!" he scoffed. "What is there to study?"

I was tempted to agree and indulge my self-pity by spending twelve months sulking in front of the television set, watching love affairs and Bedouin swordfights, but I had tens of thousands of words I needed to memorize. "I want to learn Arabic," I told him.

"*Shoo, majnoun inti*? What are you, crazy? Why would you want to study Arabic? English is a perfectly good language."

"I like Arabic."

"What are you going to use Arabic for?"

"To study the Quran."

He looked at me in horror. *"Ya Allah!"* he muttered. "Dear God!" He shook his head sadly to himself. "Well, let me know if you change your mind about the television set. I think I can find a way to attach yours to mine if you want to get cable for free."

WHEN I FINISHED WATCHING TELEVISION with my neighbor, I liked to wander from my front door deep into the surrounding Old City, where I wove through the hundreds of tiny alleys around the Umayyad Mosque, taking in the smell of olive soap and spices, the endless traffic and the clang of bells just before a bicycle whizzed past, the round circles of pita bread lifted from giant ovens, the prayer beads dangling from store windows and glimmering in the sun. My house was just a ten-minute walk from the buzz and commerce of Souq al-Hamidiye, the main covered market of the Muslim Quarter, which was not so much a place to shop as a total assault on the senses. Women in bright headscarves brushed up against Iranian pilgrims draped in long black robes, and Druze men from the countryside sauntered by in their baggy black pants. Children sold gum and chocolates beside men balancing wooden trays of sesame rolls on their heads. There was something almost theatrical about all of the costumes and colors, and every few meters great beams of light fell through the holes in the arched iron roof of the covered market and landed on the faces of men passing by like spotlights. Sometimes on a side street I would catch a glimpse of a swath of glazed medieval tiles or a caravansary from the eighteenth century casually mixed in among the stalls and pedestrians. It was just stunning.

My favorite route took me through the perfumed streets of the spice market and past the gold souk until I turned onto a small street near the back steps of the Umayyad Mosque, where a few unpretentious cafés were always full of old men smoking water pipes and reading the newspaper, pausing every few seconds to greet friends and relatives. If I timed my arrival well enough, I could catch the *hakawati*, or traditional storyteller, regaling men with a tale from *One Thousand and One Nights*, his arms gesturing emphatically through the clouds of tobacco smoke. At the bottom of the stairs, a group of young, good-looking shopkeepers loitered at the doors of their stalls, chain-smoking cigarettes and trying to look casual in their skintight jeans. They had all slicked back their hair with great quantities of gel and had clearly picked up their fashion sense from Italy, judging by the T-shirts hugging the muscles of their chests and the gold chains hanging around their necks. Every time I walked past they leaned out of their shops and called out in various languages, trying to guess my origins:

Ciao, bella!

¡Hola!

Bonjour, madame!

Do you remember me?

Sometimes one of them even called out in Japanese, just to see if I would crack a smile.

As the sun began falling in the late afternoon I made my way home via Straight Street, the thoroughfare that has connected the Eastern Gate outside my house to the city center since Hellenistic and Roman times. It turned out that Straight Street was not straight at all, but a winding boulevard dissecting the sprawling alleys of the Old City into parts and lined by antique dealers, carpet sellers, and coppersmiths. My house was on the part of Straight Street called Bab Touma, or Thomas Gate, the city's so-called Christian ghetto. Though the walls around the Old City had largely collapsed, two tall gates of white Roman stones still flanked the neighborhood, and old wooden houses and artisans' workshops filled in the surrounding streets. Here, in what must have been one of the most ancient and diverse Christian neighborhoods in the world, thousands of Arabic-speaking Christians still lived in houses piled on top of one another, near the patriarchates for the Eastern churches. They were Catholics, Protestants, Assyrian Christians, Armenian Christians, Greek Orthodox, and Syrian Orthodox Christians, and in the mornings bearded priests in long, flowing robes and tall hats passed me on the streets.

It took me a few days to realize that my house off Straight Street was not only "the most beautiful house in Bab Touma," but that it also managed to contain, in a single building, many of the Christological controversies of early church history. In order to keep my neighbors straight, I had to remember the details of the Christology courses I had taken at divinity school, which I had assumed covered religious communities that had largely died out during the Byzantine Empire. Yet apparently these Christian churches were still alive and well in Damascus, and the fact that my neighbors now washed their laundry side by side was a minor miracle, considering that their leaders had spent much of early church history calling one another heretics.

After a few days of coffee with Juanez I knew enough gossip about my neighbors, including the man himself, to fill an entire issue of *People* magazine. Juanez was an Armenian Orthodox Christian, a proud member of the sizable Armenian population spread across Syria and Lebanon, many of whom arrived from Turkey seeking refuge during the massacres and expulsions of Armenians that began in 1915. I never saw him attend the Armenian Orthodox church just ten steps from our front door, but he held all Armenians in high esteem and spoke as though he knew every single Armenian in the entire country, if not the world. He maintained an endless series of Armenian connections, known in local parlance as *wasta*, and he frequently urged me to limit myself to the Armenian cabdrivers and shopkeepers he knew. "Go get yourself a sandwich at Little Armenia, and tell them I sent you," he barked whenever I told him I was grabbing lunch. "He'll give you a discount, and the food is clean. Clean, do you hear me? *Ndif!* Do you know what clean means?"

Across the courtyard and to the right of Juanez's room, a skinny, mustachioed man and his family occupied the section of the house closest to the citrus tree. We called him *"Ustez"* or "professor," because he was a professor of Arabic literature at Damascus University. The *Ustez* was a Greek Orthodox Christian and married to the embittered and middle-aged Roman Catholic woman I often saw lurking in the courtyard each morning in her bathrobe. My guess was that when the marriage happened it had been a rather unusual event in both Orthodox and Catholic circles in Damascus, neither church having completely recovered from the split between them in 1054. So great was the tension between the churches that most years they even celebrated Christmas and Easter on different days. Still, my neighbors' Orthodox/Catholic union in our crumbling house spoke less of Romeo and Juliet than of the dismal salaries that university professors in Syria were paid. He wore the same brown suit to work every day, and in the mornings she washed out their tattered undergarments by hand in the marble fountain and left them hanging on the clotheslines for the rest of us to see.

On the second floor of the opposite side of the house, to the right of my room and above my kitchen, a family of Roman Catholics kept mostly to themselves, and I knew little about them save that they had picked up smatterings of English and French in their Catholic-school educations. They were excessively proud of their limited French vocabularies and insisted on dropping French words into their greetings even though I couldn't understand them. *"Bonjour!"* they called out cheerily when they passed me in the courtyard in the mornings. *"Marhaba!"* I called back in Arabic, until I saw them again and they called out, *"Bonjour!"*

Finally, in the rooftop apartment overlooking the city a family of Assyrian Christians lived, members of a Christian sect who survived largely in Syria and Iraq and who still spoke Syriac, a late dialect of Aramaic, the language of Jesus. Assyrians, as well as the other Syriac-speaking Christian minorities of Syria, were rather proud in those days because they could watch Mel Gibson's *The Passion of the Christ* without reading the subtitles. I, on the other hand, had the privilege of witnessing on a daily basis what Jesus might have sounded like if he were gossiping with his family about the neighbors.

As an American living in Syria during the Iraq war, at a moment when my country was largely despised in the region, I could at least find comfort when I remembered the historical circumstances of the company

I kept. Most of my neighbors belonged to sects that had at one time been embroiled in regional scandals. The Armenian Orthodox Christians, of which Juanez was a member, rejected the council of Chalcedon in 451 by declaring that Christ had one incarnate nature, which meant that for centuries they were accused of denying Christ's humanity. On the other hand, my upstairs neighbors the Assyrians, pejoratively referred to by many as Nestorians after their most famous heretical member, Nestorius, rejected the Council of Ephesus in 431 for the opposite reason, emphasizing that Christ had a duality of natures and a duality of hypostases, whatever that meant, but that these were contained in a single person. They were accused of denying the *divinity* of Christ, which managed to offend even more people than denying the humanity, and were still unfairly criticized as heretical in much of the Orthodox world fifteen hundred years later. A Greek Orthodox professor at my divinity school had once remarked sarcastically to our class that he wasn't surprised that Tariq Aziz, Saddam Hussein's deputy prime minister, "happened to be a Nestorian."

The Greek Orthodox Christians such as the *Ustez* seemed to be safe on the theology front, but they still had their hands full lamenting the fall of Constantinople, the disintegration of the Byzantine Empire, and the fact that many of the Orthodox Christians in the region had converted to Islam over the centuries. Finally, we Roman Catholics were considered suspect due to the unfortunate fact that we happened to share a history with the country's former French colonizers, as well as, not incidentally, the Crusaders.

I guess that all of us were outcasts, living in a neighborhood of exiles, for I was hardly the only foreigner in Bab Touma. As Arab Christians emigrated abroad in increasing numbers, their empty rooms were filled up in turn by hundreds of foreign students flooding Damascus to study Arabic after September 11. We made our homes among Christian families who had been catered to under the French Mandate and were now left between cultures, not French and yet not always feeling completely Syrian, minorities in a secular country that each day grew increasingly Muslim. Bab Touma maintained its own rules, and the shops sold wine and the storefronts advertised short-sleeved clothing; the women in the streets flaunted their uncovered, highlight-streaked hair. Mothers scoffed at

Arabic names and instead called their sons George and Michel. Though Syria's official day off was Friday, the Muslim holy day, the shops in Bab Touma stayed open on Friday and closed on Sunday. The Christians filled their alleyways with statues of the Virgin Mary and makeshift shrines to her, and pedestrians automatically made the sign of the cross over themselves as they passed by, often barely finding time to rest their arms on a short walk home.

I had landed in a small world, a microsociety, and there was something unsettling about that life, for like everyone in Damascus we lived in the remnants of a palace in disrepair and full of vacant rooms, at the end of an era, but this was perhaps inevitable when you find yourself living in the oldest continuously inhabited city in the world. And the city was teeming with these microsocieties. Ten minutes away by foot in the Muslim Quarter, shopkeepers sold prayer beads and Qurans, threading religious verses into their business transactions. A five-minute walk across the road, the Jewish Quarter was half populated, full of the ghosts of abandoned houses recently left vacant by Jews who fled to America, the inhabited houses occupied, in the irony so typical of Syria, by Palestinian refugees.

From Straight Street I began to feel like I had access, in some form or another, to almost every story that had ever existed in that part of the world, from holy books and holy lands. Any Arab could enter Syria without a visa, and many non-Arabs ended up there just because it happened to be the easiest place to land. The unfortunate ones from across the region fled their homes during various conflicts over the centuries and made new homes in those neighborhoods: Christians, Muslims, and Jews; Armenians, Kurds, Circassians, and Palestinians; militant jihadis going to and coming from the war, hundreds of thousands of Iraqis fleeing their homeland, and finally, little old me.

So here I find myself, in the twenty-seventh year of my life, living in a rambling house in what my government has declared to be a rogue nation. We are almost eighteen months into the war in Iraq. In two months, Americans will decide whether or not to elect George Bush to a second term as president. In the meantime, I have been sent as a "scholar-ambassador" to a country we have just passed sanctions against, and I don't think I've ever felt so out of place in my entire life.

My only friend here is Juanez, my seventy-three-year-old knight in shining polyester pants, whose door is literally two steps across from mine. In this country women live with their families until they are married, and so he seems convinced that the reason I'm alone is that I've been cast off by my relatives and possibly left at the altar, thus prompting my flight to the other side of the world. As a result of his pity and his retired status, he's made taking care of me his full-time job.

In Syria, the tradition is to call your son or daughter by your own name, suggesting that you are so close to them that, as though bound by a cosmic force, you can no longer tell the difference between your child and yourself. A mother might call her daughter "Mother," a father might call his son "Father." In the same spirit, Juanez has begun calling me "Grandfather." In fact he calls it out all day long, from morning until evening, as he increasingly forgets that I'm American and insists that I live by the morals of a Syrian girl.

"Grandfather, I saw that you didn't come home last night until eleven o'clock. Where were you?"

"Grandfather, a neighbor told me you were speaking with that boy who works in the flower shop this afternoon. What do you want with him?"

"Grandfather, did you get your glasses fixed at that Armenian shop like I told you? What did he charge you?"

"Grandfather, don't you want to stop studying and come drink coffee?"

"Grandfather, you aren't going to wear that dress outside, are you? You can see your legs!"

While I call my neighbor and guardian "Juanez" and occasionally "Grandfather," the rest of the neighborhood knows him by his Armenian title, "the Baron." The Baron carries himself as a man who was once debonair and who now comforts himself by imagining that he still lives in another era, in his case the early disco era of the 1970s. Every afternoon he changes out of his regular outfit of tight green track shorts and a white undershirt and puts on neatly pressed polyester trousers and Italian shirts to take his daily promenade through the neighborhood. If I compliment him on his clothes, he flashes a smile and says, "Yes, they're beautiful, aren't they? You know, they were imported from Milano."

I don't believe that his clothes are actually Italian, and yet I sense that the only thing of importance is that everyone can pretend that they are. And they oblige. I've watched him saunter through the narrow streets of Damascus in his pressed shirts, smoking a cigarette nonchalantly, the shopkeepers leaning out of their windows and calling out to him, "*Marhaba, ya* Baron!" He may as well be the prince of Straight Street.

Every day over coffee, the Baron tells me another segment of the glamorous story of his life. He grew up in northern Syria, where his grandparents fled the massacres against Armenians in Turkey, and at home as a child he spoke Turkish and Armenian, learning Arabic in the streets. In his youth, the Baron played semiprofessional soccer in Aleppo, a city near the border with Turkey known for its famous medieval markets and olive oil soap and containing a sizable Christian minority. He traveled throughout the Middle East in a life he recounts as if he were a celebrity, wowing spectators as he starred in soccer matches in Jerusalem during the British Mandate and in cosmopolitan Tehran, encountering stunning women at every turn. Later he married and lived with his family in Lebanon, where he made a fortune owning an upscale shoe store and had the luck of passing his afternoons sliding imported Italian heels onto women's slender feet. In his small, squalid room in our house in Damascus, just next to a poster of the Virgin Mary and Child, he has posted a black-and-white photo of himself in his late thirties in a flashy suit and wide tie posing with a beautiful curly-haired woman in front of a storefront window lined with rows of Italian pumps. He assures me, winking, that she is not his wife.

"I was gorgeous, wasn't I?" he asks every time he shows me that photo, and then he pinches my cheeks playfully. "You know, in the shoe business, you are always in touch with women . . . and their feet. Ah, ha!"

Unfortunately, stories of luck in the Middle East usually don't have a happy ending, and the Baron's life is no exception. When the Lebanese Civil War broke out in 1975, he fled with his family to Turkey, where he managed to keep working due to his fluency in Turkish. A few years later, he returned to Lebanon, only to flee again after his village was raided by the Druze—yet another of the dozens of religious sects scattered throughout the region. He might have forgiven them had they not also raided his shoe store and stolen his entire stock of Italian heels and delicate flats, ending his career in shoes forever. To him looting a high-end shoe store was as barbaric as looting an antiquities museum, and he has never fully recovered from the scandal of it. Twenty-five years later, his ravings against the Druze are a staple of his afternoon lectures, as he invents more and more crimes they have committed.

"They worship goats!" he fumes to me. "Can you believe that? Goats!"

After he lost everything, he returned to Turkey, and then like many Lebanese refugees he moved to Brazil, finally splitting the last ten years of his life between Brazil and the decaying room he inhabits in Damascus next to mine. And yet in some way I'd like to think that his fall from grace is an illusion, for he has convinced himself that we live in the finest house in all of Bab Touma and the neighbors still address him as a gentleman.

It was the Baron who first discovered the final tenants of our humble, decaying house. They are two lovebirds, with beautiful color-stained wings, who together each afternoon descend from their hours of circling the city and come to nest in the highest branches of our citrus tree in the courtyard at exactly 6:30 p.m. If they are late, the Baron starts to worry, peeking out to look for them from the doorway every two minutes or so, afraid that they have become estranged. If more than ten minutes have passed, he knocks at my window frantically, calling, "Grandfather! Grandfather! One of the birds hasn't arrived! There must be a problem!"

Half an hour later, he inevitably returns and lets himself in, certain I have also been beside myself with worry. "Oh Grandfather, you don't need to worry anymore," he assures me. "The other bird came."

3.

THE DAYS HERE LAST FOREVER. The sun rises early and stays at full force over the city until around five in the afternoon, when it finally begins its slow and gradual retreat behind Jebel Qassioun, the mountain in the distance where locals believe that Cain killed Abel by casting his head against the stones. Because daylight is excruciatingly hot, some of the shopkeepers close their stores in the afternoons, and after sunset there is again a brief silence for dinnertime across the city. Then the markets open up again in the evenings and fill with crowds of people seeing one another and being seen, the Middle Eastern version of the great Italian *passeggiata*. By the time the streets quiet down completely I can only catch a few hours of sleep before it starts all over again.

I find it hard to fill my days, and so I've started to develop a routine. In the morning after coffee I wander to the Internet café across the neighborhood to see if anyone has written to me. The café is situated in a tiny alley just beyond the only mosque in Bab Touma and is nothing more than an ancient room filled up with cheap computers and young men hopefully instant-messaging women across the globe. By now the man who works the front desk recognizes me and gives me the best computer. I never stay long though, and after seeing my empty mailbox and writing my daily letter back home I make my way toward Straight Street again. By the time I arrive at the house it is time for a second cup of coffee and a chat with the Baron. When we've finished I grab a sandwich and fries, often from the Armenian place around the corner, and then I return to my room to spend a few hours drilling myself with Arabic flash cards. I take a hot shower, have another cup of coffee with the Baron, and then wander for a few hours in the Old City, looking for a chance to try out some of the new words I've memorized.

The problem is, my attempts at learning Arabic aren't working. I'm just terrible. The words feel unnatural coming out of my mouth, and I sometimes think that my tongue isn't the right shape to pronounce them. I'm like a child learning to speak again—in an alphabet full of letters that don't exist in English, the guttural *kh* and the strange *g*, the two different letters that both sound exactly to me like the letter *t*, two more that sound exactly like *d*, and even two that sound like *th*. The *k* sounds like *q*, and I can't differentiate the two *s* sounds for the life of me. Even when I manage to sort out the letters, I can't get any of the new words to stick in my brain, because they don't sound like any words that I already know.

Almost every day I've made embarrassing, even offensive mistakes. Last week I went to buy a toothbrush from the pharmacy, and instead of asking the pharmacist if he was open, I asked him, "Are you a virgin?" Later, struggling as always to differentiate between the *h* and the *kh*, I complained to the *Ustez* that I was having difficulty pronouncing certain sheep (*kharuf*) instead of certain letters (*hruf*) and was confused when he howled with laughter. When trying to make a passionate point, I told Juanez that I was speaking with my dog (*kalb*) instead of with my heart (*qalb*). Worst of all, I keep repeating what I hear other people say to me, which always worked fine in English. Yet along with its impossible alphabet, Arabic has separate grammar for speaking to men and women, and all adjectives are gender specific. I've picked up the unfortunate habit of speaking to all of the men around me as though I'm speaking to a woman, insulting their manhood in the process. This is driving the Baron crazy.

"Grandpa!" he ranted to me after I told him that he looked pretty yesterday. "I am a *man*. A *man*. Why do you speak to me like that?"

It is time, I've decided, to return to Arabic school.

So it is that this morning I climb out of bed earlier than usual and gulp down my cup of coffee on the run. On the corner of Straight Street I flag down a taxi and hand the driver an address scribbled on a piece of paper, where the *Ustez* has helpfully scrawled in blue ink the Arabic words *The College of Literature, Damascus Autostrade*. A moment later we snake out of the intimate, known world of Bab Touma and into the traffic of the highway circling Damascus, crammed in the early hours with yellow taxis and old, exhausted buses, hordes of minivans with destinations written on placards on the roof, bicycles and brave pedestrians who put their heads down and dart between the cars. On the side of the road, a man is selling tea in plastic cups to drivers who have slowed down to pay through their rolled-down windows and chat with him, causing the cars behind them, including us, to back up. The driver turns around.

"Damascus University?" he asks for confirmation. I nod.

"Do you want to try to keep taking the highway or cut through the Old City?"

The conversation is quickly getting ahead of my ability to respond in Arabic. "I have no idea. You know better than I do."

He laughs. "At your service. Where are you from?"

It takes me a minute to understand his question, which sounds to me like he is asking not *What is your country?* but *What is your civilization?* It's the first time I've ever heard the question asked like this, and it makes me feel like an alien who has landed from another planet.

I look at him steadily in the rearview mirror. "I'm from America." I finally say in Arabic. I make sure not to say it defiantly. I just want to be careful not to sound ashamed.

An almost imperceptible look of surprise flashes in his eyes, like he has accidentally touched a light socket.

"America? You mean you're from *the* America?"

"That's right."

He breaks into a broad grin. "Welcome to Syria."

He shakes his head in bewilderment, and he continues to look baffled for the next minute or so, glancing in his rearview mirror as if to confirm that I am actually there. I imagine that he can't quite believe the first person he has ever met from the country that embodies such raw power has turned out to be an awkward, bumbling girl on her way to her first day of school. I try to imagine what would happen if I were driving in downtown San Antonio and I picked up an Iraqi refugee speaking Chaucerian-accented English.

Which brings me to another point: in addition to jumbling letters and forgetting vocabulary, I speak a kind of medieval Arabic. I mean this quite literally—the hours of Arabic I studied in graduate school were unfortunately limited to classical Arabic, which is a language not actually spoken by ordinary people anywhere in the world. I speak the Arabic of the Quran, the Arabic of newspapers and of the newscasters of Al Jazeera, but one that barely resembles the colloquial Arabic spoken in the streets. Me showing up in Damascus speaking this Arabic would be like a tourist landing in Rome and trying to get by speaking Latin while everyone else is speaking rapid, slick, and vibrant Italian. I sound ridiculous, like those people who dress up in costumes and attend Renaissance festivals, which is perhaps why when people hear me speak, they very often burst into laughter. This has not been very encouraging.

But the taxi driver, to his credit, is remaining tactfully silent despite the fact that a girl from an enemy country has just climbed into his taxi and addressed him in a dialect from the thirteenth century. In the meantime I discourage further conversation by staring out the window at Damascus flying past, and as we cross the city the ancient alleys around my neighborhood disappear and are replaced by grim apartment buildings and hotels, banks and towering mosques, all of the suburban sprawl of any Arab capital trying to contain a population of several million people.

Yet even this ordinariness is somewhat refreshing, considering the fact that ordinariness is something relatively new to Damascus. The first time I came here for a visit, in 2000, the country was still recovering from the death of President Hafez al-Assad, the man who had kept the country firmly under his thumb for nearly thirty years. The Internet was still illegal, the secret police were everywhere, and the streets were full of yellow classic cars serving as taxis that sailed down the road, flaunting their tail fins. Damascus in 2000 looked like most other countries in the 1950s.

Much has changed in four years, and now Internet cafés are visible on corners and the streets are crowded with modern taxis. On a billboard a shampoo model shows off her cascading hair, and Western-style coffee shops have opened near fashion boutiques. Outside I can see women in headscarves mixing with men in suits, all chatting on their cell phones, and old devout Muslim men still wearing traditional clothes. Yet not everything has changed, and the face of Hafez al-Assad has been largely replaced with that of President Bashar al-Assad staring down at me from everywhere, the British-trained ophthalmologist who took over from his father after he died. Here he is, smiling from the backs of taxi windows, from giant billboards: Bashar in his military uniform, Bashar posing with his wife and children, Bashar against a billowing Syrian flag, Bashar with a mountain scene reflected in the shades of his aviator glasses. The sight of him peering down at me from everywhere makes me slightly nervous.

My driver must have noticed my discomfort, because when we pull up near the curb at the university he turns around and faces me through the space between the seats and smiles reassuringly, like a father dropping his little girl off for her first day of school.

"Don't be afraid," he tells me. "You know, we love the American people here. I mean it. We just hate your government."

My shoulders relax, and I manage to smile back at him. "Well, I don't much like it right now either," I reply in my medieval Arabic.

"We know the Americans can be like that! You see?" He holds up his hand and counts off his fingers one by one. "A hand has five fingers. This one is big, this one is small, this one is in the middle. Not all of them are the same."

I hand him the equivalent of a dollar and he hands me my change, the cheapest cab ride of my life.

"Do you need me to pick you up after school?"

"No thanks."

"Then God be with you."

"Go with peace."

"God keep you well."

Then I close the door and enter the gates of Damascus University, to a sea of unfamiliar faces.

A LARGER THAN LIFE-SIZED STATUE of former president Hafez al-Assad is waiting for me on campus, standing in the center of the courtyard at attention in his suit with his hand placed over his chest. It takes me a while to identify which of the drab Soviet-inspired buildings around him is the Arabic Language Center. Finally I see a circular concrete building with a flight of stairs and an English sign over the doorway. The Old City where I live is beautiful, but hell must look like this.

Damascus University has a reputation in the world of Arabic language students for being one of the cheapest and most intense places in the world to study. Here, native Arabic-speaking teachers drill students in four hours of reading, writing, and speaking Arabic a day, allowing students to learn in a few months what would normally require years of studying. It is a matter of learning by osmosis, of being subjected to such a torrent of Arabic that eventually some of the words sink in. No one is allowed to speak any language other than Arabic during classes. Famously, the university does not care who comes to study at their institute, as long as the students have passed an official blood test given by the Syrian government certifying that they do not have AIDS. As a result, poor students from across the globe flock here for the chance to learn Arabic for around two hundred dollars a month, about what it costs for a single day of the best intensive Arabic course in America.

When I arrive, the corridors are already crowded with Shiite Muslims from Iran with full beards mixing with European doctoral students, young Western journalists checking grammar with long-robed Sufis from West Africa, Muslim women wearing *niqabs*, full veils covering their entire faces except for their eyes, chatting quietly with Mormon students in starched white shirts. It may be the most bizarre mix of students I've ever seen.

I take a placement test and am assigned to level three, which means that after two years of studying Arabic I can barely form a sentence. I stomach two hours of listening to the names of the parts of the body before I excuse myself and sneak into level four. At least I was under the impression that it was level four. I may also have accidentally entered Chinese class by mistake. I can barely understand anything the teacher is saying. It seems that in the space of a single level, students jump from talking about their fingers to discussing the finer points of quantum theory.

The teacher, a rather handsome Syrian man wearing khaki trousers and a red plaid shirt, is busy pacing back and forth in front of the chalkboard like a military sergeant. Every few moments, he taps the blackboard with a piece of chalk to command our attention.

"Today, we are going to discuss irregular plurals," he announces, scribbling a sentence in Arabic on the board.

"Now suppose you have a single dog who is chasing you down the street. How would you say 'dog' in the singular?"

"Kalb!" the class sings out in a chorus.

"Now suppose you have two dogs running after you. What is that?"

"Kalban!"

"And in the genitive?"

"Kalbeen!"

"Now what if you have a substantial number of dogs running after you?"

A devout Shiite from Iran raises his hand: *"Kilab!"*

"Now what if you have a really enormous number of dogs running after you?"

His eyes turn toward me expectantly. At which point I feign taking notes with great concentration, then stare out the window, at the floor, gaze at the portrait of Hafez Al-Assad hanging across the street, and pretend to possess the legendary powers of the Invisible Man, until at last a Turkish Quranic student jumps in and shouts, *"Ikalab!"*

And then, for a moment at least, I am safe.

4.

HERE IS THE CAST OF CHARACTERS who have joined me to study Arabic at Damascus University. There is a young American from California whom the other students secretly call "Jihad Johnny," after the American John Walker Lindh, the Californian discovered fighting with the Taliban in Afghanistan. Sporting a beard, a skullcap, and a long robe, Jihad Johnny has recently converted to a radical version of Islam, and despite his American roots, he dominates our class discussions by angrily denouncing American imperialism, quoting the Quran, and suggesting that America deserved September 11. He accomplishes this all in very poor, broken Arabic, which makes the entire spectacle that much more surreal. Our teacher Adel, whom I suspect to be a secular member of the Baath Party, also finds JJ's behavior ridiculous. Each time he makes a point about Islam in class, he wryly turns to Jihad Johnny and asks, "What do you think about that, Abdullah?" Abdullah is not Johnny's real name. In Arabic, Abdullah means "the slave of God."

Then we have a blond Canadian teenager named Christine who has somehow become fluent in an extremely religious strain of colloquial Arabic while growing up in Hezbollah-dominated south Lebanon. I am only guessing that she is blond: she possesses a Nordic face, but she has also converted to Islam, along with her whole, presumably blond Canadian family, and so covers her hair with a tightly fastened white scarf. She volunteers to read every sentence in class and, unlike Johnny, reads so quickly and flawlessly that I cannot fathom why we are in the same Arabic level. I also can't figure out what might have led her family to move from Canada to the south of Lebanon, which until recently has been the site of frequent conflicts between the Israeli military and Hezbollah, but I don't dare ask her.

There is a gorgeous Iranian student named Leila with striking green eyes who wears her sheer blue scarf draped loosely over her head and leaves wisps of hair falling from beneath it. According to the hallway gossip, she had recently been imprisoned in her country for fighting for human rights, and rumor has it she was forced by the Iranian embassy to wear the veil, even in Damascus, where it is not required, under threat of deporting her home again. Then there is the magnificent Suleiman, a Nigerian Muslim studying to be an imam, who wastes no time before announcing that he wants four wives. There is a Turkish madrassa student named Aisha, who wears a floor-length Islamic robe to school every day and has fiery opinions, and a handful of staunchly secular and verbally anti-American European doctoral students, including a German named Frida with predictably perfect grammar. Finally, a Japanese girl looks so overwhelmed by the lot of us that I keep expecting her to burst into tears at any moment. I am one of only three Americans, the others being Jihad Johnny and Michael, a quiet banker from Washington, D.C., who rarely speaks at all.

WE SPEND THE FIRST FEW DAYS OF CLASSES reviewing tedious sentences meant to teach us impossibly obscure grammar, including how the numbers one and two, three through ten, and eleven to nineteen all require different rules. But my heart is not in it, and while the teacher is writing out sentences I let my mind wander off to the streets of my old neighborhood in Boston, or the scent of food from the Chinese restaurant around the corner of my old house, the sound of the wind rustling through the trees in autumn, and most of all, the man I left behind.

At the end of the week, after working from the blackboard, we buy our Arabic textbooks at last, photocopied and bound in bright pink plastic, nothing like the gorgeous textbook of calligraphy I'd been dreaming about. Still, for a moment I'm excited enough about Arabic to pull myself from my reveries and to focus again on why I'm here. I've been waiting years to learn Arabic in an Arab country, to finally read the love poetry of the famous Syrian poet Nizar Qabbani or perhaps excerpts of a short story by the Palestinian writer Ghassan Kanafani in the original. I've always found Arabic to be a language of stunning beauty, and in poetry it becomes music. It is the language Muslims believe that God used when he revealed the Quran, choosing the most perfect language, the one that all people will speak when they arrive in paradise. For Arabs, to learn Arabic is to stumble through the language of God.

I open the first page of my textbook and run my fingers along the columns of curls and loops moving backward from right to left across the page. I have never held a book containing so much of a foreign language with the knowledge that I will actually eventually decipher the meaning of the words. When Christine, the fluent Canadian, volunteers to read from our opening text, for once I feel a surge of joy upon hearing her voice.

She reads the first sentence quickly and flawlessly, and I silently translate it to myself. Then I repeat it once again in my mind, trying to sort out where I went wrong. *Today, the distribution of food is more dangerous than the atomic bomb.*

I scan the classroom to see if the other students are also confused. My teacher is busy flashing his hands open and making explosive noises. When he says *Hiroshima*, I know that I have translated correctly. I write *atomic bomb* in English in the margin of my text before continuing on to the remainder of the article, which describes how developed countries are able to control poorer countries by cutting off their access to food.

This is how I learn that there will be no poetry, and that our classes will be an occasion to learn the language of Baathism, the story of class struggles and the cold and dry vocabulary of war. Though I still don't know how to order in a restaurant, in the next week I'll learn the words *unemployment*, *depression*, *suicide*, *famine*, and *starvation*. Instead of memorizing Arabic poetry, I'll read about the crisis of Syrians from the countryside moving to the city. I'll memorize the words *soldier* and *war*, *politics* and *explosion*, and learn my grammar through a story of a freedom fighter from Libya who refuses to be paid for his deeds.

A few days after our first text, we come upon a word that no one in the class recognizes, *fard*. My teacher is left to communicate via charades. He pretends to push the chalkboard. He presses his fist against his hand. Then, his face brightens.

"America tries to *tafrid* its opinions on the rest of the world," he announces triumphantly in Arabic.

Everyone nods and scribbles in their margins obediently. I continue looking at him in bafflement, until I finally register the meaning and rush to record it on my text. *To force*, I write down in my margin. As in *America tries to force its opinions on the rest of the world*.

5.

WHEN I RETURN HOME FROM SCHOOL in the afternoon, exhausted and deflated, Juanez is waiting for me in his green track shorts and tank top, the door to his tiny room propped open, the sound of an Arabic soap opera escaping from his television. After I have taken two steps into the courtyard he jumps out of his seat and starts gesturing to me wildly, waving me into his room.

"Hey Grandfather, were you at school?" he asks suspiciously.

"Yes, I was at school."

"Have you showered?"

I shake my head. I don't know how I could have showered if I was at school.

"Okay, *yalla, yalla*, hurry up, go take a shower," he says, dismissing me with his hand. "I heated up the water for you."

After two and a half weeks in the house off Straight Street, I still cannot determine if the Baron loves me deeply, desiring to dote on me at every opportunity to reveal his affections, or if he simply thinks that I am completely incompetent. I am confident that, given encouragement, I could heat the shower water myself. Not that I can actually call what we have in our bathroom a shower. Our old, traditional house did not originally have a bathroom, as the people who once lived here did their bathing in the *hammams*, or public baths, that were once a staple of social life in all Arab cities. In recent years my neighbors have adapted a concrete storage room in the corner of my kitchen to double as a bathroom. Yes— when the Baron told me that I had my own bathroom, he neglected to mention that I also shared it with all of the other members of the sprawling household, who enter it via "my" kitchen door. He also forgot to mention that there is no bath, no shower, and no shower curtain in this bathroom. "Bathing," in our washroom, means sitting on a red plastic stool and scrubbing myself down with soap, then filling a bucket full of hot water and pouring it over my head.

I'm actually lucky—bathing in my house works on the class system, and as a result of my inflated rent I'm allowed to bathe every single day in "my bathroom," a privilege normally reserved only for the Baron. The rest of the house can only bathe every Thursday, when they file one by one down from their rooms and scrub off a week's worth of grime and smoke. Still, it's hard to think of myself as lucky as I sit on the plastic stool, turn the rusty metal spigot, and fill up the small metal basin with the almost scalding water the Baron has prepared for me. I dip in a plastic bucket, ladle out a portion of water, and pour it over my head and repeat until my whole body is at least moderately wet. I scrub myself with olive oil soap. Then I sit for a moment, naked, covered with soapsuds, on that red plastic stool and remember what life was like not long ago, emerging from the shower and into a warm flannel robe, to drink a cup of tea and speak to the man I loved, in my own language.

When I finish rinsing off, I quickly dress, slightly suspicious of how thin my curtains have worn through the years, and then peer out of my front door and wave into the Baron's room to signify that I'm done.

"Have you finished?" he always asks, as though I might have stopped a shower in the middle because I suddenly felt the urge to chat.

I nod in reply. "Well then, *Na'iman*, Grandfather, may you be blessed," he answers, bestowing on me the traditional Arabic blessing for those who have just showered or received a haircut.

"*Allah inam aleek*, And may God give you pleasure," I respond. And then he rushes into the shower himself, before the water gets cold.

Apparently, the Baron interprets the fact that I speak Arabic at roughly the level of a second grader to mean that I actually possess the mental capacity of an eight-year-old child. He speaks to me very loudly, repeating everything two or three times. He is alarmed that I do not understand Syrian household appliances, and out of courtesy and lack of Arabic vocabulary, I have chosen not explain to him that these models have not been used in America for several decades. How can I not know, he asks me in frustration, that a toilet can be flushed simply by pouring a full bucket of water down it? How, after twenty-seven years on earth, did I not understand how to operate a central heater, called a *sobba*, powered by a small and to my eyes potentially lethal tank of slowly dripping petroleum? When my fan breaks, he calls in a repairman to take it apart and rebuild the engine. How do I not know that this is cheaper than buying a new fan with all new materials?

When the Baron finishes his shower, he knocks on my window, a sign that it is time for the second of our daily coffee sessions. Now that I am in school, we are down to three coffees a day. The first daily coffee session is for waking up, the second is Arabic pop quiz, and the third is for the evening news. The second is a cruel variation on Chinese torture.

The Baron waits until I take my seat, and then he casually pours me a cup of coffee. He turns down the sound on the television, takes a seat across from me, leans over the table, and asks, "How long have you been here? Two weeks already? When are you going to learn to speak Arabic?" He sadly shakes his head in disbelief, then reaches across the table and knocks on my skull, pretending to listen to a hollow sound. "Is there a brain in there?" he inquires. Then, without giving me time to respond, he points to the trash can.

"How do you say that in Arabic?" he demands.

This continues for half an hour. He manages, with frightening telepathy, to ask me only words that I do not know the Arabic equivalent to. What! I don't know the word for "freezer"? For "ceiling fan"?

He opens his refrigerator and pulls out an obscure Armenian pastry that I have never seen before, waving it in front of my face like a fish in front of a dolphin's mouth.

"What is this?" he demands. *Five hundred grams of fat*, I think to myself. *"Shaobiyya,"* he says. "Repeat after me." I parrot his words, and he hands me the pastry in reward. I dig in.

Five minutes pass before he casually asks, "Grandfather, what is that you're eating?"

There is no escape. Even if I do know the word in Arabic, he mocks me for not knowing the word in the Syrian dialect, which, when I learn it, he replaces with another word with a slightly different meaning, but which he insists is more appropriate.

He holds out a coffee cup for my inspection. "What's this?"

I smile proudly. "That's a *kass*."

He groans. "A *kass* is a cup. That's a *finjan*, a coffee cup. How many times have I told you that?"

He grills me on Lebanese actresses, on types of liquor, on random varieties of Armenian sausage. After the first humiliating session, I returned to my room, took out my scissors, and spent the next several hours taping up small paper squares all over, identifying wall, floor, window, salt, pepper, butter, and, of course, trash can in Arabic until the rooms around me resembled a kindergarten classroom. Now, they are the first things I see when I wake up in the morning, the slips of paper fluttering in the wind sobering reminders of just how much I do not know.

6.

MY FIRST ARABIC TEACHER once explained to me that there is more than one word for returning in Arabic: *irjah* means to simply return anywhere, but *aouda* means to return to a place that belongs to you. You can *irjah* to the supermarket, but you *aouda* to your homeland. *Aouda* has the quality of the sacred about it.

Sometimes when I trudge back to the house after school, or when I watch those two birds alighting in the tree each evening, I wonder if *aouda* can even apply to me anymore. Do I even have a home? Other than the Baron, who has nothing better to do with his time, is there anyone left out there in the world waiting for me? If I disappeared, would anyone even know that I was gone?

Every morning when I awaken in Damascus, in that brief space between the merchants shouting outside and the appearance of the Baron's face in the window, I lie in bed and think about the life I've lost. I try to picture myself a few weeks ago on the other side of the world, in a steel-blue house on a quiet, oak-lined street in Cambridge. I'm wearing a thin floral dress with small straps at the shoulders. Mark has just returned from the library. From our bedroom window I watch him park his bicycle against the tree in the front yard. Then I run to the kitchen and flip open a magazine, so that he can't tell that I've been waiting for him.

Beside me, the rings from our morning cups of tea are still visible on the breakfast table, and I rub at them gently with my fingertips. The tree outside the kitchen window is blooming white flowers. A few minutes later Mark walks in and wordlessly sets a CD of tango music into place and pours us two glasses of red wine. Then he reaches over and pulls me up from the table and folds his hands into mine.

I resist him until he pulls me up closer to him, and then I stand on top of the toes of his heavy black shoes. He moves me like that, picking me up with every step, until he finally lifts me off the ground entirely and swings me over the kitchen tiles.

"You're home early," I whisper in his ear.

He is just about to whisper something back when I hear a tapping on the window.

"Grandfather! *Yalla*, it's time for coffee!"

And then, just that quickly, my entire life is gone again.

I lived for two years in Cambridge, and one year in that house on the oak-lined street with the man I loved. In retrospect, it feels as though I spent as much time losing that house as living in it. I had just returned to America after being abroad for many years, working as a journalist and studying in several countries scattered across the Middle East, Europe, and Asia. I was exhausted from wandering from place to place without ever pausing long enough to truly rest. I had lived in eight different rooms in eight different years and traveled through more than twenty countries. By the time I settled into that final house, my body no longer even experienced jet lag, as though it had accepted homelessness as a permanent country in which it now lived.

I was in my last year of a master's, twenty-six and utterly alone. I was also diving headlong into what might have been one of the earliest midlife crises in history. My heart had torn in so many places that I had little hope of setting it right again. In the last five years, I had left behind a thoughtful French teacher with soft brown eyes on the island of Corsica, a linguist in China, a scholar of Ottoman studies on the way to Lebanon, a British historian on the way back to America, and a half-dozen other men in cities along the Silk Road. I have always loved too easily and often, and each of these loves bruised me in its own unique and particular way. The problem wasn't that I was unlucky in love—it was that I was chronically incapable of staying in place. Every year, no matter what the circumstances of my life, I woke up one morning overtaken by an almost primal desire to pack my bags and flee to the other side of the earth. It did not matter if I happened to be waking up in someone's arms, or if I had finally arrived at a place of contentment. I needed to keep moving. The men I cared about could not be blamed for not wanting to follow me.

In time, I became a master at destroying my own happiness. I traveled. I fell in love. When it was time to settle down, I packed up my bags and left again, only to wake up in another unfamiliar room, alone. I grew adept in the art of waking up in strange rooms scattered across continents. I woke up in Costa Rica, on the edge of the Taklamakan Desert in western China, along the banks of the Nile. I woke up in a village in Umbria, Italy, in a grassy field in the south of Spain, in a hotel room in Crete with my belongings missing. I became accustomed to trying to remember where I was in the morning. Sometimes it was romantic, such as when I woke up in a small hotel on the Greek island of Patmos, a few steps away from the sea. Other times it was just plain sad. One night I was jolted awake in a forty-eight-hour sleeper bus in rural China. We had just crashed into a mountain, and snow was coming in through the window. The doors had been crushed shut, and around me people were frantically climbing out of the broken windshield and into the cold. I stared at the snowflakes catching in the moonlight and thought to myself, *I don't even know where I am.* If I had died, how long would it have taken for anyone to know that I was gone?

After a few years of drifting, I was lucky enough to stumble upon a newspaper editor in Lebanon who thought of my years wandering the planet writing the occasional travel article as valuable work experience. I left another boyfriend, bought a plane ticket, and headed to Beirut for my first real job. Six days after I arrived, two airplanes flew into the Twin Towers.

I was sitting in a rooftop café having lunch, and suddenly around me cell phones were going off. Everyone kept saying *Amerka, Amerka,* and because I couldn't understand any other words, all I knew was that something had gone terribly wrong in the place where I was from. That night, I sat on the floor of the apartment of a girl I barely knew, watching television, too shocked to cry. Over and over, those two towers were collapsing onto the earth. It happened so quickly. As I watched footage of people weeping in the streets, clinging to one another, for the first time I understood how reckless I had been with my own life, how much I had taken everyone I loved for granted. They could be gone in an instant, and I would be all the way on the other side of the world.

I also learned what it was to grieve completely alone.

I wanted desperately to go home again. I wanted to be with my family. I wanted to tell them that I loved them. I certainly didn't want to be in Beirut, Lebanon, sleeping on someone's couch because I didn't even have an apartment of my own.

If I were a braver person, I would have cut my losses and caught the first flight back home again that week. But I had, unbelievably, fled two countries, three states, and four men in four months. I was too ashamed to go back. I was also just beginning to convince myself, along with those I knew, that I lived a glamorous, enviable life. The truth was, I kept running in part because I didn't have a home to go back to anymore. I hadn't been a good friend, daughter, or lover to anyone in many years. I had spent the last Christmas holidays in China, far from my family. I rarely spoke to them (much less the man I left behind in China). I had lost touch with most of my college friends. While I had collected new stamps on my passport, they were settling down to build careers and have families. And while I had spent many years thinking of their lives as boring, it was my life that had taken on a quality of the mundane. I was a professional wanderer, and though the countries I passed through were different, in time the ancient cities and foreign languages began to blend together. I sent home photos of an exotic Roman city on the Lebanese coast, and in return I received news of a friend's child being born. There was no comparison.

The boyfriend in China had said it best before I left: "You know, Stephanie, you can't go on running like this forever."

He was right. I ran from him anyway.

In the end, I didn't buy a ticket to go home. I did what I had always done and wrote to my family saying that I was perfectly safe and extremely happy, and that I would rather be in Lebanon than anywhere else in the world. But from then on I began to envy those people who managed to succeed at normal lives. I wanted what they had—houses and families, front yards, barbecues, health insurance. I wanted to stay in one place long enough to remember my phone number.

By the end of my year in Lebanon, I decided that if I was going to cut and run again, then I might as well run back to my own country. So it was that the following September I moved to New England and enrolled to study theology at Harvard Divinity School in Cambridge. Their master's in theology was only a two-year program, and I thought that, with summer vacation and a few holidays built in, I might be able to manage being settled in one place for that long. I didn't really care so much about getting a degree in theology. What I wanted was to be quiet, far away from war, and rooted again to the earth. I wanted to remember who I once had been, before I had lost my bearings.

I spent the next two years in Cambridge holed up in the divinity school library reading about God, saints, and angels and learning to find a place in my own country. I made girlfriends, and we drank cocktails together on Friday nights. I bought items too large to fit in a suitcase. I went to the doctor for a checkup for the first time in many years. I acquired a mailing address and had the newspaper delivered to the front door. Every morning I passed by the corner Starbucks coffee shop, where I ordered a grande nonfat chai latte and dreamed of the day when the barista might ask if I wanted "the usual."

I reveled in once again being around books in my own language, and often I would wander through the library and open books at random, thrilled at being surrounded by so many English words. When I needed to escape I escaped into my studies, and I used the time to finally learn about the countries I had lived in, to read the monastic texts of Greece, to study the Muslim Sufi saints who had written in Turkey and Syria. Instead of rushing away to foreign countries during the holidays, I went home to see my family. I memorized hours upon hours of Arabic verbs on the off chance that I ever needed to return to the Middle East. I managed to resemble an ordinary twenty-something student. I also watched way too many movies, sliding away from the library to catch the matinee at the Brattle Theatre off Harvard Square.

And here is where I confess what I wanted most of all: I wanted to fall in love. I wanted to know what it was like to love in America, instead of in some distant, unfamiliar country. I wanted to go on dates and chat on the phone between classes and hold hands on small streets. Well, this is not exactly true: I wanted to love like people love in the movies. I wanted to wear grown-up strappy dresses and eat dinner over candlelight and dance on the deck of a boat passing beneath the stars while a man told me that he would never, ever leave me. Still, I was willing to settle for holding hands and dating, as long as it was with a man who was willing to stay in place with me.

Even so, love managed to take me by surprise.

By the end of May, I was only a few months away from finishing my master's program. One morning I was sitting at the kitchen table of my house in Cambridge, reading the morning paper, when my roommate Mark wandered in, still wearing his plaid flannel robe, to attempt to wash some dishes. I say attempt, because Mark was one of those Harvard doctoral students who spoke ten languages but had difficulties completing simple tasks like washing dishes and stringing together words in English. He would get caught in midsentence as he pondered the etymology of the name of a certain vegetable in a recipe or began to visualize the comings and goings of the Russian court during the reign of Catherine the Great. So it was that as I was spilling tea on the *New York Times Book Review* that morning, he was standing nearby with a dish in one hand and a blue towel in the other, trying his best to bring the two together.

We had been friends all year, siblings almost, and even while he was immersed in history books about the tribulations of Kazakhstan and I was buried in monastic texts, we found time to take occasional walks together beside the Charles River to catch up on each other's lives. Yet recently I had been seeing much more of him, because we had made a pact to both wake up early and collect ourselves from opposite sides of the house in order to drink tea together. I loved our early morning routine, which felt more like *home* to me than anything I had lived in in many years. Mark would come into the kitchen at seven in his flannel bathrobe, and as he boiled water we would sit across from each other at the table and split our sections of the morning paper, wordlessly. He would briefly get up to remove the kettle from the stove, pour me a cup and then pour his own, and then we would continue reading until he emptied his mug and waved good-bye and disappeared for the rest of the day.

That particular morning when I entered the kitchen, the water was already boiling on the stove, and Mark was slowly and unsuccessfully drying his dish. He had forgotten to put on his glasses and so was presumably functioning in a world of fog, but he probably didn't even notice.

I took my seat at the table and began reading the paper, and after a while he began musing aloud over the kitchen sink.

"Do you know what I was thinking the other day?" he asked me, or himself, or the wall. "What would happen if I won the lottery? Then I thought: Maybe I would buy an enormous house by the sea. But then I thought: What would I do with a house on the sea? And what about Stephanie? Would she come and live there also? Or would I need to buy her another house next door?"

I looked up at him. He seemed to be watching his sentences form in the air, word by word as in a cartoon balloon. After a full two seconds he stared at me in alarm, having just heard the words his mouth had spoken aloud. "Why would I think that?" he asked me. At which point he dropped his dish and hurried to his bedroom. I knew that we were done for.

I fell in love with Mark hard and fast, with all of the diligence and ferocity of someone who had waited a lifetime to finally love someone well. We quickly settled into the routine of a married couple. I migrated to his section of the house, and I marked my new territory by placing my poetry and theology books on his shelves alongside Uzbek and Persian dictionaries. He woke up in the morning and made me smoky Chinese tea before regaling me with the love story between Catherine the Great and General Potemkin. We drank great quantities of red wine together. We were a couple, a real American couple, albeit with slightly quirky interests. I loved that he talked to himself in Russian. I adored the terrible lime green shirts he wore to go dancing, and his addiction to Shostakovich. I loved the fact that he left check marks next to paragraphs in *The New Yorker*, as if to tell the authors, "Bravo! Well done!"

It was what I had longed for but never thought possible—all of the flair and intensity of life abroad taking place in an American three-bedroom apartment. We could watch Iranian films and speak about Middle Eastern policy, we could eat Japanese takeout and sample Italian wine, we could rush out on Sunday afternoons to hear a Russian symphony and still be home for the evening news. I would never have to choose again.

I was quite sure that we would live happily ever after. I was counting on it.

Admittedly, we had our problems. He was quite a bit older than I was, which meant that he actually came of age during the Cold War, whereas all I remembered of it was that the Soviet Union had boycotted the Olympics I attended when I was seven years old. He could be hawkish in his politics and sometimes thought of me as naïve, which made him infuriatingly dismissive of my points of view. He was cynical where I was optimistic, and like many historians, he mistrusted claims that could not be backed up by empirical evidence. I studied faith, and he spent his life looking for answers in foreign archives.

This tension came up most often when we spoke about religion. "Did it ever occur to you that religious people might be delusional?" he asked me one morning over tea.

"Excuse me?"

"I mean, seeing as they talk to an invisible man in the sky. Don't you think that this qualifies as being delusional?"

"You know what I think."

"I was just curious."

I didn't feel like being baited into a fight, and so I took a moment to collect myself. "So you really think that a majority of the American population are delusional?"

"Well, frankly, yes."

I tried to summon up a response. Finally he smiled and tapped me on the shoulder.

"Steph, I'm just kidding," he said. But he wasn't.

I had been raised in Catholic schools, and though I rarely made it to church anymore, I was still culturally very Catholic. I studied theology. Many of my friends and family were deeply spiritual. Still, I chose to ignore Mark's words. I had always kept my faith intensely private, and lately I had felt so far away from any spiritual life that I reasoned I could live without it. If God existed, and if he was as compassionate as I hoped he might be, then I reasoned that he would understand that all I wanted was to be happy.

They were only words, after all. And they seemed so small beside everything else I knew about this man, who was passionate about food and music and somehow even about me, who spoke longingly of having children, who had once held my hands as we stood in front of a restaurant and said, *I'm so glad that you exist.*

MORE PROBLEMATIC THAN GOD, it turned out, was the fact that Mark had recently weathered a terrible, prolonged divorce. Like many a graduate student, he was also buried beneath a dissertation that he couldn't finish, and his personal life was making it even more difficult to focus. He tried to tell me gently that, while he cared about me, his emotional plate was already full with an ex-wife and three hundred pages on the relationship between Russia and the Caucasus, and that he had no desire at all to fall in love with me or anyone else.

"Steph, I really need time, to sort out being alone, to finish my dissertation, to find peace with myself after years of struggling through my marriage," he told me as I moved my belongings across the house. "I just can't see myself in a serious relationship in the next year." Over the following weeks he said it over and over again, in very clear terms, like a mantra. Yet I had no intention of giving up. I secretly believed that enough mornings of tea and omelets and newspapers would finally and inevitably add up to a commitment, even if he didn't notice that it had happened. I would simply insert myself into his life until he couldn't live without me.

So I began to make plans for both of us. I dreamed of how we would settle down and have children and buy our fabled house on the beach. I spoke of it quietly to other women in kitchens at dinner parties. I put my academic future on hold and began to search for office jobs in Cambridge so that we could stay together after I graduated. For the first time in eight years, I prepared to live in a house for more than a single year in a row.

Then an envelope arrived in the mailbox one afternoon in May with my name typed on the front. I opened it in front of Mark that evening. Inside I found a single piece of paper, which contained in painfully nonambiguous language the words that would change my life:

Dear Stephanie:

We would like to congratulate you on being selected as a Fulbright scholar for Syria, for the year 2004–2005.

I caught my breath. *Syria.*

I had applied for the fellowship eight months before and had long ago given up on receiving news. But with that one word, all of the old temptations came flooding back. *Syria.* Its almost total isolation and lack of English speakers made it perhaps the best country in the world to study Arabic. It was home to some of the oldest Muslim and Christian traditions anywhere in the world. Monasteries and Crusader castles and Roman cities lay scattered across the landscape, with some two hundred abandoned Byzantine cities sprinkled across the north of the country, just sitting there, because no one knew exactly what to do with such an embarrassment of riches. I had visited Syria only twice, and I had promptly fallen in love with its buzzing, outdated cities, its minarets and posters of the president, its crowded bazaars full of spices and scarves and meat hanging from hooks. I had often told myself that it was the one country on earth that I would give anything to spend a year in, the embodiment of all that remained exotic and unknown in the modern Middle East, if not the entire world. For the American scholar of the Arab world, Syria was the classic unavailable man, silent and brooding and impossible to pin down for a date, the kind of man who never returned your phone calls.

I had been lusting after him for years. I longed for him almost as much as I longed to possess an ordinary life.

We were already at war in Iraq, and the U.S. government had recently added Syria as an honorary member of its Axis of Evil. I was surprised that the Fulbright had not been canceled altogether and knew that the years in which Americans could obtain visas to Syria were possibly limited. I might never have this chance again.

Go, the voice inside of me said. *Go while you can.*

Unfortunately, the voice arrived right at the moment when Mark was coming around to the idea of settling down.

"It's only a year apart," I told him. "I know that it won't be easy, but there's no reason why we shouldn't try a long-distance relationship."

But I knew it was hopeless. Mark liked to refer to his "long-distance divorce" as proof of why long-distance relationships were a bad idea. I would need to make a choice.

"You can't keep living your life with the wind forever, Stephanie," Mark said. "At some point, you have to decide what you want your destiny to be."

I TOOK MY TIME, and the next months were a nightmare. We broke up and got back together again. We were engaged for an afternoon. After a terrible argument, I left the house. He didn't come after me, and after waiting in vain for days, I had to cry and plead my way back in again. I decided to take the fellowship, not to take it, to take it. I postponed mailing my acceptance letter and skipped the orientation. I woke up in the same house, day after day. I memorized what that felt like. I wore his flannel robe. Drank his tea. Became accustomed to catching him conducting a symphony in the kitchen, or with that look in his eyes that told me he was talking to himself in his head, or perhaps to the Russian ambassador to Georgia. He began to accept the fact that I was destined to leave. Then one morning I woke up, felt the bones of his chest with my two longest fingers, and I didn't want to go to Damascus anymore. I wanted to stay, and I wanted it more than I had wanted almost anything in my life. I wanted to plant roots, to hold out for the Starbucks barista to remember my order. I wanted to live in the same house for a second year in a row. I wanted him.

It was already August, just a few weeks from the day I was supposed to catch a plane to Damascus. Our relationship had become so broken that I didn't know if we could salvage it. Still, I sat down in a café, pulled out a pen and paper, and summoned up the courage to write him a letter telling him that I had made my decision.

I want to be here when you finish your dissertation. I want to be here when your brother has his child. I want to be here when you wake up in the morning, when you come home at the end of the afternoon. I'm sorry it took me so long to understand, but now I'm certain. This life with you is the only country I want to live in right now . . .

IT WAS THE BRAVEST LETTER I had ever written. I hurried home and left it on his pillow, and then I went for a walk.

The Bread of Angels

When I returned that evening, Mark couldn't look me in the eye.

"What is it?" I asked, but I was already beginning to cry.

"It's beautiful," he said softly. "This is the kind of letter every man dreams of receiving." He kept looking at the floor.

"You have to go," he said, finally looking up at me. "You have to go to Damascus."

It didn't make any sense. "Stephanie, please go," he repeated. "I'm not ready. You can't stay. I would never forgive myself for stopping you."

For the first time in my life, I had offered a man everything. And he had responded by saying no.

Two weeks later Mark drove me to the airport. We stood in the terminal, and he embraced me awkwardly and promised that he would phone me often and count the days until Christmas, when we'd see each other again.

It wasn't that he didn't love me, he insisted. He just needed time.

I left for Damascus like a prisoner exiled to Siberia. By the time I arrived, it had become the last place on earth that I wanted to be.

7.

I PASS MY DAYS WAITING FOR MARK to call me home again. I write to him every day, and every day I rush to the Internet café to see if he's responded. I endure four hours of classes and spend my afternoons sitting at my desk in front of my arched windows, pretending to flip through flashcards of Arabic verbs warning of death and destruction, war and famine, and watching my neighbors pass through the courtyard and walk up and down the stairs. I jump every time a phone rings. When the door opens, I imagine that Mark might have hastily packed a bag and followed me to the other side of the earth. But alas, it is a boy selling cigarettes, or a peasant woman begging for coins, the laundry boy with a white cloth sack slung over his shoulder, or one of ten thousand cousins coming to visit the Roman Catholic family upstairs.

I talk to him in my head all day. An entire grammar session can pass at the university without me noticing. Jihad Johnny can predict the end of the world and I don't hear a thing. In the evening, when I walk to the market downtown I can go blocks without registering faces, without even noticing the streets I've turned on or hearing the shopkeepers calling out lines in a dozen languages. Instead I rehearse my conversation with Mark should he ever call. I imagine he is telling me that he is sorry, I practice saying that it's not too late for me to come home again.

But he doesn't call, and he doesn't write, save for a few brief e-mails rushed in response to the long letters I compose to him about the loneliness of Damascus and how much I miss home. One of his earliest responses says, *I'm so sorry that I haven't written, but I've been busy working on my dissertation. I've been in good spirits lately. I am so happy to hear that you are settling into your new life.*

It brings me to tears.

I CAN'T MAKE SENSE OF IT, and sometimes I think that if I could be wrong about something so basic as being loved, then I've been wrong about everything. I had been sure. I had honestly thought that I had possession of my own life.

Yesterday evening, the doorbell rang, and as always I ran to the window to see if it might be him, but it was only a heavyset man sauntering across the courtyard toward the opposite side of the house. I thought nothing of it until the Baron began to knock insistently on my window a few minutes later, and I recognized a peculiar look of discomfort in his eyes that made me suspect that he might be calling me in for something other than coffee.

An agent of the Syrian secret police was waiting for me in the Baron's room, sitting at the table and wearing a badly cut black polyester suit, faux leather shoes, and shiny striped socks pulled up high around his ankles. Unlike the secret police in films, there was nothing sleek or even secretive about him. Instead he was busily tearing apart one of the Baron's prized pastries and licking the syrup from his fingertips.

His visit was not entirely unexpected, but I was surprised that it had happened so soon. The secret police, or *mukhabarat* as they are known in Arabic, are notorious in Syria, known for keeping files on anyone of interest and listening in on conversations. The mere mention of them can awaken fear in the hearts of locals and foreigners alike. As an American on a government program who intended on spending a year in the country, I was automatically suspicious.

I took a seat across from him and waited for him to finish his pastry. He reached over to grab a cigarette out of the Baron's pack, lit it, and left it to hang in the ashtray between us.

"Your name?" he asked me in Arabic by way of greeting.

"Stephanie Saldaña."

He pulled a notebook out of his bag and began to scribble down something resembling my name in Arabic letters.

"Where are you from?"

"America." He knew that I was from America, of course. That was the only reason I could fathom for why he had come.

"Where in America?"

"Texas."

He smirked. "Texas! Do you know George Bush?"

I didn't dignify that question with an answer.

From then on we settled in for an intense round of interrogation.

"What is your father's name?"

"What is your mother's name?"

"What is their address?"

"What does your father do?"

"What does your mother do?"

"What are the names of your siblings?"

"How old are they?"

"Where do they live?"

"What do they do?"

It was terrible to speak of my family members as though they were objects, characters in a story, and not who they are, living and breathing human beings whom I care about. Just saying their names felt like a betrayal. I couldn't understand the reason for this line of questioning, particularly since the Fulbright Program had all of my personal details, and when I was finished giving my family's background I hoped that I was done. But Mr. X picked up his cigarette and finished it before lighting another, and I sensed that he was just getting warmed up.

"Where did you go to high school?"

"Where did you go to college?"

"What did you study?"

"What year was that?"

"Nineteen hundred ninety-nine? Well then, what have you done for the last five years?"

Trying to answer his questions in Arabic was exhausting, particularly since my answers were meaningless. His purpose was to intimidate me, perhaps to see if I would trip up. I spent half an hour taking him through the list of countries I had recently visited: Egypt, Jordan, Italy, Greece, Turkey, Spain, China, and Lebanon. He asked me to name them twice. I remembered, twice, not to say that I had been to Israel. I listed all of my jobs and hoped that my prior work as a journalist would not put me under suspicion. He wrote each job down in a long list in his notebook. It all felt, very oddly, like being asked to undress in front of a stranger.

I had been guilty of so much in my past, but not of any of the things he suspected me of.

He waited until the end to ask the cruelest question.

"Are you married?" he asked.

"No," I answered softly.

"How old are you again?"

"Twenty-seven."

"And you're not married?" He looked shocked. "What's wrong with you?"

I was so taken aback that it took me a moment to answer. "I'm waiting," I said, biting my lip.

"Do you know how old girls are when they get married in Syria?"

"I don't know, eighteen?"

"Younger even. No one would ever dream of waiting until she was twenty-seven." Then he wrote down on his pad of paper *Not married*, as though it were a matter of national security.

Then, at last, he was finished. He reached across the table to shake my hand. "Welcome to Syria," he said.

I watched him walk across the courtyard with his thuggish gait, his chin raised high in the air. The Baron walked him to the door, shut it behind him, and turned the latch. Then he returned to his room with his eyes gleaming.

"Bravo, Stefanito," he said. "Coffee?"

But that time I declined. I crossed the courtyard to the washroom, closed the door behind me, and then turned the water on.

The Bread of Angels

For a moment I thought that it was not only my life that I no longer possessed—I no longer even possessed myself. I was no longer a poet, or a scholar, or a traveler; it did not matter that I loved the sea or listening to the cello. Now I was simply an American. Something bigger than me and beyond my control had become the sum of me, canceling out the rest.

I stood in front of the mirror for a long time, scrubbing myself down with hard yellow soap, trying to get clean again.

8.

BY NOW I'VE MADE A SINGLE FRIEND in my class at Damascus University: Michael, the quiet American banker from Washington, D.C. Michael resembles Alex P. Keaton from *Family Ties* transplanted to Damascus. He always comes to class wearing neat, preppy shirts and ironed slacks that look strangely comical in the midst of our class conversations about dynamite and Apache helicopters. I can't quite figure out why he's here, though I guess he could be an undercover weapons inspector—he has that responsible and earnest though somewhat lost, still-haven't-found-what-I'm-looking-for aura about him. Most Americans I've met at the university are either Fulbright scholars or Mormons studying Arabic on their mission abroad, so that a standard joke when meeting an American is "Fulbright or Mormon?" Michael is one of the first non-Mormon, non-Fulbright, non–potential Islamic extremist Americans I've met in Damascus, making him a rare and rather fascinating species.

He is my ally at school. Whenever Jihad Johnny begins one of his tirades about Americans colonizing the world, Michael looks in my direction and catches my eye with a deadpan expression before barely smiling with the edges of his mouth. *Right now we are in hell together*, his smile says to me. And thank God, because I need to know that I am not in this alone.

Michael first approached me during break at the end of our first week of classes. We had just finished a discussion session led by Suleiman the Magnificent on the subject "What are your favorite weapons?" It had been full of enthusiastic participation. Submarines, tanks, machine guns, and of course nuclear bombs had all made the list, but we never settled on a favorite. There were just too many possibilities.

Our classes had recently taken an alarming turn for the worse. A discussion session on "Is marriage necessary?" earlier in the week had led to all-out war. The secular Europeans had all said no, because marriage is nothing more than one person's desire to own another person. Suleiman the Magnificent had said of course, because if a child was born out of wedlock he could not inherit his father's property. When he mentioned his desire to marry four wives, Aisha the Turkish madrassa student began screaming at him, quoting the Quran and accusing him of never being able to treat four wives equally as the prophet Mohammed had. Though I normally kept silent in class, I raised my hand and suggested that two people might want to get married because they were in love. The Europeans all burst into laughter.

When Michael finally pulled me discreetly aside, I was deeply relieved to have another sane person in my corner. "Are you as scared as I am?" he whispered in English. English was forbidden in our class.

"I would be scared," I whispered back. "Sadly, ninety percent of the time I have no idea what's going on."

"You're lucky," he assured me, and flashed a smile.

I know nothing about Michael except for the fact that he is an American. Yet in light of my visit from Mr. X of the secret police and the rather radical nature of my other classmates, I've decided that it is enough to have a single person to trust. I look forward to seeing him every day arriving for class exactly on time in his neatly pressed shirts, some semblance of order in a world suddenly so unpredictable, his shirttail tucked in and his belt firmly fastened, not a single hair out of place or the smallest scuff on his shiny brown loafers.

Sometimes after school we sit together in a coffee shop and review grammar together, and I love the chance to speak to him in English, for all of those foreign words to be balanced out by the weight of the familiar. We splurge and buy three-dollar cups of coffee at InHouse Coffee, a new chic Syrian coffee chain with menus only in English, where the Syrian jet set gathers to drink frozen cappucinos and watch music videos flashing on giant screens. The girl behind the counter wears a green baseball cap, and when she hands me my coffee she chirps the only full sentence she knows in English: "Have a perfect day!" My days are so far from perfect that I have to try hard not to laugh at her.

The Bread of Angels

Michael is also homesick, and so tonight we've bypassed the coffee shop and decided to see a film together, less a date than our mutual attempt to engage in something reminiscent of our pre-Syrian life. I choose the closest modest outfit I have to "American girl clothes," loose khaki trousers and a long-sleeved maroon shirt, and I walk to the Sham Palace Theater to meet him.

The Sham Palace Theater is the only theater in Damascus that shows English-language movies, mostly B-list movies that barely make it to the theaters in the States. But tonight we're here to see Michael Moore's film *Fahrenheit 9/11*, which has been selling out for weeks. Though the Syrian government censors everything from books to films that enter the country, not a single moment of Moore's film has been censored. Locals have been reveling in the public blasting of President George Bush by one of his own citizens, proof that they are not alone in their disdain for him. We buy our two tickets, and when the usher in his black suit shows us to our seats, shining his flashlight on two chairs in the back, I look around and notice that we are the only two foreigners in the room.

Then the curtain parts and the credits begin. From the light emanating from the movie screen I can make out groups of teenaged girls in headscarves, a few couples, and large groups of young men seated in rows. Together we sit transfixed as we watch the war enter into the room. The screen fills up with American soldiers riding in tanks, breaking into houses. Iraqi women are awakened from their sleep. Children wail. The audience and the film seem to fuse into one, and the people around me sink back into their chairs, staring wide-eyed.

Then it comes again—that sense of being tied to something bigger than I am, something beyond my control. As the film rolls on, I start to feel claustrophobic. Each time an Iraqi speaks, there are no subtitles. Everyone around me simply understands, viscerally. But I don't—I've never heard the dialect, and they speak so quickly. It is only when the Americans speak that I understand, and the subtitles flash on-screen so that everyone else in the room begins to read. People are wounded in two languages. But for the most part, English is the language of those who are killing. Arabic is the language of those who are dying.

I sit between Michael and a Syrian man, who keeps shifting his feet back and forth on the ground in front of us. I can feel Michael responding to the English. I can feel the other man's silence and his body reacting each time an Iraqi speaks. Sometimes he hides his face in his hands. Sometimes he looks down at the floor. When a young African-American soldier in the film says that he would never return to Iraq to kill another country's poor people, he whispers quietly to the screen, *Shukran leki.* Thank you.

But other American soldiers say terrible, shocking things. Around me the people shiver. I shiver also. Most of all I think to myself, with new, uncomfortable confusion, *Listen to that. They're speaking my language.*

9.

A DAY LATER, Michael and I are studying together in his house in Bab Touma, just a few blocks down from my house. His host family is traveling for the week, much to his relief, and so we make space for ourselves in their traditional living room, spreading out our books and papers on the table. Michael rents a tiny bedroom on the second floor of this family's house, just between the rooms of several siblings, which means that he has no privacy. Perhaps I *do* have the most beautiful room in Bab Touma, after all.

He pours me a glass of tea, and I realize that it is the first time I have been alone with a man other than the Baron since I left Mark in Boston. It feels oddly intimate. "So, what do you think of the other students in the class?" he asks. "How about that Jihad Johnny?"

I laugh. Johnny had been wearing the same floor-length gray robe to class every day for a week now, and his beard was getting longer. He had recently mentioned that he planned on settling in Syria for good. Unfortunately, despite his enthusiasm for the subject, his Arabic didn't seem to be improving. As a result the Germans had usurped his role as the most vocally anti-American students. "I don't know where they dug up those people," I confess. "They're scary. I hope they wait until I finish class before they kill me. I'd like to die with at least intermediate Arabic."

He smiles, and I see his face relax into an unfamiliar, less guarded, and more human face. "I always said that you should never trust a foreigner who comes to study in Syria."

"Apparently not."

It is a common joke between us. Since, mathematically speaking, there are very few Europeans and Americans living in Syria, and we figure some of them must be up to no good, we often speculate on their ulterior motives. Pretending that our classmates are spies and double agents makes memorizing grammatical points more interesting.

I turn again to reviewing my Arabic flashcards, flipping through a list of jungle animals left over from a text of socialist parables: monkey, giraffe, elephant. I am looking at a picture of a monkey when I notice that an uncomfortable silence has settled in the room.

I watch Michael moving his pencil back and forth on the table nervously. "Listen, Stephanie, there's something I want to tell you," he says. "But I need you to keep this to yourself until I leave."

I nod, nervously. I'm not sure that I'm prepared to carry other people's secrets in Damascus.

"I'm Jewish," he announces. A weight drops off of my heart. So that was all. There are so many Jewish foreigners studying in Damascus that they may as well open up their own yeshiva. Though many of them lie and say that they are Christians, this is just to make daily life easier, not because they have some sinister, secret agenda. Damascus was once home to one of the most ancient Jewish communities in the world, and there are even a small number of Syrian Jews still living a few streets down from my house. It makes sense that Jews would be interested in Damascus, and as far as I know there is nothing expressly keeping an American Jew from studying here.

"I actually live in Israel," he continues. Now he had me. "I made up that entire story about being a banker in D.C."

"Wow." I try to think of something to say, but he has left me speechless.

Israel and Syria have been official enemies for more than fifty years, the border between the two countries an impassable no-man's-land except for the few United Nations workers authorized to travel between sides. Israelis, and anyone who has ever been to Israel, are prohibited from visiting Syria. In fact, according to most Syrians, Israel doesn't even exist, and the question on visa applications asks only, "Have you ever visited Occupied Palestine?" While some foreigners travel to Israel and Syria on separate passports, it took audacity and a certain stupidity for a Hebrew-speaking Jew living in Israel to come spend a month in Syria studying at a state-run institution. It was a miracle that Mr. X had not found out. The entire spectacle was as shocking and unlikely as a Syrian trying to slip, quietly and unnoticed, across the border to spend a few months in Tel Aviv learning Hebrew. All the foreigners at the university were so frightened of even mentioning the word *Israel* that we collectively referred to it as Disneyland. While I had often met foreigners who looked forward to visiting Disneyland, I had never met someone in Syria who worked there.

I don't want to be here. I want to be out of this room and back in the house off Straight Street again.

"You didn't guess, did you?" he asks.

"No, I thought you were a banker. I was just wondering why a banker wanted to learn Arabic."

"You know, there have been a few times in class when I said words in Hebrew instead of Arabic, and I was scared that someone would notice. But I guess no one knows what Hebrew sounds like."

"I guess not," I say. Or if someone did, he certainly wasn't about to raise his hand and offer that information in a classroom run by the Syrian state.

He is clearly oblivious to how uncomfortable I am. "You know," he continues, "I'm not a spy or anything. I work on dialogue between Israelis and Palestinians. It's just that you can't speak Arabic for twenty seconds in Israel before someone breaks in with English or Hebrew. Syria is the only place I could ever hope to actually *speak* the Arabic language."

I wish he would stop saying those words. *Israel. Hebrew.* Doesn't he know that people are listening? It would only take a bread boy walking past at the wrong moment who was paid to keep an eye out, a neighbor who coincidentally stopped by.

I turn back to my animal flashcards, flipping through one after another, with no hope of even processing the words. I can feel Michael studying me.

"Stephanie?"

I continue flipping.

"Are you going to be traveling this weekend?"

"Yes," I tell him, relieved to remember that this is true and not just a tactic to avoid him. "Actually, I am traveling to some Byzantine sites in the north."

He smiles. "Do you see how my room is inside of this house, so that everyone can see everything that I do all of the time?" I nod. Since he had uttered the word *Israel*, I have thought of little else.

"Your room has a separate entrance from the other rooms in the house, doesn't it?" he continues.

I nod.

"This weekend is Yom Kippur, the Jewish Day of Atonement. Do you think I could use your house to pray in while you are out of town? It's impossible for me to do it here, and I can't think of where else I might go."

He looks down at the table shyly. "I'm not that observant, but I've never missed Yom Kippur in my life. For us it's the holiest day of the year."

Yom Kippur. The Day of Atonement, in which God decides who among us will be written in the Book of Life.

I swallow hard and tell him that I'll think about it.

10.

I KNOW WHAT I SHOULD DO. I have read stories of Jews in concentration camps risking everything in order to complete their prayers, even when their lives were in danger. And I can't help but be moved by what Michael is asking me. He hasn't yet lost the ability to believe that prayer matters, that it is worth protecting at all costs.

I also know what part I am supposed to play. I have been rehearsing this moment since childhood, and it has been reinforced a hundred times since then, through *The Diary of Anne Frank* and the lives of the righteous among the Gentiles whose trees are planted in Israel, through history lessons and museum displays and the many stories of lives changed and saved by a single human being with the courage to stand up when it makes more sense to stay silent. I am supposed to put myself at risk. I am supposed to hand Michael the key to the door.

But the fact is, I'm not brave. I want to say, *Yes, of course, come, pray in my room, don't be ashamed of who you are*, and yet every voice in my body is screaming, *You can't do it, don't do it, don't do it!* As I walk along the streets, I visualize him in my head praying on Yom Kippur, the outline of his body vaguely visible through my thin curtains as he bows his head over his Hebrew text. I imagine the sound of his chanting leaving his mouth and escaping beneath the door into the courtyard, the voice gathering like water within the fountain for the neighbors to hear. I imagine the frame of the Baron's face, staring in through the windows, his mouth opening in awe and perhaps even fear. I imagine the horrible visit by Mr. X that would certainly follow.

I try to convince myself otherwise, and yet I know in my gut that I will not allow Michael to use my room to pray. I try to tell myself that it is for practical reasons. The mere fact of me, a single woman, giving a man the keys to my room would be enough to cause a scandal in a society where many still believe that unmarried men and women should not even speak without a chaperone. If Michael were to come alone, and someone were to look in the windows and suspect that a Jew was praying in my house, then my status in Syria would be at risk. Questions would be asked. Why was he praying in my house, of all places, and not his own? Was I perhaps really Jewish and hiding my identity from my neighbors? Why had I lied? Worse yet, what if they found out that he lives in Israel? My presence as an American in Syria was already suspicious enough. I did not need my neighbors or the secret police suspecting that I might also be a spy aiding a country they consider themselves to be at war with.

Yet I also know that five years ago, I might have let him pray in my room without thinking about it. But I was a different person then, a better person, and I don't see how I can go back again. When Michael asked that small, naïve question, he could not possibly understand how much I have worked to make my life in Syria that of an ordinary girl—for all of the strangeness and suspicion to be wiped clean of me. I can't let myself be found out. I promised myself that, if I ever decided to return to the Middle East, then I would come as a student, not someone who gets caught up in the story. That's the only way I can handle it.

When Mr. X had asked me about my past in the Middle East, I had offered up only the bare bones of my years in and out of this complex region. I did not tell him that when I had accepted a fellowship five years ago to travel in the Middle East, I, too, had first arrived in Israel, that most forbidden of countries, alone and lost. I took a flat in the heart of downtown Jerusalem, on the second floor of a loft, just above a recent Russian immigrant who kept her dog chained up all day and taught me how to separate the dishes in her kosher kitchen. A few days later, I walked to the West Bank town of Bethlehem. On the other side of the checkpoint, a local man offered me a lift, and with that brief encounter I entered the Arab world. In the town square I was offered another ride, with a man who took me door to door until a nun answered the yellow gateway of a convent of Palestinian nuns. I heard the man speaking to her in Arabic, what must have been him explaining that I had no place to stay. When he had finished, she nodded and smiled at me kindly.

"We've always thought that we might take guests here," she said. "I guess that you'll be our first."

I stayed in that convent for the remainder of my days in the city, waking up to the rosary chanted in Arabic in the chapel, and during the afternoons I walked through the city where Jesus was born. On every corner locals spoke to me: the bell keeper at the Church of the Nativity, dozens of Palestinian shopkeepers who invited me in to tea, men carving olive wood. I fell in love with them and their quiet piety and hospitality. I spent the next three months traversing my two lives, between Israel and Palestine, making a home in both worlds at once. It was July 1999.

In college in Vermont I had been a recluse, a stranger to most of my classmates, usually holed up in my tiny dorm room trying to escape the blistering winter. I had grown up middle class, around men who appreciated beer and bowling, and so I felt largely out of place among my wealthy classmates, many of whom had attended elite New England boarding schools, not a Catholic school in San Antonio whose senior class had been ruled by a group of young men in tight jeans and cowboy boots who called themselves "the Farmers." At times I was so lonely that I turned in my library books late on purpose, just so I would get late slips in the mail and could pretend that someone had written me a letter from home.

I never took chances in college or risked failure, and it was the bewildering kindness of those I met in the Middle East who finally shook me out of the protective shell I had learned to wear around myself. I made more friends in a few months than I had in four years. I had grown up dreaming of becoming a poet, and in the Arab world I found a place where everyone dreamed of becoming a poet and even shoe shiners and shepherds could recite poems to me by heart. I felt oddly at home in the Middle East, with its Texas-sized heat and enormous families and huge plates of food at dinner and religious festivals similar to the San Antonio I had left behind, with all of my fourteen aunts and uncles and thirty-something cousins. When I finished traveling in Israel, instead of heading to Italy as I had planned, I moved on to Egypt, Jordan, Syria, and Turkey. In Egypt, six Israeli boys, on their last trip together before joining the army, invited me to hike with them through the deserts of the Sinai, and we shared meals and slept beneath the sky where Moses once saw God in a burning bush. I felt so free and full of life that I wanted to cry out in thanks. I hitchhiked in Syria and slept in the houses of strangers in Jordan. I made friends at every stop, traveled fearlessly, and in some mysterious way discovered a part of myself that I was not even aware existed. "Little Flame" people started to call me, because I was full of passion. Something in the Middle East awakened the deepest core of me. It made me a better person. It made me the best person I had ever been.

I left the Middle East in July 2000. Two months later the Second Intifada began in Israel and the West Bank, and I watched the news from my apartment in China as the cities I knew were transformed into combat zones and Israelis and Palestinians went to war. Palestinian militants hid out in my beloved Church of the Nativity in Bethlehem, where I had so often gone to pray, where I had begun to recover the faith I had lost in my childhood. The pizza shop where I met friends in Jerusalem was bombed, and so was the market where I did my shopping, and the café where I drank hot chocolate. The cities of Hebron and Nablus, which had once showered welcomes on me from the street, became the sites of car bombs and killings and almost daily clashes between locals and the Israeli army. I had found my heart, only to lose it in the most violent way imaginable.

After my relationship in China fell apart, I moved to Beirut to work as a journalist. Though I wrote about music and art, every now and then work brought me to Palestinian refugee camps, where I walked with my notebook among pools of open sewage, watching young children playing in the streets with toy guns, Hezbollah bands tied around their heads. I visited a man in Tripoli, just after his Kentucky Fried Chicken franchise was bombed, simply for being an American company. Just twenty-five years old, I passed my days walking through that city scarred by fifteen years of bloody civil war, the bullet holes still visible in the sides of buildings, and at night I wrote poems about the city swimming with angels. I still loved the Middle East. I loved it as I had loved nowhere else in my entire life. But it felt like loving a man in critical condition, who could die at any moment.

At the end of every day at the office in Beirut, just after I filed my story, I used to put aside half an hour and open the news wires to look over the photographs of the day. It was my evening meditation, as the sun was falling down over the mountains and illuminating the houses looking over the sea. I would flip through one photo after another: a boy shot to death in Bethlehem, a mother weeping after a bombing in Jerusalem, the wreckage of downtown New York, the dead in Afghanistan. I filed them away in my memory, where they slipped in between images I had seen myself. At night I dreamed of all of them.

By the time I returned to Boston, I was haunted at night by those images I collected like icons of the dead. I wanted to forget them. I spent two years in the attempt, passing afternoons in cafés like everyone else, willing myself to fall in love, doing anything I could imagine to get back part of who I had once been—that girl walking between Israel and Palestine, full of passion and poetry, before the world around her began falling down.

My life was turning out all wrong. Everything had become jumbled, mixed up, the opposite of what I imagined it would be, and it had happened so quickly. I tried not to think about the fact that the first man I ever loved had been recently sent off to fight in Afghanistan and Iraq. I tried to disassociate it from my life, to forget about those he was killing, those he loved who were being killed beside him. Yet whenever I saw an image of the war in Iraq, I saw something familiar on both sides. I saw on the Arab side those who let me sleep in their homes. Behind the face of the American soldier, I saw the young man who once slow-danced with me in the middle of a street in Texas, holding me close, before handing me the tiny diamond ring that was all he could afford and asking me to marry him.

I tried to forget that those Israeli boys I walked through the Sinai desert with were now in uniform, patrolling the streets of the Palestinians who asked me in for tea, or that one of my very closest friends, an Israeli, had carried out her military service near the border of Lebanon. My friends were now all on enemy sides. And now I had become the enemy.

THERE IS A STORY I have never told anyone before—not Mark, not my family, not my closest friends—one that I have tried to forget until now. When I was a young journalist in Lebanon, after several months of reporting, I was asked to cover a story in the Palestinian refugee camps on the outskirts of Beirut. It was the week of the Arab League Summit, and the leaders of Arab countries had gathered to discuss the plight of Palestinian refugees in Beirut. I was sent to see what those refugees thought about the fact that their fates were being bartered and balanced and traded like poker chips.

At the time I spoke only a little Arabic, and I arrived with my translator. The streets had emptied, with most Palestinians glued in front of their television sets, still hoping that their fate would be decided after more than fifty years in uncertain exile. Security around the camps had been tightened to prevent riots from breaking out.

After a few minutes my translator led me into a tiny, very poor house. Inside a woman, her husband, and several children were standing together. And in the woman's arms, a baby was wailing.

I tried to interview them, but the baby kept wailing, then coughing violently. She screamed herself into such a fit that her face turned bright red and then darkened toward blue.

"She's sick," I told the mother awkwardly, and she nodded.

"The roads are closed," she said. "I can't get her to a clinic until tomorrow when they are opened again."

The baby wouldn't stop screaming. I was suddenly anxious that something might truly be wrong. I thought that with my press pass, maybe I could get them to a hospital. At least I could try.

But then a voice in my head said, *Don't start getting involved now, Stephanie. This is none of your business. If you start, when will it ever end?*

I left, and I never saw that family again.

SOMETIMES, WHEN I RETURNED TO AMERICA, I would dream of that baby screaming. Or the thought of it would come at the strangest times, when I was sitting down to coffee in Boston or looking out a window of the library at the falling snow. That child screaming. And it seemed to me so strange, so utterly surreal, that in the same space of time I could be reading a book and somewhere on the other side of the earth a man was being shot, or a child was in pain, when everything in front of me looked so still and quiet and even, for a brief moment, entirely beautiful.

Now, two and a half years later, Michael is asking to pray in my room, asking me to help his name to be written in the Book of Life. But I still can't do it. Part of me hates him for even asking. I'm exhausted now, too tired from the simple weight of being in this world as it is to go about trying to change it. I'm tired of passing the corner store selling pictures of Hamas leaders alongside posters of Egyptian rock stars. I'm tired of the portrait of Hafez al-Assad staring down at me from the roof of the building across from our classroom window. I'm tired of wondering which shopkeeper is watching me for the secret police. I just want something resembling a carefree day. I want to walk home without thinking about militants in neighboring countries. I want to catch a taxi without being asked why women and children are dying in Iraq. Michael has ruined my last bit of ordinary life, a room in a house with windows and laundry and showers in the afternoon. Mark is gone. Home is gone. Even the Middle East that I once knew is gone. And the person I once was—that girl crossing a desert with her bag on her back, radiant and full of hope—she is gone beyond retrieving.

So I refuse to give Michael an answer. Every day I slide out of class as quickly as possible and into the street. I know that he must be hurt that his closest friend in Damascus no longer acknowledges his existence. It hurts me, too.

11.

At night, I walk through the alleys on the other side of Straight Street where thousands of Jews had lived until just over ten years ago, when they were allowed to immigrate, provided that they did not move to Israel. Their streets look ghostly now, the alleys of empty houses with their windows sunken in, full of trash and old wood, the still-bright light of the summer casting strange shadows against their back walls. I cannot blame Michael for coming to Damascus. The Jewish community in Syria was once one of the oldest in the world. Jews had lived for such a long time here that St. Paul himself came to preach to them in the synagogues nearly two thousand years ago. I don't believe for a moment that he came here to study Arabic—he could have studied Arabic anywhere. Maybe he came here in search of a missing piece from his own past. Or maybe he is just as I was once—young and daring and full of reckless hope.

I keep walking, turning into an almost invisible street, and after climbing over piles of tree limbs I find myself standing in front of an old abandoned synagogue, locked up behind bars. She looks lonely. Her enormous brass doors are sealed shut. Across them, a menorah stretches out beside an engraving of a Torah scroll, two birds with their wings spread open, as if to embrace me. She is one of the last left. I almost cry, confronted with that empty building, with all that it represents, like the Jewish cemetery I once stumbled across in Beirut on the border between East and West, its tombstones engraved in Arabic, French, and Hebrew, the only remnant of an entire community gone.

Yom Kippur passes, and I never tell Michael that he cannot use my room to pray. I am too ashamed to speak to him. Instead, I mark my own quiet Day of Atonement, considering the sins I have carried that year and have not asked to be forgiven.

As the semester comes to a close, I take a long evening walk, out past the Old City and into the broad streets of new Damascus with its banks and flashy hotels, not far from where Michael and I once sat side by side to watch a film together. Then suddenly, he is there, looking at me, across a lane of traffic, startled and trying to balance a pile of mail in his arms.

"Stephanie!" he calls out, and he crosses the street, dodging cars, until I have no choice but to talk to him.

"I've been trying to track you down. I want to exchange addresses before I leave."

He stops in front of me, and I have a chance to study him. Something looks different. His shirt is still ironed, perfectly tucked in, but something about him looks off.

We're standing on one of the busiest streets in Damascus, but I know that this is my only chance to apologize. "Listen, Michael. I'm sorry that I never, um, spoke to you about um, you know." I look around the street anxiously. "About Yom Kippur. I couldn't. The neighbors would have had a field day if I gave a man the keys to my room. I'm sorry. I should have said something."

I'm ashamed at my cowardice. He smiles weakly. "Don't worry about it. I understood."

We stand there in the street in silence.

"So, um, for that day." *That day.* "Did you find anyone to help you?"

"There are still Jews in Damascus, you know," he says softly.

Yes, I know.

"I found the address of a rabbi from a contact I have in America."

I look at him, standing in the middle of the street, the mail still halfway out of his hands. He looks like the picture of sadness. Like the sadness contained in those van Gogh paintings of shoes, which have walked beyond their capacity and now want to fold, quietly, into themselves.

"The night before Yom Kippur, I called him up and asked to meet with him, to see if I could spend the holiday with their community. We met for a few moments in the street. He looked frightened. He barely spoke a word to me. He simply gave me the holy books and then asked me to go away and pray on my own. He said that he was too scared to let me pray with them."

He stops for a moment, not to look at me, but to look somewhere else, an invisible point in the air. "When he said that, I actually felt tears come up in my eyes. It was the first time in my life I have been turned away by another Jew."

I want to tell him, *He didn't turn you away. Neither did I. We were turning away from something inside of ourselves.* But I say nothing.

THEN MICHAEL'S DESK AT SCHOOL IS EMPTY. When classes are over, I don't have to rush out the door to leave first. There is no one hoping to speak to me.

So I make my way outside slowly, through the crowds of Syrian students, and instead of fighting for a taxi I stand on the edge of the highway, looking out, until a driver stops of his own accord and rolls down the window. I tell him my address, and then I keep my silence in the backseat, looking at the streets blurring past. After a few moments, he attempts to start a conversation.

"How do you like Damascus?" he asks.

"It's fine."

"How long have you been living here?"

"Just a few weeks."

"Oh, really?" His face brightens. "Are you here with your children?"

"No," I tell him quietly.

"Why not?"

"Because I don't have any yet."

He looks confused. "You mean, you're not married?" he asks. There is a tone of honest surprise in his voice, a tone I'm not expecting, and suddenly, and completely without warning, I begin to cry in the back of his taxi. "No," I tell him. "Someone in America is waiting for me."

But it isn't true. No one is waiting for me. The driver pulls up to the edge of my neighborhood, bewildered by my tears, and looks at me kindly. He refuses to accept my money when I try to pay my fare.

12.

October

I CONTINUE ATTENDING ARABIC CLASSES, but by early October I simply sit behind my desk, counting the minutes until I can leave. Something has changed ever since Michael left to return to Israel. I sometimes think that, even though I did not let him use my room to pray, he managed to take it away from me anyway. I can no longer live obliviously. All of the conflicts I want so much to avoid press up against me in streets, like beggars who corner me in the most isolated places, hitting me up for all of my spare change.

By now there is no use avoiding the war in Iraq, trying to pretend that it is someone else's war playing itself out in a distant country. It appears everywhere. I glimpse it on television screens flashing behind open doors: wounded children, men on stretchers bleeding from the head, a body part visible beneath a pile of rubble. On the front page each morning, funeral processions wait for me, women weeping, cars bombed and smoking on the side of the road, families mourning at the hospital, infants killed by mistake. We are only a day's drive away from Baghdad, less than the distance between San Antonio and El Paso. It feels almost close enough to touch.

The more of the Arabic language I understand, the more I can pick up the conversations between shopkeepers, the background noise of the radio in the taxi each morning. Only then do I recognize that the war is slowly closing in on us. We are three and a half weeks away from the American elections—and my neighbors are afraid that if George Bush is reelected, then America will invade Syria, and the war that has been whispered about for so long will come to the streets in which we live.

Look at yourselves, I want to tell them. *Stop waiting. The war is already here.*

BY NOW THE STREETS ARE SWELLING with Iraqi men and women wearing flowing black *abayas*, carrying their tired eyes and strange accents from the places they fled. I watch them every afternoon, standing in line to buy bread, or disappearing into the Shiite mosque in the Old City to pray, and it often strikes me how easy it is to spot those who find themselves out of place in the world. *Hundreds of thousands of them*, the neighbors tell me, with still more arriving every day. I hear them speaking in the streets, in their dialect full of consonants we drop in Syrian, calling out greetings I don't recognize. I try to stop myself from shuddering when I hear that dialect. It sounds harsh. It sounds like war to me.

My neighbors warn me to keep my distance. "I heard a woman had her handbag stolen by an Iraqi on a bicycle just last week," the *Ustez* clucks, shaking his head. "Now when you walk, you keep your purse close to your body. Do you hear me?" In a café, as a man begins strumming the strings on the oud and singing a folk song, the girl next to me leans over and whispers in my ear, "He's Iraqi. I don't like the sound of his voice."

In my years in and out of the Middle East, I have learned the particular logic of life on the edge of war. An Iraqi from Baghdad once told me that, on the eve of the American invasion in 2003, his neighbors had convinced themselves that war was impossible because they were still drinking tea in cafés and eating pastries. *Who would be drinking tea on the night before an invasion?* they asked one another. *That just wouldn't happen!*

Yet the invasion came despite their pastries, shocking and awing all of them, just as the bombing of Poland happened in September 1939, despite the fact that locals could not believe that it was possible, for it was such a sunny day.

I'd like to think that after one man learns that his fluffy pastry is no match for an air raid, he might think to pass on the news, but so far my neighbors remain oblivious. They have honestly convinced themselves that they can hold the world together by maintaining their routines and habits, as though they are the Jewish sages who keep the world from collapsing because of their prayers. The Baron's routine borders on the obsessive. In the morning he wakes up and drinks a cup of Turkish coffee before watching the news. At exactly noon he makes a cup of Lipton tea and eats a piece of cake. In the afternoon he changes into his pressed clothes from Milano and takes a walk through the neighborhood, where he joins his elderly friends for exactly two glasses of tea taken with spiced bread. He returns home, takes a shower at two in the afternoon, and then has a nap. When he wakes up he drinks a single Nescafé. Then, in the evening after dinner, he sips watered-down whiskey and allows himself the pleasure of smoking French cigarettes. Not a single detail varies from one day to another. "I have discipline," he tells me defensively when I tease him. "*Discipline.* Do you know what discipline is?"

The *Ustez*'s wife washes out her laundry every morning. The bread boys traverse the courtyard, the *gaz* vendors ride their ribboned horses through the streets, and the two lovebirds come to meet us at six thirty in the evening. We rely on one another's fidelity, for a change in the routine might mean that something has tipped off balance and that the entire world as we know it might collapse.

I check my mail every day for letters. Hold imaginary conversations in the morning with Mark. I go to school. I drink coffee with the Baron. Most of all, I've started taking photographs.

Every evening, just before five o'clock, I abandon my notebooks at my desk and snake through the crowded markets of the Old City, sliding past the gold markets and spice shops, carpet stalls and cafés, past the Azem

Palace with its inlaid tiles, the sweets stores with their candy-coated almonds and Turkish delight, the curtains of Islamic headscarves hung in long, flowing rows, and down a broad, cobbled street where the western gate of the Temple of Jupiter once stood. At the exact heart of the Old City, I turn right and push through a black metal gate and take a moment to cover my long brown hair with a scarf. I then remove my shoes and allow my bare feet to press onto the cold marble tiles. Sliding my shoes into my backpack, I walk straight ahead until I am staring up at an enormous brass door that stands at least four times the height of my body and is pushed wide open. Once I have crossed the threshold I am within the courtyard of the eighth-century Umayyad Mosque, the fourth holiest site in Islam. It always succeeds in taking my breath away.

The Umayyad Mosque is the most beautiful place I have ever been in my life. The front facade resembles a Byzantine church, covered in dazzling mosaics depicting paradise, fruit trees and flowing rivers, celestial cities sparkling in the sun. The lower portion of the mosque is covered in marble tiles, the wooden doors carved geometrically by artisans. Yet it is not simply the building—something about the space it occupies seems to form some holy link to heaven, which is why I am not surprised that it has been at different times the site of the Temple of Jupiter, the Temple of Hadad, the Church of John the Baptist, and now one of the most stunning Islamic buildings in the world. For the most part, Syrians do not come here to pray—they come here simply to *be*, to walk hand in hand through the courtyard, to picnic and play with their children.

I come to the Umayyad Mosque to witness a miracle. At around five o'clock every evening, the sun begins to set over Damascus, and the light gathers in a pool over the white marble courtyard, illuminating the tiles, until everyone walking on it appears as though they are angels. Light reflects from the ground up into their bodies. They look weightless. Each time I witness it, I am almost moved to tears—at the sight of humans so ethereal, so transcendent that they might have wings, might press their toes against the ground and then lift off, away from all of this madness. Nothing appears sinister in that light.

Every evening, I remain for an hour or so, sitting anonymously in a corner of the immense courtyard, a sudden quiet and open space in the midst of the crowds of the market. I watch the couples holding hands, the women carrying their husbands' shoes, the children who open their arms like wings and race out to join the flocks of pigeons taking flight. I snap one photograph after another, of human beings like that, caught in a moment—beneath the marble pillars and great glistening mosaics, near the tomb that still holds the ancient bones of St. John the Baptist, in this beautiful haven where locals say that Muslims and Christians both prayed in the earliest years of Islam. When the call to prayer sounds, it is the loveliest I have ever heard in my life, three voices instead of one, all singing together in harmony.

For just an hour a day, the war disappears, the war and any possibility that it might come to us. There is only that white space of light, and the laughing faces of children, and the trees and rivers of paradise shining down on me from above.

When I return home, I enter the images into my computer, and I spend the early evening zooming in on the photographs and trying to discover details I had missed in life. Here in the corner of a photo, a woman clutches her handbag, her fingers holding on with a ferocity that had escaped me earlier. Now I can see a boy walking past, sneaking a forbidden glance at two girls cloaked in white gowns. A Shiite woman, entirely covered in black except for her eyes, lifts a child to her mouth to be kissed, his yellow overalls flashing against her gown. Syrian soldiers walk arm in arm, their heavy army boots filling their empty hands.

I sometimes smile when I think about returning to America a year from now, armed with those photographs, how I will show them to Mark and to my family. I won't need to tell them about the other parts of my life—about the loneliness, about betraying Michael, about the refugees in the streets and the war pressing down on us in the air.

"Isn't Damascus beautiful?" I'll say. "I've just never been in a place with such remarkable light."

Today at the mosque it is raining, and still the light remains. Children are sliding on the wet stones, with their pants rolled up to their knees. I take their pictures.

A group of four young boys run up to meet me. "Take our photos!" they call out. "Here! Here!" I do, over and over, capturing the ridiculous beauty of them, wet and messy and laughing at the rain, playing hide-and-seek among the red marble pillars of the mosque.

One of them approaches me. He must be nine years old, and he is absolutely arresting, with blue jeans, a denim shirt, and a look of innocence in his eyes I have rarely seen in anything, human or animal. He sits down beside me, like I have known him all his life.

"Are you a Muslim?" he asks.

"No, I'm a Christian."

"Then why are you here?"

"I like it." I smile at him. "Do you know that John the Baptist is buried here?"

"Yes, Yahya, the son of Zachariah. But he's a Muslim!"

"He's also a Christian."

He looks at me in curiosity. "Do you pray?"

I have not thought about prayer in such a long time that his question awakens a sadness from deep inside me, the kind I feel when something reminds me of the dead. "Sometimes, I guess."

"Show us how you pray."

I am embarrassed. Then he kneels down in the mosque courtyard, makes the sign of the cross, and folds his hands together.

There are dozens of people in the courtyard. I reach out and touch his shoulder. "Please stop. I don't want people to think that I'm converting you."

He laughs. His friend is standing behind him now. "Can you tell us part of the Bible in Arabic?"

I only know one part in Arabic, a paragraph I memorized years ago. I take a deep breath, and whisper, "In the beginning, God created the heavens and the earth. And God said: Let there be light. And there was light. And God saw that the light was good. He separated the light from the darkness. The light he called day, and the darkness he called night. It was evening, and it was morning. The first day."

The boys nod their heads. "We know that one. We have it, too."

I let them use my camera for a few moments, watching them capturing birds, taking photos of one another, rushing back to see those images appear on the camera screen like miracles, faces called into existence by their own hands. I remember that in Arabic, the word *sawwir*, meaning "to shape or form," is the same as the word "to take a photograph." It is the word used in the Bible when God creates man in his image.

The light begins to fade and the children walking darken into shadows. The call to prayer lifts out from the minaret. Before I leave, I turn to the boys one final time. "Can you tell me about Jesus?"

The boy with the blue shirt and shining eyes points to the sky. "Do you see that minaret? That is where Jesus is going to come at the end of time." Yes, the famous Jesus minaret, where Syrian Muslims believe that the prophet Jesus will descend at the end of the world.

"What will happen?"

"Everyone will be gathered up."

"Gathered to what?"

"To God."

I imagine people, like flower petals spilled out over the earth, gathered again into larger hands. It must be nice, to be gathered into the hands of the infinite. "Do you think it will only be Muslims who are gathered, or Christians also?"

The boys consult between themselves, in a football huddle, then pull apart and smile at me. "I guess it will be everyone."

Then I want to embrace them. I feel as though they have blessed me, the way my grandfather blessed me when I was a child, pressing his thumb on my forehead and forming the sign of the cross, to keep me safe.

They rise to leave. "I hope we see you again," they call out.

"You can find me here."

The boy in the blue shirt, with all of his startling innocence, turns to me and asks, "Are you a holy person?"

I don't think so, I start to say, but then I stop myself. "I don't know," I tell him instead.

13.

I'M ON MY WAY HOME from the mosque the following evening when I notice a shop I've never seen before, a tiny stall displaying colorful oil paintings of the Old City and a few painted portraits. Near the entrance, a thin, slightly nervous man is painting on an easel with a metal palette knife, moving between the canvas and the paints with such speed one might think he was afraid they might dry without warning. Beside him, a heavyset man with thick, wavy black hair slicked down on the side and impossibly dark eyes is inviting passersby into the shop.

I stop in front of the store and they greet me excitedly.

"Welcome, welcome. Come in! Come in!" The skinny, nervous one pours me a glass of sweet tea before I have time to stop him.

"You're new here?" I ask. "I never noticed your shop before."

The heavyset man walks over to shake my hand. "We're fresh from Iraq," he announces. "Allow me to introduce myself. I'm Hassan, and that there is Ali."

Ali salutes me. "At your service." Hassan pulls a stool from the back of the shop and places it in front of me, and I take a seat.

"Where are you from?"

"From America," I say shyly, looking down.

He doesn't even flinch. "Then welcome," he responds, with his great eyes gleaming. "It's very nice to meet you."

Hassan and Ali's place looks less like a shop than a walk-in storage closet, with every available surface covered except for the ceiling. On the walls, paintings of old Ottoman houses stare in on me, their roofs folding onto one another like those in my neighborhood. Piles of old postcards are stacked behind an easel in the back. It smells like oil paint and cardamom and cigarette smoke, mixed in with the faint scent of their two bodies, sweaty from sitting in that small room all afternoon in the heat.

Hassan fetches me a cigarette, lights it, and hands it to me, and I accept it gratefully, despite the fact that I don't really smoke. Silence seems less awkward with something in my mouth.

"How's Iraq these days?" I ask hesitantly.

He whistles under his breath. "It's *fawda*, chaos. Every day there's another kidnapping, another car bomb. That's Iraq."

It's what I've already suspected from the flood of images I've seen on the news at night. When I'd first arrived here, there had still been the faintest possibility that Iraqis might be better off because of the American invasion. But lately insurgents had been setting off bombs in the cities, so that people in Baghdad could no longer walk to the market without worrying what might happen on the way. From their first names I could guess that Hassan and Ali were Shiites, which meant their neighborhoods might be particularly at risk of falling prey to bombs from Sunni insurgents.

"You still have family there?"

"Of course, all of my family and friends are still there." He shrugged sadly. "What do you want me to do? Thank God I talk to them once a week to know that they're okay."

I want to apologize, but I don't know how to begin. Nothing in my life has prepared me for sitting down to tea with a man from a country my country is at war with. I drink my tea quietly. "How is life in Damascus treating you?"

Hassan avoids my eyes, and I know then that I have asked the wrong question. "I feel a bit lost here," he answers, finally. "In Baghdad, I was a poet and a professor, an artist. If you mentioned my name to intellectuals, it would mean something."

He casts a resigned look at the paintings of Damascus surrounding him. "I never would have believed that I would one day be working in Damascus, selling cheap paintings to tourists."

I stand up to examine Hassan's "tourist paintings" hanging in long rows, the lines of houses and streets forming a kind of neighborhood on the wall of their shop. Each painting has been made with extraordinary attention, emphasizing some small detail that one might normally overlook—a lantern hanging in front of a doorway, or a blue shirt drying on a line of white laundry. I can almost imagine opening the canvas and walking inside.

"They're beautiful," I insist.

"That's not painting," he says, and I am surprised by a sudden bitterness in his voice. "That's just making enough money to survive."

Until this point Ali has simply been listening, but now he jumps into the conversation, trying to change the subject.

"I'm sorry. What was your name?" Ali asks me.

"Stephanie."

"I'm sorry, Stephanie. Please, let us give you a painting as a gift."

I shake my head.

"We want to," Hassan says firmly. "It's nice to speak to an American trying to learn Arabic."

I wonder then if I am the first American they have ever spoken to who is not in the military, not occupying their country and carrying a gun. They, too, are the first Iraqis in Damascus I know like this, smoking cigarettes, drinking tea. Not the anonymous, exhausted refugees I pass in the streets, or the wounded children I glimpse on the news at night. Just people.

I scan the paintings on the wall, my eyes settling on a painting of a narrow, cobbled street winding through an Arab market, with a few vaguely outlined figures rushing home. "I want this one," I decide. "Where is it?"

"That's this street, here." Hassan points outside.

I peer out the door to the street outside. The painting looks nothing like it.

Ali glances up from his easel. "Don't be ridiculous, Hassan. That's not Damascus. That's Baghdad."

He shrugs. I point to another painting of a cityscape. "Is that Damascus or Baghdad?" Hassan examines it closely.

"Damascus?" he asks helplessly. Ali shakes his head.

Then Hassan shrugs his great, broad shoulders again and laughs. "Do you know what the truth is? I can't tell anymore which ones are of Damascus and which ones are of Baghdad. I start painting a main street in Damascus, but then one of the alleys off the main road belongs to my old neighborhood in Baghdad. A courtyard in Damascus might suddenly belong to a house from Iraq. A window might be from Damascus, a door from Baghdad. After a while, the two become one city in your head."

Ali fastens a new canvas onto his easel. "Listen—let me paint a picture especially for you, so that you'll never wonder if the painting hanging in your living room is one of Damascus or of Iraq."

He squeezes a tube of burnt sienna onto his palette, and then dipping his knife into it, he begins to gently press one spiral on top of another on the canvas. Soon I can see a tower, built in a spherical cone pointing up toward the sky, and in time I recognize the famous Malwiya Minaret of the Great Mosque of Samarra, built in the ninth century in Iraq and one of the masterpieces of Islamic architecture. He moves the tip of his knife swiftly, until an old man trudges across the landscape in front of it, leaning on his cane.

Ali smiles and salutes me once again. "Always at your service, *ya* Stephanie," he announces playfully. "Come back and see us in a few days, when the paint is dry."

14.

I DO COME BACK. I return to retrieve my painting, then the next day to smoke a cigarette, until soon I find myself stopping by Hassan and Ali's shop every afternoon on my way home from the mosque. Hassan is always waiting in the same place, pacing in front of the storefront chain-smoking, looking out with a worried and slightly perplexed expression on his face, as though he can't quite remember where he is.

The second time I came to visit the shop, I realized that Hassan and I were both slightly limping through our conversations with each other, trying to speak in a foreign language, since I wasn't fluent in Arabic, and he didn't know the Syrian dialect.

"Now, if we are going to be friends, then you will have to teach me how to speak the Iraqi dialect," I told him.

"*Moo ma'oul!*" he laughed. "Impossible! An American speaking Iraqi?"

"I insist."

"Okay then. Every time I see you from now on, I am going to call out, *Shlonitch!*"

I grinned, hearing the colloquial greeting colored by the famous Iraqi *itch* at the end of words addressing women. "Then what do I say in return?"

"You say, *Zweena!* That means 'I'm beautiful.'"

"What if I don't feel beautiful?"

"It doesn't matter. Say you're beautiful."

So, whenever Hassan sees me approaching from down the street, he calls out *Shlonitch!*

I'm beautiful, I answer, and take my place beside him.

Until just a few years ago I had imagined that I would one day be a poet, and Hassan reminds me of that former life. Since he was once a literature teacher in Baghdad and a published poet, imprisoned under Saddam as a dissident, we feel right at home with each other. All he needs is a tweed jacket and we could be two old friends, drinking cappuccino and sharing poems at a New England coffeehouse.

Today, like every other day, we sit down to discuss poetry, switching between three dialects of Arabic and English, which he speaks almost as formally as I speak Arabic, with an Iraqi, slightly British accent. With one eye out on the street to look for potential customers, he turns to me and says, "I've been meaning to ask you: Who are your favorite poets?"

For the past years, I haven't read much at all other than the front page of the newspaper and academic texts, but I try to dig back to the poems I used to read in another life. "I don't know. I've always liked T. S. Eliot and Rainer Maria Rilke, Czesław Miłosz. From the Arabs I like Mahmoud Darwish and Nizar Qabbani, and of course, Abdul Wahab al-Bayati."

He knows all of them well—in fact I have never mentioned a poet that he isn't familiar with. But his eyes shine when I say the name of the Iraqi poet and master of Arabic free verse al-Bayati, who recently died in exile, right here in Damascus.

"And you, Hassan?"

"Me, I love Baudelaire and Rimbaud. But you know me. I read Yannis Ritsos and Nazim Hikmet."

I laugh. The Greek writer Ritsos composed many of his stories from exile on an island in Greece; Hikmet had written much of his poetry from a prison in Turkey. Two perfect companions for a man who once spent time in an Iraqi prison cell, waiting to see if he would emerge dead or alive.

HASSAN IS SLOW TO TALK ABOUT HIMSELF, but I'm fascinated by his history, and my delicate prodding slowly uncovers the miraculous story of his past. His life was literally saved by poetry. In Baghdad he had been an intellectual dissident who protested against the reign of Saddam, which not surprisingly landed him in an Iraqi prison. Yet instead of collapsing into despair, he had transformed the prison into his own private classroom. Every night he gathered the prison guards around him, and he spoke to them about poets like Shakespeare, Dante, and Cavafy, filling the cold cell rooms with the sound of his voice, singing out verses.

In Arabic, the word for "home," *beyt*, is the same word used for a line of poetry, and Arab poets often speak of making a home in language. Maybe that is what led Hassan to begin giving his daily lessons—whatever the motivation, those poetry sessions gave him the strength to remain sane. Eventually he became very close to one of the young guards, who came to him alone and asked him about poetry. The relationship between guard and prisoner gradually changed into that of student and teacher and, finally, to one of friendship. It was this guard who finally helped Hassan to escape. One day the guard gave him permission to leave the prison grounds and go for a walk but said that in the evening he should return again. So Hassan left, wandering through the landscape near the prison, but in the evening he returned. The next day, he did the same. Day after day, he walked out of the prison gates and into the free world, and in the evening he returned and spoke to the guard about Yeats's "Lake Isle of Innisfree" or the way Qabbani described the women passing him on the streets, who smelled of jasmine. In the evening he finally fell asleep in that lonely cell. And I think that it must have been this—the fact that he always returned at the end of the day, that he remained faithful, even when he could have simply disappeared—that made the guard decide to let him go free.

One morning the guard came to see Hassan in his cell. *Please,* he said. *Today do not return. I cannot bear any longer to participate in holding you here. But I cannot set you free myself. I can only let you escape on your own.*

So Hassan walked out of the prison that afternoon and never went back again.

That afternoon he walked into exile. As long as Saddam was in power, he could never feel safe in his former life. Now Saddam was no longer in power, but the insurgents had forced everyone else he knew into exile. The streets of his paintings are the only home he has.

It would be easy for me to dismiss Hassan's story as fantasy, and maybe it is. Perhaps it is a story he tells himself because the truth of his past is much too difficult to bear. Or maybe in the telling of a story in three languages, it is I who misunderstood the details. But I don't think so. I think the story is just as he tells it, and just as I understand it. Long ago I decided that war is a collection of stories that don't make sense. Besides, Hassan doesn't seem proud of having survived Iraq. He seems ashamed of it.

The Bread of Angels

"Exile is my homeland," I quote from al-Bayati. "Words are my exile."

"No, you, *habibti*, you make my exile so much easier," he tells me. "I had no one in Syria to talk to about books before I met you. Please come by more often, if you can. I miss talking about art and literature when you are gone."

I quietly finish my tea, and he excuses himself for a moment, to sell a tourist painting for ten dollars.

"What is this painting?" the man asks, inspecting the alley of blue and white laundry hanging over roofs.

"That's Damascus," Hassan answers.

Now I know that he is lying. He only paints Baghdad, all day long.

15.

I HANG ALI'S PAINTING OF THE MOSQUE of Samarra in my room. Soon I buy a second painting from Hassan, of an anonymous alley in old Baghdad mixed with an alley in Damascus, and I set it on the sill of the window looking out toward the Baron's. For now, those paintings are the only decorations I have on my walls. Before I go to bed at night I look at them one last time, a final reminder that we can't run away from our lives. They follow us. They show up in the most unexpected places—in front doors, in alleys, even in someone else's laundry hanging out to dry.

It's been almost ten years now since I left home, and in one way or another I've been running ever since. I've even tried escaping into other people. Maybe Damascus is the end of the line—maybe this is where we all end up when we've run out of places to disappear. The legend says that when God created the world, he made Adam from the clay of the nearby Barada River, and that it was to somewhere near Damascus that God cast him and Eve after they lost paradise.

Sometimes when the Baron has finished one of his stories, about kissing a blond customer in the storage room of a shoe store in Lebanon, I ask him, "What are you doing in Damascus? Your children are still in Lebanon. Your city is there. Your entire life is there. Why are you here, in this tiny, forty-dollar-a-month room in Damascus, in a neighborhood that has nothing to do with you?"

"Forget about it," he tells me. "What do I want with that place anymore?"

It's not that he no longer loves Lebanon. It's just that he can never forgive it for having once been so good.

HERE IS THE DREAM I sometimes dream at night in the house off Straight Street: I am twelve years old again, vacationing on the Texas coast, on a pristine expanse of beach, and everything is still as it should be. My grandmother Elida is sitting behind me on a blanket, tanning her long, beautiful legs and braiding my hair. I lean back and kiss her cheek, and for a moment our faces touch each other and I can sense the resemblance between us. She points in the distance where my grandfather Enrique, with his shiny silver curls, is building a sand castle, digging his fingers deep into the sand. Behind them my aunt Loretta is holding hands with my mother, and they are walking together in the low tide, bending every now and then to gather seashells. My mother, thin and lovely in her red bathing suit, notices me watching her and smiles.

I know it is a dream, because almost all of the people in it are dead. It can't be real because my mother is happy. Still it keeps coming back to me, my mother looking up from the beach beside her sister and smiling an honest smile at me, a smile I don't think I've ever seen in my entire life.

16.

TODAY THERE WERE BOMBS IN BAGHDAD. I heard about them on the way home from school, on the radio in the taxi, the word *Baghdad* and then *infijar* and then the number of the dead, the taxi driver shaking his head sadly in the midst of traffic. I always remember the word for "explosion" in Arabic, *infijar*, because it sounds just like *mufaja'a*, the Arabic word for "surprise." And I imagine that they must be the same, a walk down the streets and then the feeling of surprise as the world around you explodes into a thousand pieces and suddenly goes dark.

Lately there have been bombs every day—car bombs in Baghdad, in Mosul, in Samarra, in cities I've never even heard of until I learn that they have filled up with the dead. Five churches are bombed in Baghdad.

Woman and children waiting at checkpoints are thrown from the earth by roadside bombs. Iraqi officials are executed, foreign and Iraqi journalists kidnapped and killed. Translators are shot as collaborators. Dozens of Iraqi recruits are murdered in an ambush on their way back from training. A British engineer is beheaded. Mass Kurdish graves are uncovered. A roadside bomb kills eight American marines. An explosion kills Iraqi policemen relaxing at a snack bar. In Falluja American forces bomb from the air, while families flee for their lives.

Today it was a car bomb against an Arab television station that made the news. As happens so often, it didn't kill those it was meant to kill. Instead the gardener died, a security guard, and members of the kitchen staff. And so it goes, all of this horror finding its way into sunflowers and gardenias, kitchen forks and spoons.

When i arrive at hassan's I find him smoking on a stool in the corner of his shop, letting his ashes collect in a small gray pool on the floor. He looks exhausted, and I know that I should not have come. I can almost feel the dead in the air around him, unmentioned and heavy.

It's been harder and harder for me to come see him these last weeks. It's not his fault. After all, we never actually talk about the war. We talk about poets who write in cottages beside the sea, or Degas's paintings of young ballerinas. We speak about Rilke's angels, or the suffering of Nikos Kazantzakis's Christ. But beneath this lurks all that we refuse to speak about. Hassan carries the war inside of him, and I can feel it building more and more each day, threatening to break through the surface. By the time I leave Hassan and make my way home, I've lost all of the shining I stored up from taking photographs in the mosque. Just the fact of sitting across from him makes me tired. He is like a letter sent from the war into my own life, and now I have to read it, whether I want to or not.

Now i take my seat beside him and he offers me a cigarette. After he lights it, we begin to speak about poetry.

"Do you know what I've decided, Stephanie? There are two kinds of poets. The good poet is able to put beautiful words on paper. But the great poet doesn't need words, and he doesn't need paper. The great poet sees that there is poetry in everything."

He steps out of the store and begins pacing back and forth in the alley. I can see him as a professor again, laboring over a particular point, pacing in front of the chalkboard. "I've decided that poetry is best considered as a science. So, just as hydrogen and oxygen are bound together to create water, the force that binds them can be compared to poetry. Poetry is an invisible energy that exists between everything, holding it together, giving it meaning. The job of every human being is to search for the poetry hidden within the midst of things."

Something about him sounds desperate. He keeps pacing. "So, this brings us back to the role of poets in society. Some people write poetry, and some people live poetry. The man who lives poetry is the greater of the two."

He meets my gaze from the street. Behind him I can see the Minaret of Jesus, and the piece of sky behind it turning gray as evening continues to fall over the alley. Flocks of birds perch at the top of the minaret, and we can hear them calling to one another from below. In the street a small breeze builds, lifting dust from the ground and then setting it down again.

"Poetry exists in everything?" I ask. "Even the war?"

"Even the war," he answers.

Suddenly I'm so utterly tired, and I can actually feel it—my heart breaking in half. He's lying to me. There isn't poetry in the midst of any of this. There's no poetry in that man, whoever he was, who collapsed in the midst of his roses this morning. There's no poetry in the soldiers who were blown in half in Falluja. There is nothing beautiful about the killing and nothing beautiful about the dying. The most stunning language in the world won't set it right again.

"Then why don't you go back to Baghdad, Hassan?" I finally ask him.

I know that my question is unfair, that I'm hurting him by asking it. But I can't stop.

"Why don't you go back, Hassan?"

He looks at me for a long time. Behind him the sky has already settled into gray, so that the minaret is a tall black shadow reaching up to heaven. His eyes go even darker than usual.

Finally he sighs. "Go back where, Stephanie?" he relents. "You know I can't go back. How do you return to your neighborhood, when everyone you know has gone away? When my family and friends have all left? Where is my home? My Baghdad doesn't exist anymore."

He looks away from me, and his last sentence is spoken softly, to himself. "My Baghdad is gone forever."

I stand up to leave. He stops me. We remain for a moment, face-to-face, just in front of the door, and he places his hand on my shoulder. "Wait for a moment," he says.

Then he turns and walks to the back of his small shop and reaches behind a painting to take out a shoe box full of old, outdated postcards. He shuffles through them, delicately, quietly glancing at one after another, until he stops at a bright, almost Technicolor postcard of Baghdad from decades ago. He hands it to me.

"Take this. I want you to keep it."

I finger it gingerly. A line of tall buildings is set against a vast and clear blue sky. In the foreground, a bridge runs over azure waters, and a bush of white and red flowers is in full bloom. Brightly painted classic cars and a British red double-decker bus cross over the bridge. I turn the postcard over. "Ahrar Bridge," it says on the left-hand corner in German, English, French, and Arabic. In the right-hand corner, a square waits for a tourist in Baghdad to purchase a postage stamp and stick it in the mail.

"When you remember Baghdad, I want you to remember it like this," he tells me. "Like it was, when it was paradise."

When you remember Baghdad. As though I have already been there.

God be with you, he says as I leave. I go home. I sit on my bed, with his postcard in my hands, and I cry like a child.

17.

November

THE NEXT TWO WEEKS pass quickly.

By the end of October, Syrians have become obsessed with the American presidential elections. My neighbors stay up late glued to their television sets, watching round-the-clock coverage of John Kerry and George Bush, debating what each man might mean for their lives.

"Maybe it would be better if they just elect George Bush again," a driver grumbles to me on the way home from school. "At least we know that he's terrible. I always say it's better to have the devil you know than the devil you don't know."

Predictably, the Baron is less interested in the politics of the elections than in finding yet another way to taunt me.

"*Ya*, Stefanito, are you all set for four more years of Señor Bush?" he asks me one afternoon after my daily Arabic pop quiz. I have no idea why he's given the president a Spanish name.

"How much do you want to bet that Kerry will be elected?" I chide him.

"A bottle of whiskey," he counters.

"What will I do with a bottle of whiskey?"

"You won't need to worry," he sings sweetly. "You won't be drinking it. Bush will win."

On the evening of November 2, I stay awake in an all-night café and watch the states turn red one after another as George W. Bush is narrowly reelected to his second term as president. When it is finished, I pay my bill and set out on the long walk home. It is early morning when I arrive in the Christian quarter and men are wearily sweeping their storefronts and opening the doors. I stop inside a liquor store and buy the most expensive bottle of Jack Daniel's I can find.

When I return to the house off Straight Street, I hand the brown paper bag over to the Baron. "Merry Christmas, Grandpa," I mutter. He giggles like a child.

A weight falls over the city with the knowledge that the war in Iraq will only get longer, an invasion of Syria will only be more likely. A kind of existential exhaustion sets into the eyes of people, like men who had set out for a long, four-year journey, only to be told at the conclusion that they are only halfway there.

The following night, I summon up the courage to finally phone Mark. I buy several cell-phone cards and dial the thirteen digits of his number while lying across my cold, narrow bed, listening as the phone rings and rings, the sound echoing.

"Hello," he mutters, his voice cased with sleep. "Oh God, Stephanie. Do you know what time it is?"

I know that I should hang up, but I can't. I'm just so impossibly tired, and I need to believe that something in the world can be good again. So I speak to him of my Arabic classes and my room off Straight Street, the loneliness of Damascus, and how many hours I have passed longing for home. "I love you," I finally tell him.

"No you don't," he answers in an even voice. "You don't even know me. And I don't think that I was ever in love with you."

I say nothing. He might have discovered the one sentence in the world to which there is no adequate response.

I hang up the phone and spend the rest of the day in bed, staring up at the spearmint-painted ceiling, trying to find some way to measure what I've lost. That street in Cambridge, that mailbox with my mail, the kitchen table where I drank my tea, and the box of my clothes in the basement waiting for the day when I would come home to retrieve them. His voice. Pieces of music I might never recover again. The only place I had planned on returning home to, if something in Damascus goes wrong.

The next week the American invasion of Falluja begins. Then Yasser Arafat dies, *of poisoning*, everyone whispers, opening up a political vacuum in the neighboring West Bank. My neighbor bawls in front of her television screen when I visit her. "He was a good man," she insists. "You know, he married a Christian." But when I pass by a Palestinian merchant near the Eastern Gate and offer my condolences, he looks up at me with an utterly blank expression in his eyes.

"God have mercy on him," he mutters in a quick, clipped voice and then goes back to his work.

I take my final exams, and I never return to the university again, not even to see whether I have passed or failed. Instead I find a travel agency and change my destination from Boston to San Antonio for Christmas, go home to the house off Straight Street, pack a single bag, and drink a last, strong cup of coffee with the Baron.

TODAY IS NOVEMBER 14, the end of Ramadan, and more than two months after my arrival in Damascus. I have crossed some invisible line in myself that I cannot go back on again. I wake up in the morning, and I don't even remember who I am.

And so I make my way to the bus station and buy a ticket north.

The ride out into the desert feels like coming up for air, like watching the earth strip itself clean and become new again. From the window of the battered minibus, Damascus gradually gives way to bare stones alternating between shades of brown and hewn red, the sky becoming blue. Outside in the desert, empty black trash bags swell with air, the open spaces appearing as though they are clogged with phantoms. We are already on the edge of winter, and I have packed no winter clothes for what will be a month spent in the desert. In fact, I have brought no real clothes at all: two pairs of pants, two shirts and a jacket, a pair of sandals and a load of books, as someone who hastily flees in the middle of the night with no thought of what they might require for the journey.

Even i do not know what I am running from. I suspect that it is not only Damascus, not only Mark no longer loving me, but another, more complex and unnameable thing—a series of places or lives abandoned in the middle, stories ruptured before completion. Maybe that's the only country I have left to flee from, this house of memories appended one onto another, each room a different country, a street, the name of a man I left standing in an airport, a fraction of myself.

If I were a better person, it would be God's voice haunting me as I watch the buildings disappear and the landscape bleed to bone dry. But it is not God's voice. It is the poet Rilke's voice haunting me, the words he had written in the last line of his poem "Archaic Torso of Apollo": *for here there is no place that does not see you. You must change your life.*

Part Two INCARNATION

Last of all, as though to one untimely born,

he appeared also to me.

—1 CORINTHIANS 15:8

1.

FROM THE FOOT OF THE DESERT VALLEY, I look up to see the ancient monastery of Mar Musa staring down at me from its perch on the cliffside, majestic, suspended in the meeting point between two mountains, no logical line marking the separation between mountain, monastery, and sky. The light on the stones turns them to a deep rose, so that the scenery as much as the monastery itself reminds me of what Moses might have felt like standing in front of the mountain of the Lord. The medieval builders piled walls the color of baked clay one behind another, each ascending floor of the monastery built deeper into the face of the mountain. From a distance, the monastery clawing to the side of the cliff gives me the discomforting sense that at any moment it might collapse and tumble into the valley below.

There are some three hundred and fifty steps winding across the mountainside, and it takes half an hour to climb the mountain. I begin slowly, my bag digging into my shoulders, pausing every so often to catch my breath, my body exhausted and cold, my lungs weak from pollution. Something about this staircase makes me think of the Spanish medieval mystic St. John of the Cross, writing of his anguished dark night of the soul, the space of pure despair before the soul climbs the ladder leading back to life again. He promised that, after climbing, the soul reaches God and attains stillness. "The ladder rests in God."

I have no idea how I succeeded in falling so far, from God and from myself. How much I also want rest.

In damascus i lived in a room, in a house, which was placed on a street, which was then in a neighborhood located in the Old City. If those had been the only circles of my life, then perhaps I would not have fled from Damascus to the desert to start over again. Yet I carried still another world inside of myself, a world as real as the war that Hassan carried within his body to Damascus and could not escape, no matter how far he fled from Baghdad.

Damascus was not the first place I had lived with violence. Nor was the Middle East. I have been running from a different story of violence for a long time, and that was the deeper reason why I couldn't go home again. On the surface, there is nothing in common between my story and the events I experienced in the Middle East. Perhaps the only thing that ties them is my growing knowledge that once history decides to unravel on you, there is very little that you can do to change its mind.

I was born into a family with such a strange and cruel history that I was raised to believe that we were cursed. My mother's mother, Elida Magdalena Calderon Cantu, was born on March 2, 1930, in San Antonio, Texas, to a family that owned a series of mom-and-pop grocery stores on the Mexican west side of the city. She was beautiful in the way only women from that particular era were beautiful, her face narrow and always smoothed white with powder, her long hair often pulled back and fastened with a flower. I have seen that face so often in photographs, and I like to imagine that she held the same allure for my grandfather when he first met her that a film actress might hold if caught unawares in her everyday life, walking down the street in the late afternoon sun. The truth, though, is that I never learned how they met, much less if they were ever in love, and I received no stories that hinted at whether they shared any happiness between them.

By all accounts, my grandparents were an explosive couple. My grandmother Elida's personality hovered between mesmerizing and eccentric. She had a penchant for turbans and lipstick and brightly colored dresses, along with a collection of peacocks that sauntered beside her through her San Antonio backyard. Yet with all of her glamour, she was also tragic, frequently thrown between bouts of mania and despair, and late in her life she was finally diagnosed as manic-depressive. Her husband, my grandfather Enrique, had no idea how to cope with her mood swings, and in his own right was said to have been a difficult man to love, one who too often judged his children and his wife harshly.

In 1950, Elida gave birth to my mother, the oldest of her six children, who despite the tensions of her family grew into a precocious and exceptionally bright dimpled child who loved to paint and sing, and who dreamed of one day traveling beyond the confines of her small neighborhood in San Antonio. In the following years, four more girls and a boy were born, all of them gifted in the arts and more than a little melancholic. Madness and music, they used to say, were the particular gifts that my family carried.

Growing up in the 1960s, my mother watched as her mother became increasingly unbalanced. She developed an obsession with death and attempted to take her life several times. Eventually she began electroshock therapy and woke up in a mental hospital, many of her memories gone. My mother's own memories of these moments remain traumatic. "Oh God," she once told me. "I know that they were trying to do good in theory, but it was as if you could eliminate just that part of the brain that would make her want to destroy herself. To me it was torture."

In 1973, two years after my parents were married and four years before I was born, my grandfather Enrique Cantu filed for divorce from his wife Elida, a predictable act after many turbulent years, and yet one full of shame for our conservative Catholic and Hispanic family. On March 2, my grandmother celebrated her forty-third birthday with her children. Two days later, the day before her divorce would have been finalized, she laid out on her bed in loving detail the clothes she wished to be buried in. Then she laid herself down also, on the sofa in her living room, and swallowed enough pills to move her body into sleep forever. She died a married woman. That afternoon her brother discovered her body lying in the living room as though dreaming, the empty pill bottles beside her.

DESPITE HIS REPUTATION AS A DIFFICULT MAN, my grandfather Enrique Cantu adored me with a peculiar tenderness. After his wife's death, he lived out in a small Texas ranch house set among high grass, bluebonnets, and Indian paintbrush, and in my eyes his rough, fierce features and ability to shoot and skin rattlesnakes made him almost superhuman. On weekends he sometimes took me fishing on the San

Antonio River, which ran through his property in the dry brush and cacti of south Texas. He knew I hated the sight of anything dying and would always bait the hook of my fishing line for me, passing his hand through the water afterward to rinse away the blood.

He called me his "little runner," encouraging me by giving me money every time I won a long-distance race. He cooked scrambled eggs with bacon and baked beans. I loved him dearly. When I was thirteen years old, my grandfather Enrique was discovered in his Texas ranch house one afternoon in March, shot in the back of the head with his own pistol. He had been tortured: beaten and gagged, shot execution style at the base of his skull. In a less tragic family, he would have died instantly. He did not. The bullet ricocheted in his brain and killed him slowly. He somehow freed himself from his bonds, called one of his daughters, and mumbled the words *I've been shot*. His brain was filling with blood. I do not know why he could not summon the strength to say another word, the name of the man who shot him.

I visited my grandfather that night in the hospital, his face blue and swollen to twice its normal size, the thoughts asleep in his head. Beside him, a machine quietly drew the lines of his breathing. I took his hand, and I remember finding his face to be beautiful, the way something familiar can change so quickly that it startles you into consciousness, seeing it as though for the first time. My grandfather's face remained a flower in bloom, and though he stayed alive for two more days, at last they unplugged him.

After he had died, someone handed me the green rosary beads my grandfather held in his hands while dying, and said, "Take these. You are the only one of us who still believes in God." I grabbed hold of them tightly.

Or did they really say that? Where are those rosary beads now? Perhaps I have only invented the memory to give myself a purpose in that brutal, terrible story, to make my role more than that of a bystander. The police never discovered who executed him, or why. I have spent the last half of my life wondering. I am plagued by the realization that, walking among us, in our daily life, there are present those who are capable of unspeakable crimes, and we have no way of knowing who they are.

I was barely a teenager, so confused with my changing body and hormones that I did not know how to make space for an executed grand-father in the narrative of my life. My family tried to pretend that nothing had happened at all. It was as though my grandfather woke up one day and simply disappeared. There was no funeral held to honor him. No one could explain why he had gone. We simply took the ashes of his body and poured them in the river, afterward wiping the white chalk and dust from our hands. It was seventeen years, almost to the day, after his wife's suicide.

As a teenager i talked to flowers, carved names into my bed, and became a novice in the madness I believed was my birthright and destiny. I saw trees morph out of walls, with long, terrible limbs reaching out to tear me apart. By age fourteen I was chronically depressed. Despite the fact that my psychiatrist always insisted that I was not crazy, only deeply sad, I had grown up with the shadow of my grandmother's life as such a heavy presence that I could not help but conclude that I had inherited her disease. Though I never met her, in some ways she seemed closer to me than most of the women I knew—for though I was one of four children, I was that child who inherited the "Cantu genes," playing the piano since my childhood, speaking with imaginary friends, living in not quite the same world as my classmates. My mother and I grew increasingly distant after her father's death, and as she coped by escaping inside of herself, I escaped into terrible dreams and visions and became obsessed with the legacy of my grandmother. I began to suspect that we possessed some special kinship of understanding that tied us beyond time and the dead.

I am sure that my mother was afraid of me. My life was a story that she had seen before, and she knew how it ended. I was already writing poetry, and I soon discovered the confessional poets, memorizing the verses of Sylvia Plath, staying up late reading Anne Sexton, Robert Lowell, and Theodore Roethke beneath my sheets each night. I became mesmer-ized by their descents into depression, madness, and addiction. In my mind my grandmother was my own link to these people, the human embodiment of all that was sad and passionate, and I alternated between wanting to be her and wishing that I had been born earlier, so that I might have learned how to save her life. I secretly believed that surely, if she would have met me, she would have recognized herself in me, would have wanted to live to see me grown. But she was dead, and I wasn't planning on staying alive much longer.

When I was fourteen, I swallowed so much aspirin that I was sent to the emergency room. A few months later, I found myself checked into the psychiatric ward of Santa Rosa Hospital after swallowing thirty-five Tylenol. But unlike the hospitals of poetry, there was nothing romantic about the lonely white room I inhabited and the fists pounding against the neighboring walls. It was the most humiliating moment in my young life, and I was angry and frightened. The two weeks I spent living among child drug addicts, victims of sexual abuse, and teenagers hallucinating and screaming in the middle of the night proved to be so traumatic that I vowed never to try to die again. It wasn't exotic—it was horrible. My fascination with death very quickly transformed into a total commitment to staying alive, which I executed with determination and vengeance, not through any love of life, but from the simple fact that failing at death had proven to be such a brutal and terrifying alternative.

Not long after my stay in the hospital, my parents divorced, and I stayed with my father, who quietly helped nurse me back to health. I willed myself into being well enough to play varsity sports, to go to the prom. I graduated from high school and moved from Texas to Vermont, distancing myself from my past as much as possible, not letting anyone know that the ordinary girl who wore Birkenstocks and composed essays on James Joyce had in another life been holed up in a mental hospital, chatting with phantoms. I became a model student, studied poetry and religion, hiked in the mountains, and gradually allowed my family history to fade into the background of my mind. I told almost no one about my past. Still, it seemed that the moment I stopped chasing after death, it came to chase after me. I was rescued in the waters off Costa Rica a few moments before drowning, miraculously walked away from a car accident unscathed, and was pulled through a window to safety after nearly being crushed in the crowds of President Hafez al-Assad's funeral procession. Despite the fact that I often found myself falling into depression, I told myself that I was through with courting death—and if death was intent on finding me, then I was determined to give it a run for its money.

Then, in March 2003, in the same month in which both of my grand-parents died, my aunt Loretta, the second daughter of Enrique and Elida, walked outside of her house in rural San Antonio to check her mail. As she lifted the letters from the mailbox, the driver of a school bus full of young children suddenly and inexplicably pulled into reverse and drove over her. She was killed instantly, the letters falling like leaves from her open hands.

My family, when we spoke about our secret history, christened our past *the March Curse*. No one would admit it aloud, and yet I knew that each and every one of us worried that one day, it might come in the morning, quietly, and take us. We were educated people, and none of us really believed in curses, of course, except in very exceptional cases. Even the most cynical people would admit that the Kennedy family was cursed, for example. And due to certain unexplained cosmic circumstances, so were we.

For years, while walking down the street, I would sometimes be seized by a sudden fear that someone was following me. Doors creaking terrified me. I was afraid to be alone in houses. Every few hours, I would think that someone had found his way inside.

I was afraid that gunmen would climb through the window. I was afraid every time I saw a parent spank a child, I was afraid of too-violent films. I was afraid of driving a car, afraid that I would lose my way, lose the keys, hit someone accidentally. I was afraid of ordering pizza on the phone, or of asking salesclerks for help finding my size. I was afraid of deli counter men.

I was afraid of leaving the stove on. Of acquiring a disease that could go undetected. I was afraid that death might come when I least expected it, in an Express Mail envelope delivered by post, in the folded pink pleats of honey-baked ham.

Somewhere, in the midst of my fears, as I increasingly traveled abroad, I came to feel at home in countries with a history of war. That is why, even after the Middle East fell apart, I couldn't stop coming back. At least there, I knew that I was not crazy. I was right to be afraid. Everyone was afraid.

So I bought my first copy of *The World's Most Dangerous Places*, and in the conflict-ridden world of the Middle East, to my surprise, I reinvented myself. In America, I couldn't talk to salesclerks, but in Lebanon, I could interview refugees. In America, I was so frightened and disoriented that I often lost my way home at the end of the day, but in Turkey I could hitchhike alone to a site in the middle of Kurdistan and arrive at a village not even marked on the map. My family's past made me an expert at navigating chaos, in surviving in the wild on my own, in connecting with those people strangled by the fear that everything might be lost to them— suddenly and completely without warning.

Life made sense in the Middle East. It was simply the ordinary, human world where I was accustomed to feeling lost and exposed, now made visible.

Until, after a year of reporting in Lebanon, I packed up my bags one day and told myself, *Stop it. Stop it stop it stop it. This isn't life you're living— running from one country and one house to another, living out of suitcases. At least try to live like everyone else.*

And I had tried, with my entire heart, moving to Boston, living in my own language, renting a house, falling in love, until I was placed on an airplane straight back to chaos.

Before I left America, when people learned that I was moving to Syria, they all said the same thing: *You are so brave.* It made me want to cry.

I am not brave. I only want to live long enough to be an old woman and have babies. I want an impossible life.

2.

AFTER TWENTY MINUTES OF WALKING, the monastery is finally hanging over me, suspended on the other side of the cliff and just beyond grasp. I try to finish the last flight of steps at a half run, my heavy breaths merging with the sounds of clanging goat bells and the incessant barking of dogs. Finally, human voices. How strange, to hear anything alive in this dead, silent place.

I reach the top of the steps, running my hands along the rough outer walls of the monastery, glad to have something solid to place my weight against. My hands follow hewn stone all the way to the edge of a front entrance, a miniature iron door half the size of my five-foot-three body pushed open, revealing a tiny passageway designed to make those who enter bow in penitence. *Doors of humility*, they are called, and I remember the famous narrow gate to the kingdom of heaven, mentioned in the Gospels, and explained by Amma Theodora, the desert mother:

> *Let us strive to enter by the narrow gate. Just as the trees, if they have not stood before the winter's storms, cannot bear fruit, so it is with us; this present age is a storm.*

I bow deeply and enter the narrow passage, the back of my head grazing the stone ceiling. When I raise my head and lift my body to its full height again, I am standing within the monastery walls where I will spend the next month of my life.

As luck would have it, I have arrived on the second day of Eid, the Muslim feast marking the end of the month of Ramadan, and the monastery is flooded with Arab Christian pilgrims taking advantage of the days off from work, giving the monastery more the air of a picnic site near fairgrounds than a house of pilgrimage. Mixed groups of teenagers are flirting together in Arabic, tourists snap photographs, while dozens of women run back and forth from the monastery kitchen to low tables placed outside, laying out dishes of thick yogurt, olive oil, flatbread, goat cheese, fresh green olives, and sweet black tea for the afternoon meal.

The intimidating shadow of a six-foot-four Italian hovers over the masses, watching them carefully. Father Paolo Dall'Oglio, the famous abbot of the monastery, manages without difficulty to look over their heads and glimpse me standing at the edge of the courtyard, no doubt looking slightly overwhelmed by all the commotion. He lumbers at me with outstretched arms that nearly cover the entire span between us. It seems impossible to me that a single human being can occupy so much space.

"Stephanie! *Ya Ahlan wa Sahlan!* We were waiting for you to arrive! How are you, fine?" His voice booms, his Arabic carrying a singsong cadence, his English affected by so many other accents that its source is impossible to place, though his overenthusiasm certainly hints at his Roman origins. He smiles behind his graying beard and throws his arms around me, his hands making two solid thumps on my back. Then he takes a step back and sizes me up like a rugby player. "So, are you ready?"

I smile, blushing. I'm not ready.

I had met Paolo for the first time five years before, during my first, brief trip to Syria, and a second time two years later while I was working in Lebanon. A giant, Arabic-speaking Jesuit parading about in the desert is not easy to forget, and he quickly won me over with his bellowing laugh and deep passion for the local people, encouraging me to learn Arabic and pursue my studies in Islam. I had always admired him, particularly his fluency in Arabic and his engagement with local Muslims, and though he had suggested that I do the monthlong Spiritual Exercises three years before, it had taken a broken heart, a brutal election, and a war in order for me to finally take him up on his offer.

I have always been somewhat shy, making Paolo an odd choice for my spiritual guide. An Italian who has lived in the Arab world for some twenty-five years, he is a bear of a man, with a giant frame and a voice to match, which can often be heard delegating twelve tasks at once in the local village dialect of Arabic, which he speaks perfectly along with French, English, and his native Italian. He looks less like a priest with a doctorate in theology than the patriarch of a traditional Arab village. On this particular afternoon, he is wearing a black *keffiyeh* wrapped around his head in the style of local villagers, and beneath his green shirt and smudged khaki pants, his bare feet slide back and forth in cheap brown plastic house sandals one normally wears only in the shower. Every so often he puts on a pair of glasses with enormous, boxy frames, the lenses so thick that they comically magnify his eyes.

Paolo is legendary in the region, a man famously eccentric, unquestionably brilliant, and most controversial for his insistence on the Christian vocation to love Muslims and Islam. His close friendships with sheikhs from various Islamic schools, his thorough knowledge of the Quran, and his open-door policy toward the thousands of Muslims who visit the monastery each year earn the admiration of many, and the scorn of many others. Some Syrians don't trust him, thinking that any European who chooses to spend his life in a desert valley in the Middle East is either crazy or a Zionist spy. Other Muslims and Christians alike call him a mystic and a saint, *majnoun b'Allah*, crazy with God, one of the holy fools famous throughout Eastern monastic history. Some local Christians, suspicious of his relationship with Islam, think that as an Italian he can never truly understand how vulnerable it feels to be a Christian native in the Middle East as Islam becomes increasingly radicalized, and as Christians are targeted in Egypt and Iraq. I have never agreed with all of his opinions, yet I admire him deeply and have always viewed him as my spiritual father and inspiration, sharing his fear that if Christians in the Arab world do not develop a new approach to Islam, their already shrinking communities will soon be in danger of disappearing forever.

Perhaps I love Paolo most because he embodies the rare faith that life can be built in the ruins of history, that the tragic story of the modern Middle East is not a tale without ending or beyond repair. In 1982, he was a twenty-seven-year-old Jesuit student living in Beirut in what was one of the most terrible years in modern Middle Eastern history. At the height of the already devastating Lebanese Civil War, Israel invaded southern Lebanon and then Beirut in an attempt to battle the PLO, and thousands of civilians were killed in air raids. That same year, terrible massacres occurred in the Palestinian refugee camps of Sabra and Shatila on the outskirts of the city, where Lebanese Christian forces protected by Israeli troops killed at least hundreds, possibly thousands of civilians. In Syria, President Hafez al-Assad responded to a rebellion by the Muslim Brotherhood by sending Syrian forces into the city of Hama, where they killed thousands in a matter of days. And throughout Lebanon, members of warring factions continued to slaughter one another.

In the midst of this, Paolo experienced what he calls a death in his heart. Searching for a place to retreat in silence, he fled to rural Syria, where he hiked through the desert mountains in search of the fabled abandoned ruins of the ancient monastery of Mar Musa al-Habashi. There was no clear trail, but after searching he came upon what appeared to be the path of the monks who had lived there hundreds of years before. He followed the indentation in the rock until he arrived at the top of the mountain, carrying clean water, candles, and a flashlight. The door was locked shut. It was a night with no moon, and sunset had fallen by the time he finally forced the door open. The crumbling church stood before him, the roof destroyed, giving the structure a new roof of thousands of stars. When he cast his flashlight along the walls, he was astounded to see the faces of medieval frescoes, illuminated in the dark, staring back at him.

Paolo remained in the ruins for ten days of prayer. He climbed the mountains surrounding the monastery and meditated in the grottoes once used by ancient desert monks. Finally, in the midst of his prayer, he received a revelation that he would rebuild the monastery out of the ruins, creating a new order of monks and nuns who would live in a shared community, dedicated to prayer, silence, and hospitality, a shared witness in the heart of the violence of the Middle East. Yet they would add to their vocation something not found in the rules of other monastic orders: the promise to dedicate their lives to dialogue with Islam and to the millions of Muslims living in their midst.

More than twenty years later, his small community of monks and nuns make their home in this monastery nestled between Iraq, Israel, and Lebanon, where they receive thousands of Muslim and Christian visitors each year. The magnificent eleventh- and thirteenth-century frescoes in the chapel have been restored, the faces of saints and angels Paolo had witnessed that first night now recognized as some of the most important frescoes in the Middle East. While the region's Christian minority disintegrates and an increasing number immigrate abroad, the monastic community remains, often fasting with the monastery's Muslim workers during Ramadan, praying the Mass in Arabic, and enforcing Arabic as the common language of the community. After September 11, the community changed their name to al-Khalil, the name given by God to Abraham in the Quran. Abraham—the father of Muslims, Christians, and Jews, who one day opened his tent to welcome strangers and in doing so welcomed the angels of God.

Father Paolo believes that if Muslims must suffer because of their own bad clerics, the tragedy of fundamentalism, and the growing stigma against Islam worldwide, then he will not allow them to suffer alone. To remain Christian in the Middle East means to live as a witness in the heart of violence, to choose to be among those suffering, and by that choice to transform suffering through love. It is his refusal to see Muslims as "others" that makes Paolo a scandal, and when he declared to an American magazine after September 11 that "I cannot but declare that I am a Muslim," many church officials believed that he had gone too far. Yet I had been deeply touched when he had explained his reasoning to me. "When you love someone else, you appreciate his way of sitting, eating, drinking, you hope his hopes, you excuse his difficulties, you recognize his gifts," he said. He explained that he could not but be a Muslim, because the Muslim world he had lived in for the last thirty years was now more familiar to him than the world of his youth, and we offer our hearts to those we love. Love, he taught me, is never abstract. It is always searching for a body.

This is why I have come to him. I know that Paolo will not allow me to escape the reality of what I have experienced in the Middle East these last years, just as he will not allow me to escape the story of my own family. It is against his theology to turn one's back when those we love are suffering. If I am going to face my life after all of these years, then it is probably best to do so in the middle of the desert in Syria, where I have nowhere else to run.

No, I am not ready for the Spiritual Exercises. What I do not dare tell Paolo, at the onset of a month of silence and prayer, is that I no longer pray at all, that my afternoons in the mosque in Damascus are the closest I have come to seeking guidance in as long as I can remember. For the most part, God and I are no longer on speaking terms.

I eat lunch quickly, gather some bedsheets, and pull my backpack onto my shoulders again. Then I cross a bridge, ascend another hundred stairs, and arrive on the other side of the valley at the women's monastery, where I look for the room that will become my new home.

PAOLO HAS ASSIGNED ME the "bishop's room," a kind of deluxe suite in the monastery, named so because it is usually reserved for the bishop when he comes to visit. The simple, spartan room is built directly into the cliff face, and a large chunk of mountain juts through the far wall, creating a makeshift altar holding an icon of the Virgin and Child. The rest of the room consists of a bed, an oil heater, and a bathroom also built directly into the cliff face. The windows look out onto the mountain and into the valley below, where a line of red desert hills remains visible in the distance. "This is not just any place where we live," Paolo reminded me. "Remember that hermits once spoke with God in the place where you use the toilet."

The bishop's room is the architectural opposite of my house on Straight Street, for here everything looks not inward, but out toward the desert, making me completely invisible in my room. Here there is no need to hide from the world outside. No one can watch me from my windows, save for birds or angels, which are the only company I am prepared to receive just now.

I unpack my belongings and place the few books I have brought with me on the windowsill: the Quran, the writings of St. Ephrem the Syrian, the chapters on prayer by the Egyptian hermit Evagrius, Origen's writings on the creation of the world. Two out of the three Christians have been declared heretics. In my impulsive preparation, I have forgotten my Bible, a notebook, or a change of socks.

Who would have guessed that I would end up here? Growing up attending Catholic schools, I thought that nuns were limited to old women with wrinkled hands who drilled us in arithmetic and who monitored my clothes to make sure that my maroon plaid uniform reached my knees. I never had aspirations to imitate their spiritual lives, just as I had no real desire to acquire a spiritual life of my own. My religious upbringing was in many ways more one of identity than of belief. I carried a glow-in-the-dark rosary in my pocket and made the sign of the cross before I shot free throws in high school basketball games, but these were mere superstitions. I very rarely prayed. I was raised to be fiercely independent, and to ask anyone for help, even God, had seemed to me a betrayal of my Girl Scout pledge to be prepared to survive in the wild all on my own. I also, deep down, refused to believe in a God who required my prayers before he would help me. Then as time passed and more and more tragedies streamed in from all directions, I no longer cared if God existed. I came to feel that a God who would cast so much horror on a single family, and on the life of a child, was not worth believing in.

Only two exceptions remain in my mind.

For a brief period, when I was eleven years old, every day after school I walked to the grotto behind my school and I waited to see if the Virgin Mary would appear to me. In religion class we had watched a film about Mary appearing to a group of children in Medjugorje, and I thought that as long as she was visiting other children she might make time in her schedule to come see me one afternoon. I went every day for weeks, but she never came. Several years later, I confessed these afternoon vigils to my father, and he admitted that for years he had also waited in the garden outside of his high school seminary, hoping that Mary might arrive.

The second exception was more recent. After I graduated from college, I had decided to celebrate by traveling to Costa Rica for a month. One afternoon I was wading in shallow waters on a beach in Montezuma, and I looked up to realize that I had been sucked out away from the coast.

I was stranded, trapped simultaneously in an undertow and a riptide. It was impossible to swim against the current, and so I treaded water, helpless as my body was sucked under and out, toward the line of the horizon. As the waves washed over me, I ducked below the water and held my breath for as long as I could, coming up between waves. My thoughts became fuzzy, the world around me dimming like a lightbulb going out in a room. I knew that I was almost out of oxygen and that I would soon pass out and slip beneath the surface.

I looked straight into an oncoming wave at my final meeting with the Divine.

That's it? I asked him. *That's really it?*

It was almost anticlimactic. I had been waiting all of my life for that moment, fighting against the inevitable. It had been written in my destiny like the stars. Like the others in my family, I would die in a tragic and untimely accident.

That's it? I asked him again. There was no tunnel of light, no vision of my life passing in front of me. It seemed that death was only a quiet passing into the dark.

No one answered. And yet when a man on a bodyboard miraculously managed to fight against the tide and rescue me, I found the strength to cling to his neck with a ferocity that I had not known that I had.

I have never forgotten that afternoon, facing God, and asking him, *That's it?* Maybe that miraculous rescue should have been the answer. But it has always remained a question, for all of these years, as I traveled through the war-torn regions of the Middle East, through ancient monasteries and sacred places now scarred with far more suffering than solace. I had carried that question in my heart day after day as I holed myself up in a library in divinity school, flipping through ancient texts, hoping to come upon a God I might recognize hidden somewhere in a story, a prayer written a thousand years ago, a word.

That's it? I can't stop asking. It is as much a challenge as a question, as though I am somehow still that same eleven-year-old girl, waiting to see whether God will abandon me or save me.

I REST A FEW HOURS, and as the light fades, I hear the bells clanging across the valley to announce the evening prayer. I descend the long flight of stairs to the monastery, climb a dark and narrow corridor, and arrive at the door to the ancient chapel. Here I remove my shoes, as I would in a Muslim house, and lift the door cloth to enter the dimly lit church. All around me, the faces of those at prayer are illuminated as they sit quietly on carpets with only candles for light, above them the ancient, astonishing frescoes staring calmly ahead. I could be in the eleventh century. We all stand, as Paolo and the monks and nuns face the altar and bow down and put their heads to the floor, three full prostrations, an ancient Eastern monastic tradition, the same prostrations that Muslims perform in the mosque. I cannot make myself bow with them. I am not ready to face God again just yet.

They look so serene, those monks and nuns, so full of purpose. The Eastern legend says that the monk leaves the world to take on the cloak of a stranger, to become nobody, that he becomes a stranger among strangers, a desolate wanderer who carries the entire world within his heart. It is in this sacrifice that he is given a particular gift, to transform the entire world within himself through prayer. So he walks, alone, carrying the world within his broken body, connected to others through breath and dreams, separated from all and united to all.

As for me, I lack the courage to make a decision as radical as living my life in a monastery in the desert, and yet I have still managed to end up almost completely alone, a stranger among strangers, carrying the broken world inside of my heart.

3.

MASS IS FINISHING INSIDE the ancient church, the smoke and incense clearing from the air. Paolo takes his place near the iconostasis and calls the names of those who will soon begin the Spiritual Exercises, and we gather around him in a circle, rubbing our hands together, shivering. The sun has fallen, and in the heart of the desert the monastery is freezing.

We are four. Dima is a Syrian novice at the monastery, loud and boisterous, with long, wavy locks of brown hair. At twenty-four, she has been in the monastery for two years, the only two years she has spent away from her family, who live in the nearby city of Homs. She will use this next month to decide if she should take her final vows. Earlier that day, as I had watched her cradling a visitor's baby, I wondered briefly if she wouldn't be just as happy as a mother, teaching English literature, which she had studied in university. She is deeply religious, but also, like many female nuns in the Arab world, she has found in the monastic life a freedom to chart her own destiny, in a world where choosing not to marry is always revolutionary.

Rania is a Damascene icon restorer who spends her days peeling back layers of smoke from the blind eyes of saints. Quiet and unsure of herself, and still recovering from the loss of a dear friend, she is also considering the novitiate. The last of us is Charles, a Lebanese novice monk who had left the monastery and is now trying the monastic life a second time, and myself. I try not to focus on the fact that everyone around me is contemplating a monastic vocation. Paolo hands us our copies of the *Spiritual Exercises of St. Ignatius*, and I wonder how it is that I have decided that a dead man who lived in the sixteenth century should play such a critical role in my life.

St. Ignatius of Loyola, the founder of the Jesuit order, designed his famous Spiritual Exercises in an attempt to place Christians in line with their destinies. He believed, and Jesuits today still believe, that all human beings have a calling and that the purpose of each human life is to discover a vocation. The Exercises move through four stages: the Fallen World, Incarnation, Crucifixion, and Resurrection, and in the coming month we will experience each of those events in full. In the second week of the Exercises, each of us will make a choice that will change our lives forever. Thousands of priests, monks, and nuns have chosen their religious vocations during their month of silence.

The Exercises are also famous because they demand a highly unusual, exhausting form of prayer. At the monastery I will suspend time and space for a month, gradually relinquishing my hold on the exterior world, and enter into the landscape of the Bible. I will leave the scenery of Damascus behind, its Ottoman houses and arching windows, the Baron and his endless cups of coffee, imagining instead the places in the text, the Roman roads and ancient markets, the Sea of Galilee and the desert near Jericho, trying to live inside of them as I would walk on any road in ordinary life. I will occupy my own mind, perhaps a more frightening terrain than any country to which I might travel.

The rules are uncompromising. We cannot speak, except to Paolo every evening, for an hour. We must eat apart from the rest of the visitors, in the kitchen alone, in silence. We should each keep a notebook of our thoughts, our fears, strange dreams we have at night. Despite monastic tradition, we should not fast, at least in the beginning, because we will need the energy that food provides to pray, for lengthy meditation is both rigorous and exhausting.

"Everything you do this month—your sleeping, your reading, your walking—will become holy," Paolo says in his loud, deep voice. "Think of this month as an appointment between yourself and God."

Unfortunately, God has a track record of canceling our appointments, taking a rain check so that he can oversee a war in the Balkans or create a new species in the Australian coral reefs. He doesn't even call to reschedule, leaving me waiting at the corner café all afternoon, near tears. What will I say to God should he choose to arrive now, after all that has happened? Should I ask him why? Attempt to forgive him? Have I collected enough rain checks by now to ask him to resurrect the dead?

"Don't read the Bible too quickly," Paolo is saying. "Read just one or two sentences, and then sit down with those words. Close your eyes. Then breathe. Wait for the characters in the story to appear, slowly, in front of you. Then, once they have settled down, ask them questions. Then wait until they give you a response. This month, you will live inside of the text. You will travel on the same roads that Jesus traveled. You will drink the same water and eat the same bread. You will walk beside the disciples. Then, in the midst of all of this, you will be allowed to walk into your own pasts."

I spend the next several days walking alone in the mountains, trying to teach myself to pray again, to accustom my body to silence, the way a climber might go early to base camp to prepare his body for the altitude. *Riyadat al-Ruhiyye*, we call this month in Arabic, which can be translated not only as "spiritual exercises," but also as "spiritual sports." As if to acknowledge what a toll it can take on the human body to simply open one's eyes.

It is the evening before the Exercises will begin, and the late afternoon sun is already falling over the distant hills. I walk out into the desert alone and lie flat against the red stones dividing the mountains in two, letting the cool rock beneath me press into my back. It will snow soon. The desert is waiting for it. All around me the desert is empty and silent, an absence more than a place, the ancient hermits' caves staring down at me with their hollow, vacant mouths. I open the Bible to the book of 1 Kings, to the story of the prophet Elijah fleeing Jezebel and escaping into the desert, and begin to read.

> Elijah was afraid and ran for his life. When he came to Beersheba in Judah, he left his servant there, while he himself went for a day's journey into the desert. He came to a broom tree, sat down under it, and prayed that he might die. "I've had enough, Lord," he said. "Take my life. I am no better than my ancestors." Then he lay under the tree and fell asleep.
>
> All at once an angel touched him and said, "Wake up and eat." He looked around, and there by his head was a cake of bread baked over hot coals, and a jar of water. He ate and drank and then lay down again.
>
> The angel of the Lord came back a second time and touched him and said, "Wake up and eat, for the journey is too much for you." So he got up and ate and drank. Strengthened by that food, he traveled forty days and forty nights until he reached Horeb, the mountain of God.

I close my eyes, waiting for the memory of the desert to peel away from the backs of my eyes. After a few moments, only blackness and silence. I have never known such silence could exist. Slowly, the air fills up with shapes, and the vacancy becomes a battlefield, a vast open space of bodies and red dust, and through it trudge hundreds of angels, exhausted, yellow with fatigue, their wings torn and barely hanging on their backs. They carry baskets of bread, covered with small blue napkins to keep them warm. The smell of the loaves is barely discernable, the smell of my mother's hands when I was a child.

The wounded bodies on the ground have lost their color, and against the red ground they look strange and ash gray, as though they have inhaled some terrible poison. The angels lean over them noiselessly. Every now and then a hand touches a face and I can see the contrast, life against death, until the body beneath that hand warms for a moment and leans again toward the living.

I see myself among the dying, lying on the ground.

The angels continue their slow, anguished walking, weighed down by their wings. The desert changes shape. They walk through the streets of Bethlehem. They walk through a portrait of Baghdad. In front of a refugee camp in Lebanon, strewn with sewage, one of the angels stops and simply stares.

I open my eyes and hurry back to my room. Tomorrow, the Exercises begin.

4.

AT SEVEN THIRTY THE NEXT MORNING, I throw on my clothes and scurry down one hundred stairs as the bells commence in their clanging. It is still dark, and Paolo and the others are already waiting in the ancient chapel, wearing long white gowns. We begin: the sign of the cross, three full prostrations all the way to the ground, the head pressing lightly against the floor, and the single plea in Arabic. *"Rhamna."*

It is the Prayer of the Heart, the prayer Eastern monks repeat all day long, silently to themselves, until it becomes as close to them as their own breath. Again and again, the monks and nuns call out the line until the words disappear and change into a cry. *Rhamna*, known to me in my childhood as *kyrie eleison*. Have mercy on us.

I take my place on the floor, listening as the prayers I have known my entire life are recited quietly, transformed, bathed in incense and sung out beneath the frescoes of the Syrian Catholic Church, the Our Father in Arabic, the Gospel of Mark in the language of the Quran. It is only in hearing them like this that I remember what these exhausted words mean: *"Atina hubzina kefafi yoomina,"* Give us this day our daily bread. As I translate the words I learned in Arabic for the marketplace, suddenly made holy, I am startled to realize that for my entire life, I have been hearing this sentence incorrectly, inserting a comma in my prayer and so changing the meaning entirely, so that the sentence became a plea that I would not die before it was my time. *Give us this day, our daily bread*, I had always prayed. As though in my mind, each extra day God allowed me to live was a gift, a piece of bread. This was the prayer I had memorized since childhood. *Lord, let me live another day.*

Now, after all those hours of learning the Arabic words for guns and atomic bombs, I am so moved to hear Arabic prayers—to hear in that language some measure of my more intimate self. How strange, to find this language, the language of Islam, of the Quran, and of Al Jazeera suddenly spoken by the voices of my own life! How strange to hear Jesus speaking Arabic, for the Psalms to find their subtle music in a new voice, so much closer to the Hebrew. As if everything taken from me is being given back a second time, new and unfamiliar, stumbling in my mouth.

After the prayer, I eat a meal of bread and goat cheese quickly, before disappearing behind the chapel into the vast silence of the desert mountain. The prayer had brought with it a small solace of being among other people, and the walk into the desert now feels solitary, like I am leaving the entire world behind. The desert, in the monastic tradition, does not function as a landscape. The desert is instead a mirror, where the silence and emptiness become so vast that the only things left to meet there are the self and God, lurking in every corner. Here is the strange world where the blue line between the interior and exterior world collapses, where the imagination is given a body. Our thoughts take on flesh in the empty air, they leave our bodies and become visible, until the body physically inhabits the interior world. The early desert monks spoke of our thoughts as angels or demons, with heavy, tangible bodies. Until we wrestle with them they will not leave us alone.

And so I lie down in the cold stone valley and read the First Contemplation of Ignatius, the story of the angels who turn their back on God and are cast from heaven to hell. I close my eyes. And then I wait.

THEY COME QUICKLY, as though they have been waiting behind the stones for decades and are only now being given permission to escape. Refugees, fleeing down the mountain, startled and unhinged. The angels.

At first, I can't make out just who they are. But then I see their faces. A boy, dressed in a pale blue suit, his wet hair pressed against his head, parted perfectly off to the side so that the comb lines still show. I can't tell how old he is. Eight perhaps. He has taken on the posture of a grown man, as though he has been asked by his mother to be brave. A girl of about six walks beside him, a small frill gathering at the bottom of her white dress. Maroon satin, a bow tied just beneath her chin, her curls fastened behind her ears with barrettes.

The mother and father stare ahead resolutely, though death is written in their eyes. And strange, awkward wings are strapped to their backs, rustling in the night air.

I do not know them or know where they are from. There is no one to tell me, and I don't dare ask, for fear of making them disappear, though I hear them whispering to one another in a language I can't understand. I know that they are Jews and that time has collapsed for a moment and they are fleeing somewhere. There is no sense of where that could be, or where they are ultimately going—I have only this single moment with them, between spaces. They walk past me, through ash and coal and a gray sky, and the sound of glass breaking.

I open my eyes, the white light of the desert shocking them. I am only dreaming, after all. These are simply the terrors of my imagination, my own ghosts conjured up into the physical world. Still, I'm frightened, frightened of myself. The mind and the heart have their own landscapes, and perhaps they are more terrible than anything we could actually meet in the desert were we left alone. I remember the words of Satan, cast out of Milton's Paradise: *Which way I fly is Hell; myself am Hell.*

I close my eyes again, waiting. Now I am no longer in the desert—I am in the midst of war. In the distance, the burned-out buildings of Beirut stand, riddled with bullet holes. Weary women sit in cafés in the midst of the rubble, smoking absently, their mouths imprinted in lipstick on cigarette filters left burning in ash. American soldiers in these streets, no, in other streets, knocking down doors in Baghdad, rehearsing under their breath the few, faulty words they have memorized in Arabic for this moment, *Yalla, Yalla, Nihna Jeysh Amerki*, the screaming inside, the bodies tearing themselves from sleep, the woman caught with her hair uncovered, tumbling down, exposed.

I have never been to Baghdad. Then how do I recognize the street, and the house, and the women inside and the men outside? I don't know their names, and still they aren't strangers. I watch them. I could reach out and touch their faces. Most of them have no wings. But I know that these are the angels I asked to see, refugees, stranded on earth. I am supposed to ask them questions. But I have no desire, no right.

These are the angels St. Ignatius said had been cast from heaven to hell, burning, for so much less than I have ever done.

NIGHT FALLS. In the church, I read the Gospel in Arabic silently to myself, following the lines from right to left and waiting for my nightly meeting with Paolo. He calls my name, and I slip out of the church, passing Rania in the courtyard. She has a look of fear in her eyes. I climb the stairs, taking my place at the end of a long table. Paolo quietly chants the Hail Mary in Arabic.

Assalamu Aleyki, ya Maryam . . .

Something about hearing that prayer from my childhood, so many years later and after so many losses, makes me begin to cry.

He looks at me gently, smiling. "You don't waste any time, do you?" he asks. I choke on my laugh.

It is cold in the room, and I move closer to the stove, then take out the small green notebook I carried with me into the mountain that morning. I begin to read softly, in an even voice, the chronicle of my day in the desert, about the refugees in the mountains fleeing war, the burning buildings, the women awakened in their beds, the angels walking with their baskets of bread. I read strangely, articulating every vowel and consonant, as one reading to a blind man. I need him to understand, to tell me that I am not crazy. Except—perhaps I have once again gone crazy, as I had always known, in the back of my head, that I would.

I finish, finally looked up again to meet Paolo's gaze. *Help me.* I came to the desert in search of God, and he was nowhere in anything I saw this morning, nowhere in any of those visions of war. How do I know that it is only the angels and not God who is in exile, that he has not cast himself out from our presence? How do I know that he is not also wandering in the desert somewhere lost?

Paolo takes my hand. He tries to speak in a low voice. "Stephanie, you must believe that God is like a child before violence. You must believe that he didn't create this, but that he is wounded and grieving to see the world as it is."

I imagine God as he describes him, with his face in his hands, weeping, like Michelangelo's Jeremiah in the Sistine Chapel at the sight of Jerusalem burning.

"But then, what is this talk of a wrathful God? What is this talk of God exiling people to hell? Why am I here in the desert, reading Ignatius? You can't have it both ways. And I'm sorry, and I know I'm not supposed to say this, but I'm not afraid of hell. I'm afraid of a God who would send people to hell. Even more, I'm afraid that if hell exists and I don't go there, then someone else will go in my place. Then all of our talk about Christian compassion is crap."

I wait for him to answer. He doesn't look alarmed, just tired, almost existentially tired. I think about those who watched as the Jews were shipped off to concentration camps, those who sent off the poor from my city in Texas to fight in Iraq and stayed at home and hung their heads. We walk on the bones of the suffering of others. How is that different from taking a place in heaven while allowing others to burn in hell? There was a famous story of a Jewish prisoner in the concentration camps who asked his rabbi for advice. He had learned that he could bribe a guard and obtain his son's release. He wanted to know, was that morally permissible, knowing that if his son went free, another man would be sent to die in his place? And is not that the larger question of desiring salvation?

Paolo takes a deep breath. I have thrown him into anguish. Somehow I don't care. I am tired of carrying my anguish alone.

"Stephanie," he begins, "we must believe that God dreams of the salvation of all mankind, that creation and salvation are a single act. Nothing else works. Otherwise, we dream that we go to heaven while others go to hell, and that our going to heaven participates in sending others to hell. If that were true, then our only choice would have to be to rebel against God, to voluntarily cast ourselves into hell in solidarity with the banished ones, because we would refuse to participate in the suffering of others."

He pauses, looking up at me. "I just can't believe that this is what God wants of us, for the faithful to burn in hell. The only thing remaining for us to do is to believe that, in some way we don't yet understand, all of this chaos will one day be swept up and everything will be transformed."

I want so much to believe him, and yet it seems too easy.

"You know, the Muslims have a saying," he finishes. "They say that no one can escape from the power of God, and the power of God is his mercy."

I write his words in my small green notebook. *Everything will be transformed.* What does that mean? Like water lifting out of clothes left out to dry, becoming steam, cloud, no recollection of the heaviness it once added to a body? Like sailboats stripped of old blue and white paint and cast out again to water? What transformation could happen to our bodies to make us forget these terrors we have witnessed, which we have carried for such a long time? And could such forgetting begin to justify the journey?

I have one last thing to ask. Tomorrow, I know I will journey into the most infamous day of the Spiritual Exercises, the journey into hell, where Ignatius asks us to lie down among the burning and the damned, to "smell the smoke, the brimstone, the sewer filth and putrid things" of hell. I have come to the desert to escape hell. With my psychological history, to place myself in hell on purpose seems like madness, no different than a scarred war veteran attempting meditation on a shooting range, a recovering alcoholic working a season in a vineyard.

"I've been running away from visions my whole life, Abuna," I tell him. "I need to know if it is safe for me to go."

He sighs a deep sigh, all the way from his chest. "It's true," he admits. "I still remember my day in hell, from when I did the Spiritual Exercises over twenty years ago. It is a very powerful event. You only wish to experience it once in your life and never again."

It doesn't matter. I have to stay. What do I have to return to?

He sees the decision in my eyes and says calmly, "Don't worry, Stephanie. I don't think that God brought you all the way to the desert to leave you stranded in hell."

5.

IT IS MORNING, after the prayer. Last night the wind turned cold, rattling the windows near my bed. Now it moves like a knife through my body with every step, sliding down my throat and traveling into my chest each time I inhale. I climb the mountain, rising higher above the valley, passing beneath the large hermit's cave, and then descending into a narrow gorge torn open when water once flowed. The wind dies down for a moment, but I can hear it passing in other places, whistling across the stones. I close my eyes.

Soon, the desert slips away, and I know that the other world is coming. I wait. Now I am standing at the top of a flight of stairs, the railings dripping with water. I descend, trying to keep my balance, into the dark. The walls are almost ice, wet and frozen, like an underground cistern. There is a faint light. And then I see my mother, crouched against a window, shivering and cold. It takes her a moment to recognize me. Then she calls my name. I reach out to her, but our hands are both damp and she slips away. She keeps calling my name, as though I am still a child, and I answer her as though I am a child. She keeps calling for help.

"Stephanie? Stephanie Celeste?"

"I'm sorry," I say, and I don't even know if she can hear me. "I'm so sorry."

I stare at her for a long time. "Let me see," I whisper, trembling. She disappears, and I take her place, shivering in the cold and in the dark. I am watching her life through her eyes. Now I reach out, pressing my hand on her mother's dead body. Kissing her father's face, wounded and blue as the sea. Watching her younger sister passing beneath that bus.

I cannot look anymore. I open my eyes and walk out of that gorge in the mountains, nauseous. In the Exercises, I am supposed to thank God for the fact that he has had pity on me and mercifully not placed me in hell for my many sins.

I am not thankful. I can't bear to see my mother like this, alive in hell. I want to take her place.

6.

THE DAYS CONTINUE PASSING AMONG THE RUINS, and I live with my mother and the exhausted angels. I sleep, and I awaken, and I find myself becoming grateful for the silence I once feared I would dread. Sometimes, when I am alone in the desert and my body swells up with visions to the point of breaking open, I can believe what the ancient mystics said, that the body contains an entire world. I feel as though my interior self is much older than my body—like I have inherited the past of the woman who gave birth to me, just as in some way I carry the past of the places I have chosen to live. When those visions come to me in the desert, many of them don't belong to me. They are ancient squatters who come to inhabit my life, and because I cannot hope to evict them, I learn to live with them, to listen to them.

Then there is memory. When I first met him, Paolo told me the story of the church frescoes, of how they had been uncovered after having been abandoned in the dark for so long. It happened slowly, over time. For many years, the frescoes were hidden beneath a layer of whitewash and forgotten. It was only when the locals burned the roof of the church for fuel, allowing the rain to come inside, that many of the faces were washed clean, staring out again.

When the restorers came, they found one layer beneath another, and they peeled the layers back slowly. When the frescoes revealed themselves, they came back wounded. Some of the eyes had been cut out. In some places, the bodies had been scarred by the names of those who passed beside them to pray and carved their initials into their skin. Hands were missing, parts of bodies. They carried the stories of all that had happened in those hundreds of years since they were painted, they wore the smoke from the candles of those who had prayed beside them. They carried those prayers.

"A resurrection," Paolo had said about watching them, rising from beneath the surface. "A resurrection, with the wounds still there."

During this first week of the Exercises, I have sometimes felt the same thing happening inside my head. The desert is washing my mind clean again, and I can finally remember my entire life, the details of faces I have not remembered since I was young. My grandfather follows me everywhere, with his silver, curly hair and leathery skin, and so does my grandmother, whose face I remember perfectly despite the fact that I never met her. My mother calls out to me, using my full name, and my aunt speaks to me also, along with the rest of my family, their faces staring out in the dark. But now the memories are scarred by what has passed since my childhood. They come back carrying new wounds, the wounds of all I have seen and lost in the Middle East. When I remember them, I also remember streets in Jerusalem, I remember Hassan, I remember refugee camps in southern Lebanon, that baby crying, I remember those images from Iraq flashing on Damascus television screens. They become one memory, the past and the present. The two worlds I inhabit carry each other inside of themselves.

Now I understand that hell is not being banished from God. Hell is the inability to save those you love. Hell is that helplessness in front of God and history, the face of a woman you love in the dark, calling out for help.

It is the end of the first week of the Exercises. This morning I sat down and wrote out all of the sins I've committed in my lifetime to prepare myself for confession. I returned to my room after the morning prayer, huddled beside the gas heater, and began to write in a torrent. I wrote all morning and all afternoon. I wrote until the gas in my heater ran dry and I had to fill it up again. I wrote until I filled ten long hand-written pages, a catalog of all that I had ever done wrong, until my arm hurt and the pen was empty so I could write no further.

It began at the age of seven, when I was mercilessly cruel to a girl in my class, who soon after was killed in a car accident.

The list goes on. I isolated myself from my family. While they were wounded, from one death or another, I pulled away and fell into depression.

I failed one lover after another. This accounts for several pages, and I was, I admit, trying to be brief.

Then there was Mark, who deserved his own section: Mark, whom I had somehow been unable to make happy—whom I had made so unhappy that he had finally sent me away.

I detached myself from my friends.

Despite all of my years in the Middle East, I did little to work for peace.

For almost an entire lifetime, I never really prayed.

When I was finished writing, I sat next to the black heater in my room, and I felt a tsunami of grief welling within me, a grief I have rarely allowed myself to feel in my lifetime, and I sobbed. My body trembled, and I let it tremble, I let the tears fall in enormous torrents from my eyes. At that moment, my life was a series of failures, ten pages long. I suppose that Ignatius had wanted us to understand that the world had fallen because of our sins. I would never believe that, never believe in a God cruel enough to let that happen. Yet the world had never seemed so fallen to me as it did right then, and I could not help but wonder if those faces appearing to me in the desert might have looked different, had I acted more compassionately. Would they be so scarred? Would they carry so many wounds? How many of those were my doing?

I suppose it is inevitable to wake up one day and ask how much of the chaos around us is of our own making, and what exact role we had to play. I wonder if I asked those phantoms in the desert for forgiveness if that would be the same as asking real people, face-to-face. Where would I begin? I can't blame myself for the wars surrounding me. And yet what of my first real boyfriend in high school, who had once dreamed of becoming a priest, but who was now a tank commander in Iraq? If I had done something differently, might some of the people he killed still be alive? Might he have been spared the horror of standing in front of that violence, might he be somewhere else in a quiet room, praying alone, or sleeping peacefully beside his wife at night?

I cannot blame myself for the tragedies of my mother's family. Yet why had I flown so far from home? Why had I left her? How had so many years passed without me consoling her in her grief?

Why had I walked away from Hassan? Why had I closed my door to Michael? How do these small, daily acts multiply and extend themselves into eternity?

7.

LAST NIGHT IT RAINED. I heard sheets of water falling outside my window against the mountain. I felt it in the desert air, within my body, which has grown sensitive to everything around me. This morning I look over the cliffs to see that the earth has changed color, dark and deep orange, the stones shining in the light.

I can bear it no longer. I leave the Exercises behind. I leave everything in my room, my notebooks, my Bible, the instructions of St. Ignatius. I walk out along the narrow path into the valley, turning left instead of right, following a new trail, a path I have never walked on before.

Wild dogs are barking across the valley. I pick up stones to carry in my pocket. I could be Jacob, fleeing overnight, who is tackled by the riverside, forced into a wrestling match with God. I know his frustration now, his insistence on finding out why this stranger has come and attacked him while he had been walking alone. "Tell me your name," he begs.

I am fed up with God, fed up with the terrors I have spent the last week remembering. I climb a mountain face without a path, stumbling on loose rocks, the earth still wet from rain. The sky is alive with blue and fierce clouds that keep changing, rolling in and departing. Everything around me is writhing and alive. I lie flat, pressed against the mountain, and crawl on my stomach, afraid of the earth giving way beneath me. When I finally reach the summit of the mountain, my hands are caked with earth, and burning. I sit down to rest, with a view of the mountains on every side of me.

And then I begin to speak aloud, to the sky. I speak about all of the people in my life, my family, my great loves, everyone I have ever kissed or lay down beside, each city I have lived in. I speak of a man I once loved in Kashgar, the way we held each other in a room set high above the market-place, hovering over thousands of scarves and carpet stalls, donkeys and wagons being carted through the streets. I speak of the sea in Tyre breathing against Roman ruins, of my father. I speak of Mark, beautiful and asleep in his bed. I tell the air the story of my life. It comes out like music. I don't know to whom I'm speaking, but I feel someone listening. It must be God. It can be no one else.

The clouds are wild, breaking off from the sky and walking across the open space between the mountains and the horizon. I keep calling out to them. Maybe for years I had only needed to say it all out loud. To admit that those lives, those cities, those stories left unfinished exist for me. I need them recorded in the Book of Life. If God is listening, I need him to know. I need him to witness my passing, so that I can at least know that it was not all for nothing. I am no longer ashamed in front of God—I am full of rage and awe and even a quiet pride, and despite any sorrow I refuse to see the world as fallen. I had loved in that world. I had loved in that stupid, hellish world, and it is beautiful despite everything, even though I cannot begin to understand how or why. I speak to the sky, and the sky listens, and the world takes me into its arms and welcomes me home again.

It is already late when I return to my room. I shower, washing the mountains off my skin, put on a clean blouse and a long yellow skirt. When I walk outside to descend the stairs for my nightly meeting, something is falling, catching in the moonlight. It is just beginning to snow.

I run down the long flight of stairs to confess my sins.

8.

FOR DAYS, THE SNOW KEEPS FALLING. The world takes on a strange, muffled sound, so that the imprint of my footsteps, my own breathing becomes magnified in space, every movement becomes pronounced. The stairs between my room and the chapel disappear in whiteness. I can barely see beyond the step in front of me. Even the mountains are gone.

After the first week, I rest, taking a few days off from the rigor of Ignatius's daily schedule of prayer and meditation. Sometimes I wake up early in the morning and walk alone through the desert valley, my hands clasping the red stones that are still cold from the crisp desert night—and in these moments it seems that nothing separates me from those who came here almost fifteen hundred years ago. I can reach out and briefly touch eternity. The desert is an endless, quiet room. A white canvas, so that any object placed against it takes on a startling fierceness—olive trees, thistles, a single blade of grass.

At night, when the clouds clear, the sky fills with more stars than I knew existed. Behind them sleeps darkness so dark that it makes the brightness of the tiny lights brighter still. When the moon swells to its fullness, the stones inhale it, and I can walk the steps from the chapel up to my room without a flashlight.

The time is becoming long. None of us manages to keep the silence. Dima knocks on my door at night and pours me a cup of tea, sitting beside me, huddled next to the stove. Rania stops me in the valley to talk before I climb the mountain. We carry the exhaustion of soldiers who have just survived a week of battles, reaching out to one another for some small solace. I have rarely been so thankful for the presence of other human beings.

The snow continues. There are no visitors at the monastery now, just us, the workers, the monks and nuns and volunteers who live here. Even with our few words, I never knew silence like this could exist. God placing his hand over our mouths, saying, *Hush. Just listen.*

9.

IT IS THE TENTH DAY OF THE EXERCISES. I walk into the desert to meditate on the story of the Annunciation, when the angel Gabriel appears to Mary to tell her that she will give birth to a child. I have been waiting for this moment since I arrived, the promised moment of salvation, the moment in the Exercises meant to redeem all of the hells of last week. I close my eyes and wait for the characters to appear. I witness them briefly: Mary trembling in front of the angel, and Gabriel trying to comfort her, whispering, *Do not be afraid, Mary, you have found favor with God.*

In truth I feel nothing at all. It isn't real. I look down at myself as from a distance and see the fool that I am, a child, summoning phantoms up in the desert. I am not sure how my life has come to this—twenty-seven years old and in the desert, talking to my imaginary friends.

I stay up all night, listening to the wind beating against the windowpanes, and by the time I climb from bed the next morning I am so tired I can barely move. In the chapel, we pray the Psalms in Arabic, and the words are far too difficult for me. They swarm through my ears like a river of noise. I begin to cry. Someone motions to me to light the candles behind the iconostasis, but I can't do it. I motion them away with my hand, exhausted.

After what feels like eternity, the prayer finishes. Paolo calls my name. I stay huddled in the back of the church, against the fresco of paradise. He asks what is wrong. I look around; there are still others in the church, kneeling in front of icons, warming themselves beside the oven.

"Out," he calls. "*Yalla*, everyone out." They leave—his voice carries that kind of authority, somewhere between an abbot and a cop. He follows the last of them, closing the door of the church, and bolts it shut. Only the two of us remain, locked inside, with the endless faces of anonymous saints staring down at us.

I find a place beneath the enormous thirteenth-century fresco of hell. Appropriate. Paolo sits across from me.

"What is it?" he asks gently. No more bad cop now.

I still don't know what *it* is. I have reached a space bolted as tightly shut as the door just beyond us, a space where I can no longer pray. I have arrived at a dead end, and I can't go forward and never want to go back again. I'm simply lost.

"I'm supposed to meditate on the Incarnation today," I say quietly.

"Why is that making you cry?"

I consider for a moment, and then I turn my face away from him. "Because I don't believe that it's true."

There are few more blasphemous things a Mexican Spanish Irish girl brought up in Catholic schools can say to a Catholic priest. I'm shocked by my own words. Until that moment, I have never had the courage to think them, much less say them aloud. *I don't believe in incarnation. I don't believe that God became man.*

I begin shaking, tears running down my face. He takes my face in his hands, looking into my eyes. "Remember these tears, Stephanie," he whispers. "These are the sweetest tears of your life."

THAT AFTERNOON, I climb to my secret place, where even the mountains disappear and there is only the red stone beneath my feet and sky stretching out in all directions. No one can ever find me here. I open my Bible and read the passage from Luke again:

> *The angel went to her and said, "Greetings, you who are highly favored! The Lord is with you!"*
>
> *Mary was greatly troubled at his words and wondered what kind of greeting this might be. But the angel said to her, "Do not be afraid, Mary, you have found favor with God."*

I close my eyes, and wait for Mary to arrive. She is alone in her room, barely a teenager, quietly folding her dresses into a neat pile and stacking them on her bed. She hums absently to herself. Now she looks up and finds an angel in front of her bed. She drops everything, looks at him.

What does it feel like, to see him standing in front of her, Gabriel in all of his strangeness? Does she look at his hands? His wings?

No, she doesn't even ask his name.

She just listens to his voice, a voice like water. Like cold water against her trembling.

Look at Mary in front of the angel, Paolo told me. *Notice how afraid she is when she learns that she is pregnant. This is how we feel the story to be true. We should be afraid. To not be confused, uncertain over something as enormous as the presence of God in our lives is not to be human. And Mary is human.*

The miracle, then, is that she still says yes.

The truth is, I have been up on this mountain for more than ten days, and I have yet to meet God. I have forgotten how to speak to him. He is like a lover whose life has gone in such a different direction that I am left to sit awkwardly across the table, silently watching him. I can't even remember when I lost him. I can only guess that it didn't happen at once, that my faith eroded slowly, over time, like a wall left exposed to the rain. Perhaps it began when I was that young teenager watching my grandfather's face turn blue. When I was in the hospital, listening to patients screaming. Later, as I saw the Middle East crumbling in pieces, perhaps another piece fell away, until when Mark told me I was delusional for believing, I could laugh and pretend that there was nothing wrong with describing the dearest longings of my heart as childish, ridiculous. Jesus was simply a man, a historical person, because God could not be here. God was in exile. He had lost his interest in my life long ago.

But then a voice from within me speaks:

Weren't there moments, almost invisible, when he appeared, briefly, like a figure passing quickly by a window? Surely, you remember. When you looked at the color of blue hand-blown glass. When a poem arrived, unbeckoned, in the middle of the night. Fireflies. A morning in the subway in Paris, when the sound of human voices hit you with such fierceness, humming against the rails. Tangerines. The eyes of pregnant women. There were moments, even if they were never articulated. When you felt: someone is here.

And now this, God becoming man, the timeless entering time. Which is worse, a God who remains distant, or a God who enters the world, a God who exists in war? A God who must now also be in anguish?

. . .

I sit on that mountain for a long time. And then I decide to give myself over. It is against every natural instinct in my body, every desire for self-protection, and yet I let go of myself. *Here*, I say to God. *Do what you will do*.

At first, I don't feel anything. It is simply a door opening. Nothing more. It isn't sadness. It is more like coming up for air. Something inside of my chest breaks open, unleashing an aching, a longing.

My eyes are closed, but they feel as though they are open. I ask to see the Incarnation. The next moment I watch a collapsing of opposites, as if one world is falling into another. The unknown falls into the known, infusing every object with light. Everything becomes electric. Everything feels full to the point of brimming over.

When I open my eyes, the desert, the trees, the stones—everything is magnified, expanding beyond themselves. All of them contain a *suchness*, as though I can look within them and view their essence. The world reveals itself from the inside. Gerard Manley Hopkins once called it "inscape." For me, it is simply as though I am looking into the soul of each thing.

Everything appears different than before, as though I haven't seen anything prior to this moment, as if I have been closing my eyes for an entire lifetime. For an instant, everything feels vivid, illuminated. As though the world is stained glass, and the light is coming in.

I close my eyes again and wait.

Now, I am looking through a window, and the other side contains several worlds at once. Beirut. Bethlehem. Baghdad. The buildings riddled with holes. And my family, my poor, exhausted family. Yet something is different now. A strange light breathes beneath the pavement, illuminating everything. Something else is present, beneath the surface of things.

I remember the story of Mary, trembling in front of the angel.

I look to the sky, and I whisper, *Yes*.

10.

A few days later, Jesus is born in the desert. I watch his arrival from my cold, barren room in the monastery. I am exhausted, and barely find the strength, and yet he comes. A snowstorm blocks the road to

Damascus, and held up in that room I pray. I light a candle, and in my heart God comes into that bruised and terrified day, he comes as a child and he keeps crying, and I hear him.

"Christ put on the body," the Syriac church fathers wrote to describe the Incarnation, so that I imagine him sliding on this new skin like a terry-cloth robe after a warm bath. Yet to me it feels more visceral and profound. I try to conceive of what it means concretely, for God to be present in the world. If he is truly embodied on earth, eternally, then this means that he is contained in everyone, in Hassan and Ali, in the Baron, in Michael, in those refugees pouring into the streets. Then he is also in the war, he is contained in the bodies of those who are dying, and even in those who are killing. My mother holds him closely, just as he had been contained in my grandfather's body as it swelled and changed color and drifted toward sleep.

For the rest of the Spiritual Exercises, I will be reading only a single Gospel, meditating on the text line by line, imagining the roads and hills and Roman markets so completely that I will live inside of them. Dima, who was raised as a Greek Orthodox Christian, has chosen the Gospel of John, whose emphasis on mysticism makes him particularly beloved by the Eastern churches. Rania chooses Luke, who legend says was not only a physician but also a painter of icons, tying his life to her own work as a restorer of frescoes and religious art. After some thought, I choose the Gospel of Matthew. Though I certainly tell no one this, the truth is Matthew's Gospel makes me smile. I appreciate his depiction of Jesus as a radical, rabbinical Jew: awkward, brilliant, and misunderstood by even his closest friends. Matthew's Jesus is so incredibly human. He reminds me of Woody Allen, or someone equally unlikely to be God, a man who in my mind has brown, curly hair and certainly would have worn glasses had they been invented. Despite the fact that he is a carpenter I still see him wearing corduroy. He is charming in his own way, charismatic and yet overwhelmed by the circumstances of his life, unable to express his thoughts directly, resigned to using parables no one understands. He is the Messiah, and at the same time marginally like almost every man I ever met as a graduate student at Harvard. I feel like I might have run into him in the Judaica section of the library at 2:00 a.m.

Yet despite his familiarity, there is something strange about him, from the moment he first appears to me in the desert, real as any human being.

I watch him baptized, see his long and lean body shivering as he emerges from the water, his hair dripping, and there is something I cannot touch. I see him hungry in the desert, tempted by Satan, his landscape mirroring my own landscape, his haunting language: *Man cannot live by bread alone.* And I know that I am watching someone who is more than human. And who, though he allows me inside of the room, will never be mine.

Sometimes, I feel like a mother, watching Jesus appearing out of the bones of the desert each afternoon. He grows up so quickly. One moment I am in the stable in Bethlehem, surrounded by animals, a few shepherds looking on, as he is born, and before I know it he is fully grown. I can barely touch him as his life moves by me—and I find myself wanting to hold on to it, want to slow it down, to claim him. I feel a kind of longing, a regret that so many chapters of his life go missing, for here in the desert those missing pages become concrete, years in a human life I will never witness. I want more time to know his laughter, to memorize his way of walking, his turns of phrase, to ask him if he ever fell in love. But I will never know Jesus at fifteen, or at twenty-five. I will only know him at the beginning and the end of his life, when it is still too early and already too late, and time for him to go.

Today, I sit and watch him as he passes by James and John in their boat on the Sea of Galilee with their father Zebedee. They are preparing their nets for the day's work. I can smell the sea, can feel the waves swelling up around them, the wind skirting across the surface of the water.

Jesus calls to them. They go.

It is just like that, a brief moment. "I'm just getting my nets ready," I whisper to Jesus. "I'll leave the boat and my father, I'll come soon."

But I don't. I just sit and watch him. I watch him all day long, wandering from village to village, the sick rising beneath his hands, the crippled walking, and those with seizures shaking and trembling until he holds them like a storm-trodden sea and begs them to rest.

11.

I HAVE COME TO THE END of the second week of the Exercises, the week of the famous choice. I'm nervous. What if I make a choice that hurls my life in the wrong direction? But I need this moment. I'm tired of living like a gypsy, moving from country to country every few years, and I need to root myself in a life. And yet what life will I possibly find happiness in? I have lost any faith in poetry and have little desire to return to school. I was never a particularly good journalist, and the idea of daily sifting through images of bombs and natural disasters doesn't really appeal to me. A career in Arabic translation is certainly out of the question. What's more, the last time I made a major choice was when I decided, against all odds, to stay in Boston and try to make a life with Mark. I don't have a very good track record when it comes to choices. *I* don't even trust my own instincts. When I used to get lost in Jerusalem, I would ask myself which way my gut feeling suggested I should go and promptly walk in the opposite direction. It normally took me straight home.

So it is that tonight, when Paolo raises the question in our meeting, I have little to offer him in response. I was hoping that he might suggest something.

"I could be a writer," I say. "I could go back and get my doctorate and become a professor. I could continue journalism. I could become a nun."

As I say those last words, I try them out in my mouth for the first time: *I could become a nun.*

It seems an odd suggestion. And yet not unnatural, coming from my mouth, with all of the casual tones of any other sentence, phrased slightly in the form of a question, the last word lilting up. *What do you think, should we catch an afternoon movie? I could become a nun?*

The idea has been secretly forming in my mind ever since the Incarnation, and I suppose I say it aloud to try it out, to see if it sounds ridiculous. It is not as though I am the first person in my family to consider a religious vocation. There is something in my solitary nature that suggests monasticism, so that my theology professor had told me just before I left for Syria, "To be honest, I would much rather see you become a prioress than a professor." Besides, I am slowly finding a home in the monastery, and I have not felt at home in any place in a very long time. I relish the underground library with its dusty books, the hermits' caves hidden in the mountains. I am growing to love that church with its ancient frescoes staring down at me, the fresco of the angel with a towel in his hands, the painting of St. Simeon the Stylite, the famous local saint, sitting atop his pillar in the sky. On a few nights I have even slept in the church and awakened in the morning to light flooding in from above the altar and landing on my face.

Most of all, I love the possibility that I might have power, that I might play a role in that history that until now I have always witnessed from the wings, the tragedy of my family, the larger tragedy of the Middle East. The miracle of the monastic life is the belief that as humans we are not spectators, but that we can engage and struggle with God—that perhaps we might even change his mind.

I was half expecting Paolo to burst into laughter at my suggestion, but he doesn't seem surprised by my words.

"I was hoping I could study," I hasten to add.

"Don't let that worry you. You can finish your studies first, or study in Rome with the others in the community. You could even teach sometimes if you would like."

"What could I offer to the monastery if I stayed?"

"Don't ask what you can give," he tells me. "Ask what you can receive."

I smirk. Sometimes I am not in the mood for his Sean Connery wisdom.

He smiles. "You think about it for a few days," he says. "And then you ask God to give you an answer."

I THINK ABOUT IT. In fact I think about almost nothing else. There are no answers for a long time. Instead, whenever I close my eyes, I see an endless desert road stretched out in front of me, with someone waiting on the other side. I stumble along it, exhausted, and beside me walks the angel with a basket of bread.

"Get up and eat," the angel keeps saying. "The road ahead of you is long."

Something about those early visions in the desert, of devastated cities and people in hell, makes it difficult for me to make an ordinary choice, to decide to return to life as I had previously been living it. I can't just become a tax attorney or even write novels when the world is falling apart. I can't turn my back on them. I can't live as though those images never existed. They demand something from me, and I don't think they'll disappear from my life in the desert until I discern what that something *is*.

Yesterday, after dreaming of that same desert road, I thought I had found the answer to my searching. Perhaps it was a real road—not metaphorical, and I was supposed to walk on it. "I want to go to Baghdad," I announced to Paolo. "I want to walk from Baghdad across the Middle East, without money or food, as a witness to peace in this time of suffering."

He sighed into his hand, and then looked at me sternly. "You'll be killed, Stephanie. I know that you don't want to hear this. But that would be a spectacular waste of your gifts."

Perhaps I am beginning to lose my grip on reality. How can I know? Watching visions in the desert all afternoon is not exactly normal human behavior.

So I read the Gospels. The days pass by without an answer. I think about what it means to be a monk or nun, the stories that said they take the entire world inside of themselves and transform it through their prayers. I still carry those visions of devastated cities, of my mother in hell, and I want to do something. I want to fix some of what has been broken.

Sometimes I lay in bed at night, and I remember my mornings with Mark in a room in Cambridge, drinking smoky Chinese tea. They seem part of another life now. I think of him in the way I think about the dead, or about a country I have lost forever. I don't long for him, because there is no use in longing for a past that can never be retrieved. I only regret what I might have done differently. I might have been kinder, more understanding, more able to forgive. He is gone forever now. But the desert allows me to watch over him from a distance, to take care of him, to make amends. I can love him from the desert in a way I never could when I was by his side. That comforts me.

Paolo asks me every day, *Where do you want to go from here? What do you want?* I don't know how to answer. I want the war in Iraq and the war between the Israelis and Palestinians to end. I want people in my family to stop dying. I want to right the wrongs of my past.

Are there limits to the question? Must the answer be grounded in reality? I want to be a saint. I want to transform rooms I enter, to make the world whole again. I want to take the world into myself.

Sometimes, when I am alone out there in the desert, I see them all at once, lined up in the desert in front of me: Iraqis, American soldiers, Palestinian refugees, Israeli soldiers. I look at their faces, one after another, and then I ask myself, *Stephanie, suppose you could, even for a day, make some of their sufferings disappear. Would you say no? Would you even dare?*

Then I summon up all of the faces of my family. I summon up Mark's face. I look at them, at those blessed, dear parts of my life, of my heart, and then I ask again: *Stephanie—what if you can give them life? Would you say no?*

Paolo once told me that the world is anchored by our souls, that if one person finds God, finds prayer, then they become a link in a chain that helps to heal all those who came before and will come after them. I have heard this before in Syria, from Muslims and Christians both, a local legend. *A person who finds God can intercede seven generations in the past and seven generations into the future.*

An impossible sentence. And yet.

What if what the ancient monks said remains true and we can transform the world inside ourselves? What if by offering myself, I can truly save them?

12.

December

I HAVE BEEN LIVING WITH JESUS for more than two weeks now, and I can hardly remember what life was like before I came here. There is no space between us any longer. I walk in the Roman markets with him and his disciples. I watch him speak on the mountaintop, real as any human being, reciting his bizarre parables: *the eye is the lamp of the body, see how the lilies in the field grow, enter through the narrow gate* . . . I see him calm storms. Remove demons. Bring a girl back to life.

He seems content to let me watch him. He even seems lonely, like any man walking through so much confusion without a companion.

He sometimes calls to me. As though he needs to be seen. As though he needs me to witness the leper's hand unwithering, the paralytic rising from his bed.

I watch him moving beside people, anticipating their gestures, the way they change in his presence. I watch his hands. He is so quietly beautiful. I try to keep from thinking while I watch him: *Please, don't die*.

Now, Jesus is walking through the streets when he sees the tax collector Matthew. "Follow me," he tells him, and Matthew gets up and follows him.

I am shocked at the speed at which it happens. I forget to be shy and pull Matthew aside. "Why did you follow him?" I ask.

"It wasn't me who followed," he says. "My heart listened and followed his heart."

I don't believe him, and so I ask Jesus, "Why did you call him?"

"I didn't call him," he says. "I was simply walking by, and my heart called him."

13.

EACH EVENING, I tell Paolo about my visions in the desert, noticeably avoiding any talk of making a choice.

"Do you still want to choose a vocation?" Paolo asks.

He doesn't know that I am terrible at making decisions. I have no way of knowing whether or not I am supposed to be a nun. It takes me an hour just to pick a video at Blockbuster.

Put it before God, he says.

He makes it sound so easy, as though a monastic vocation is a recipe we need to try, to see if it is hopeless or perhaps just needs more salt. I can't blame him. His own choice to become a priest came when he was still a teenager, and he had never lost the conviction that he had been called. I had met many other monks, nuns, and priests who had received their vocations in much the same way, a miracle that stayed within them, a kind of love at first sight moment between them and the Divine. Yet I am not accustomed to letting God participate in my choices, and since he has not taken the initiative to call out to me like he did to Charlton

Heston in *The Ten Commandments*, I don't know how to begin asking him what he might think.

I'll just ask God for a sign, I decide. *If God really wants me to become a nun, then he will give me a sign during the Mass tonight. There will be a sign in the moment when the bread is raised to the sky.*

IT IS ESPECIALLY DAMP AND COLD when I take my place that night in the back of the church. Outside, the wind is howling. We light the candles and make our prostrations to the ground.

As the readings in Arabic begin, I watch closely and wait for a sign. Yet the Arabic vocabulary of the Mass is too complex for me, and I understand nothing. The first reading passes, and then the second, and I have no clue from which books they are taken or what they are about. I am as lost as I was when I first arrived in the Middle East years ago, not knowing a word.

I won't lose hope. As the Communion approaches, I still wait for the smallest possibility of a miracle—a flicker of light, even a deep feeling in my heart. Paolo lifts the bread into the air, imitating the words of Jesus to his disciples: "Take this, all of you, and eat from it. This is my body."

No, there is nothing, nothing at all. Not even a faint gleaming.

Though it hardly seems possible, the Mass gradually becomes increasingly baffling, a Monty Python skit of the nonmiraculous. During the Communion hymn, everyone sings so off-key that they finally begin the song from the beginning, trying to salvage a tune, to bring forth at least some semblance of music. Again, I do not recognize the song and cannot join them. If it were not so depressing, it might be funny. It is not simply that God will not give me a sign. I am beginning to wonder if he has made everything deliberately obscure, as if to warn me never to ask for one again, as the words of Jesus in the Gospel of Mark: "Why does this generation ask for a miraculous sign? I tell you the truth, no sign will be given to it."

After the Mass, I barely eat. By the time I return to my room, night has already fallen. I lock the door behind me, feeling, in that quiet room, betrayed. It is not so much that I desire to be a nun. I want to know that God is listening to me. I want for my life not to be anonymous, for it to be witnessed by someone else. I want to know that I am not still that eleven-year-old girl, waiting all afternoon, speaking to the empty air.

I climb into bed and then, changing my mind, climb out again, standing in the center of the room. *Listen, God*, I whisper to the walls. *I am going to give you another opportunity.*

I remove an icon of Christ from the wall and take a candle to light in front of it. I find the box of matches, only to realize that they have all become damp during the course of the day. I strike one match after another and watch as the ends crumble into powder. Finally, the last match lights—catching the wick just in time.

I sit down in front of that candle, in the dark, and read the story of Abraham's sacrifice of Isaac. I have read that story so many times, but only now do I touch the agony it contains. I ask them to appear to me. I watch Abraham saddling his bags onto his donkey, his fingers stumbling over the knots, the way he places his head against the saddle just for a moment, breathing. I follow his slow and tortured walk up the mountainside with his son, pressing the brush aside so that it will not scratch against the child's face. I can see it in his eyes, his desire to give up everything in obedience to God. I stand beside him as he lays his son down on the altar. I close my eyes, seeing the faint candlelight through my eyelids, and pray. *God, I am offering a second chance. I am willing to give you everything. I only ask for a sign.*

I wait. And wait. I wait until the wick wears down to nothing and the night is finally drowned in darkness and silence. The last thought I have before sleeping is that even God no longer wants me.

14.

I SLEEP LIKE A STONE. In the morning I awaken to a pulsing of joy and relief flooding out of my heart. The storm has passed, and now light is coming through the windows in full force, illuminating everything in the room. From my bed, I look down at the candle wax on the ground and remember the events of the night before. Suddenly it seems so very long ago. Perhaps God has not abandoned me after all. Perhaps he simply sent an angel to me in my sleep to whisper in my ear, *Don't worry. You don't have to go through with this.*

After the morning prayer, Rania intercepts me in the dry riverbed on the path to the mountain, clearing a flat stone so that we can sit side by side to talk. I reason that God must surely understand that, even during a month of silence, women in their twenties sometimes have to process.

"What happened last night?" she asks. We are following the same schedule, both of us in the section of the Exercises where we are asked to make a choice. Like good Syrians, Dima and Rania always manage to know what is going on in their neighbors' lives. I would not be surprised if they met my Jesus on the way down the mountain, just to press him for details.

"I waited for a sign to see if I should become a nun," I tell her. We live in a bizarre microsociety, where one can mention waiting for signs and witnessing visions with the same nonchalance normal people use to discuss the weather.

"And?"

I smile. "Nothing happened. I mean, many things happened. But none of them were good."

Rania wrinkles her brow in confusion. I am sure that she thinks I have said the opposite of what I had intended in Arabic. It wouldn't be the first time.

"But you look so content today," she says. "I haven't seen you look this happy in a long time."

She has a point. Why has God giving me the silent treatment put me in such a good mood? Could it be that I simply love the rush of impossible relationships? Yet for some reason, this relationship doesn't feel at all impossible anymore. It feels so manageable. So fitting to my life.

"I think I know what I want to do in my life," I say, realizing this is true even as I say it. "I want to have children. I want to fall in love. I want to get married. I want to become a writer, I want to find poetry again. I have just been so scared of wanting anything, for such a long time, that I haven't been able to admit this."

She squeezes my hand. "Well, isn't that a calling?"

I'm not sure yet, but I do know one thing—that last night was the first time during the Exercises that I truly prayed. And I had told the complete truth, for perhaps the first time in many years. That call in the dark was less a prayer than a full confession to whoever was out there listening that I had hit rock bottom, that my life had lost its meaning.

Help me, I had prayed. *Give me proof that I am not completely alone.*

Maybe what I'd needed was not an answer, but simply the act of the asking.

Today in the mountains, something changes in the Exercises. When I close my eyes, the entire desert is on fire, everything appearing with new and startling clarity. I watch as John the Baptist is killed. I watch Jesus walk away with his head hanging, like a man collapsing into himself. I watch him disappear into the desert to pray.

Don't worry, I whisper, as I discover him crying in the desert beside me. *I'm here*.

I watch him feed the five thousand, the bread and fishes born again and again against the flesh of his hands. I walk beside him on the dusty road from Jericho and listen as two blind men call out to him, loud as hell, loud as the gas sellers in my neighborhood in Damascus. Everyone in the street tells them to shut up. Jesus calls them over, has pity on them, presses his hands over their eyes, and gives them sight.

I'm amazed. "Why did you have pity on them?" I ask Jesus. "Because they were blind?"

He grins at me like a schoolboy. "No. It was just because they kept shouting my name even when everyone told them to stop."

I'm not satisfied. "If they were blind, then how did they know you were coming?"

He turns to me and says sharply, "When you were blind, how did you know I was coming?"

15.

Someone once told me that we know that the Spiritual Exercises are authentic when our visions start telling us things we would rather not hear. I hope this is true, because these days, Jesus is taking on a life of his own and seems entirely not of my own making. Today I watched him turn over tables and cast out the moneychangers at the Temple. He has quite a temper suddenly. I was tempted to read him the line from his very own Sermon on the Mount about the blessed peacemakers.

Paolo is also confused. He is not sure how God could not give me a sign, I could choose not to become a nun, and then, in response, receive days of baffling and highly powerful visions.

"It's just like St. Francis," he tells me. "At the end of his life, he felt that he had been abandoned by God, and so he retreated to Mount La Verna in anguish. It was there, when he was most abandoned, that God gave him the stigmata. The moment he felt most alone was the moment God was closest to him."

But what does that mean? Part of me wants to believe that my visions carry some deeper significance. It's true that I want a family and that I want to write and return to the world I left behind. But if a firefighter has to choose between his own desires and the vision of a house in flames, won't he always run into the house to put out the fire, even if every fiber in his body is asking him to run in the opposite direction? I have stood and witnessed tragedy so often in my life without being able to intercede, and it seems impossible to imagine turning that possibility down if it presents itself.

Could I have misunderstood—could it be that I have finally received the sign I was asking for that night in my room, in the moment I thought I had been left behind?

"Do you still think you aren't called to be a nun?" Paolo asks.

"I don't know," I admit.

"Think about it for a few more days."

16.

NOW I AM BACK AT THE BEGINNING. I still wake up from my dreams and see that vision of an endless desert road, stretching on forever, fading from the backs of my eyelids. I remember the story of Elijah collapsing beneath the broom tree, kept alive by the bread of angels.

I am supposed to be advancing through the Exercises, and still I have not made my choice. Dima has already chosen to become a nun, and Rania paces all day in the valley, struggling as much as I am. I cannot put this off forever.

So, after waiting a week for a revelation, I give up, and I try the old standby. I make a list.

NUN	MARRIAGE
To heal myself	To love someone for my entire life
To heal my family through prayer	To have children
To heal the world	To be part of something that
To live a life creating hope	remains on earth forever
To spend my life learning to pray	To have a partner in loneliness
To find poetry again	To take care of a family
To make God the center of my life	To become greater than myself
To make love the goal of my life	

I want both lives. They both promise solace, at last, and the thing I long for more than anything else: a home.

But because I cannot live both, I choose the monastic life. The list is so much more selfless. And it is slightly longer, after all.

17.

I ENTER THE WEEK OF CRUCIFIXION, after some twenty days in the desert. The Jesus I have come to know will soon be gone. I know that I should be grateful for the hours I have passed with him, but still I'm angry. It has taken me half a lifetime to find him, and now he is going to die. I came to the desert knowing how his story would end, and yet for once in my life I wish it could be different. It would be nice to love someone without counting the days until he died tragically. I would have liked to save a life. It is right, I realize, that saying in the Talmud and the Quran. Whoever saves a single person, it will be as though he saved the entire world.

On Holy Thursday of the Exercises, I hike with Jesus up the Mount of Olives until we come to rest at the Garden of Gethsemane. Among the ancient olive trees I sit beside him as he weeps and begs God that he might live. His hands cling to each other until his knuckles turn white, and sweat pours down his face. *Let this cup pass*, he keeps begging. *Let this cup pass from me*. He is beyond comfort. I have never seen a man so weak— and yet there is something touching in that moment, in Christ confronting God, in asking him, *Is suffering necessary? Must the story be like this?*

Watching him, I am embarrassed and quietly in awe, the same feeling I had the first time I saw my father cry, realized that he was not invincible. I keep my distance. I don't think this conversation was meant for my ears.

I am in the desert, hidden in a valley of hermits' caves and empty spaces, lying on stones. I watch Jesus weeping just a few paces away from me, too far away to touch. Then, something in his grief hits me—the reason why he is crying. He is about to lose everything. He is about to give everything away.

Oh no. I'm giving away everything—my family, my friends, the streets I love.

I sit with that.

I am never going to have children. I am never going to conceive a child.

Suddenly, my stomach feels like it might burst open.

I look over at Jesus, weeping. Until now, I've never had the courage to think about being a mother. I have not been close to my mother for such a long time that I assumed I had missed out on that essential transmission needed to become one myself. Being a mother has always in my mind meant passing on curses, not passing on life. Every one of my sunken relationships has only reinforced that I lack the ability to nurture. I kill plants that can survive alone in the wild. Whenever there are problems I run away, which does not bode well for the life of an infant.

I have always felt that I wasn't made for motherhood, that I would never manage the tasks of doing laundry, of making school appointments, when I can barely balance the details of life on my own and tremble with anxiety over the prospect of speaking with the deli-counter man. Yet now I want children. I want them with a ferocity I have never felt before—my twenty-seven-year-old body is literally crying for them in the desert. I want to be a mother. I want it more than I have ever wanted anything in my life.

I remember the verses from Jeremiah: *A cry is heard in Ramah—wailing, bitter weeping. Rachel is weeping for her children. She refuses to be comforted for her children, who are gone.*

Yes, they are gone. It is too late. I already made a promise to God, and now I lack the courage to undo it. I whisper in the valley, "God, let there be another way."

A few strides away, Jesus whispers, "Let this cup pass."

I feel closer to Jesus than ever before, the two of us among the olive trees, collapsed in our pleading.

I cry all afternoon in the desert. I must exorcise this demon from my body completely if I hope to continue down the monastic path.

LATER THAT NIGHT, I tell Paolo about my afternoon in the desert.

"Stephanie, it's true that someone who chooses to be a nun only because they feel they cannot be happy being married has no religious calling," he says. Then he looks at me with strange eyes, as though he has been granted a glimpse of me from the inside, as if he knows how small his words sound in the face of this moment.

"To be honest, I think you're being very brave," he finally admits. "I can't imagine what you're going through. Because it seems to me that to have a child is as big as God."

He is right. It is as big as God, made concrete in a tiny, living person. It is to give birth to an entire, new world.

We sit there together, Paolo and I, staring at the walls. I know that he is worried for me. But I have been clear about my desires. I want to join the monastery.

He looks at me across the table, and when he speaks his voice is full of tenderness. "Who knows? Perhaps, if you do choose to become a nun, then thirty years from now you will be here, sitting at this table. You will be sitting across from a young woman who is considering becoming a novice. And you will suddenly look at her with surprise and think to yourself, *Where did she come from, my daughter?*"

18.

AT NIGHT, I HAVE A DREAM. There are no images, just a great violence coming over me, and a voice saying, *You don't have a calling.*

It is not a kind voice. It keeps me up all night. Which makes me wonder why, if it is God, he decides to speak to me only when I don't ask him to.

In the morning, before the prayer, I stand outside and look out across the desert, my eyes stinging from lack of sleep, watching the sky and earth fold one over another like a blanket of light and red spaces. Paolo comes up behind me, equally exhausted.

"You had a dream, didn't you?"

I nod. "How did you know?"

He looks out across the railing. "I felt it. I had it too."

Studying monasticism in a classroom does nothing to prepare one for moments like these—for meeting the angels and demons the ancients write about, but that we take pains to convince ourselves could never exist. I am in over my head—and I no longer know what voices I am meant to believe. Who was that voice calling out to me in the night? Was it God? Could it have been my own voice? Or did it belong to some darker force? In Arabic, there is even a special word for that voice, *waswas*, meaning "a devilish insinuation," "a doubt," "a misgiving," and a special Quranic verse asking to keep it away. It is related to the Arabic noun *waswasa*, meaning "a rustling," as in a whisper of leaves.

It doesn't matter. It is too late to change my mind. I walk into the desert after the prayer, as deep into the desert as I can manage, and I ask the stones to cleanse from my mind any voices that might steer me from my purpose. I ask for a blank slate. It is my mother's birthday, and Good Friday in the Exercises. After weeks of walking beside him in the desert, it is time for me to go and watch Jesus die. It has taken me so long to believe that he might exist, I can hardly bear that I have to let him go. I promised myself that on this day, as he dies, I will formally give my vow to God that I will become a nun.

What is there to say? I watch them bind his body. They put him up against the light. He looks terrible and beautiful. He opens his hands to the air.

The chief priests say to him, *He saved others but he cannot save himself.*

I look at him, and I remember how hard he wept in front of God, how much he had clung to life before finally relinquishing it. Yes, life will be like that after all. To save others means to not save oneself.

He is gasping in the desert. Looking straight ahead and gasping.

We had always been taught that Jesus is not alone in that moment, that we can also carry the cross with him and take the burden of the world onto ourselves. I need to believe that this is possible. I need to believe that we can participate in transforming hell.

My mother is fifty-four years old today. She had been my age, half a lifetime ago, when she had given birth to me.

I look up. Jesus is slowly hanging his head and going silent.

No, I will not have children. I will carry this knowledge within me instead of a child—the knowledge that I will save others. I fall down on my knees in the desert, and I pledge my life.

19.

WHAT TO SAY ABOUT THE HOURS since he died? He is gone now. The desert feels so empty without him. I keep expecting him to appear, suddenly—for me to catch a glimpse of him sleeping beside a stone, or screaming at a fig tree in frustration, to once again walk with him beside the sea. Instead the desert stretches out, and it has never felt so lonely as this.

He took all of the miracles with him, all of the light that used to lift from beneath the earth, all of the angels. He packed them in a small cloth and carried them away, with his wounded body, into the bowels of the earth.

Ignatius has put aside an entire week to experience the Resurrection. But I don't have the heart to go there, to pretend that this death never happened. I skip those pages in the Exercises, now that the Crucifixion is done. It's still too soon. I know the man I learned to love in these mountains will rise someday. But for now I simply walk in the desert, missing him.

20.

I HAVE ONLY A FEW DAYS remaining in the monastery—at least until I return. I still can't get used to the idea that this place might become home forever.

After four weeks I've had my fill of meditating all day, and so I've spent today waiting for a man whom I barely know to appear—not Jesus this time, but Frédéric, a young French novice who has been living in the monastery for three years now. All month, he has been away on retreat at Mount Athos, a peninsula in northern Greece full of monasteries, monks, and hermits, one of the holiest places in the Orthodox world. I was nearby once, but no women are allowed to enter the monasteries—including females of all animal species except for cats, who are useful in keeping the mice population down.

Everyone is waiting for Frédéric, not just me. I have met him, and he is terribly charming, the kind of man you meet in storybooks and old films but never expect to encounter in real life. He is a real desert monk, with this mane of wild, curly, blond hair and sparkling blue eyes the color of cornflowers. He speaks his Arabic softly, tinged with a French accent, so that he comes off as a cross between a hermit, Lawrence of Arabia, and, well, basically every woman's fantasy of an incredibly handsome French-speaking poet, which he also happens to be.

The local people think that he is a saint, and I have often heard him compared to St. Francis. I am of the opinion that very few people on earth can be compared to St. Francis, but in this case even I think it is warranted. For one thing, Frédéric talks to cats, goats, birds, and every other animal, in French of course. He is also beloved by children, who grab on to his legs and climb into his arms at every opportunity. He is a musician of great talent, playing the guitar, the Chinese flute, and singing with that tenor that God seems to bestow on monks more often than other people. Then, there is of course that shining—that classic otherworldliness that one sees sometimes in Buddhist monks—that transcendence that is instantly recognizable. Frédéric is to monks what Julia Roberts is to film stars. I look at him and think, *A calling looks like that.*

Though I barely know him, I keep glancing every few hours down the long flight of steps to the valley, wondering if I might see him, leaping in his joyful way up the stairs. I'm not sure why, but I have a feeling that this Frédéric has something to teach me. We are going to spend the rest of our lives together, after all, a monk and a nun working through life in the land of the angels. Only he has a three-year head start.

By evening, he still hasn't arrived, and so we begin Mass without him, lighting the candles and singing the Alleluia. His voice takes us by surprise, sewn in with our poor and trembling voices in the middle of the song, swelling with the tones and richness of the monasteries in Athos, and our song takes on a beauty it has never possessed in the month I have lived in the monastery.

It feels like new life. Frédéric, back at last, from the Holy Mountain.

21.

I HAVE BEGUN WATCHING HIM. In the afternoons, I still take my long walks into the mountains, and when the evening falls and the light begins to fade, I find a stone midway up the mountain and watch from a distance. After a few moments, he always arrives.

He does not know that I am watching. By now I have mastered the art of watching unnoticed, from all of those hours of standing back and watching the angels. He is that much more beautiful, not knowing that I am there. He walks with the grace of an animal, as though he belongs in those mountains, his feet moving from one stone to another the way a man's hands might caress the body of his wife after a marriage so long that they have witnessed grandchildren being born. He never looks down. His right hand slowly makes its way across a *masbaha*, a string of black beads, and I know that under his breath he is chanting the Orthodox Prayer of the Heart, the prayer said over and over until it becomes as regular as breath, allowing the monk to pray without ceasing.

After watching so many terrible things this last month, it is comforting to see a human body, a man in the flesh, a man I know won't disappear into the air a few moments later. He gives me the small comfort that I am not alone here as the darkness falls each evening—and that I am not alone, completely, in this solitude I have chosen.

Tonight, I am late walking down the path to the mountain at last light, just before prayer, and I hear his footsteps behind me.

"Stéphanie?" he whispers. And because in this month of silence, I have heard my name spoken so rarely aloud, it causes me to shiver.

I turn around, looking up at him, at those blue eyes. I don't know what to do. I am still not supposed to be speaking, and I don't even know how to pronounce the *r* needed to say his name in French. I stand in front of him, stupidly, a frightened animal.

"It's strange," he says softly, as regularly as though I had asked him a question, "I traveled all the way to Athos to understand that the desert at Mar Musa is the quietest place in the world."

He fumbles in his pocket. "Wait, I brought something back for you."

I watch as he fishes out a tiny rosary, smaller than my palm, tied in black thread, separated by knots. Each knot contains a prayer.

It is like a single, fragile sentence, strung together and separated by commas, with no beginning or ending.

He places it in my hand. I close it, hold it tightly. "Thanks," I whisper. He stays behind me, and our steps fall in line together as we walk the last path down the hillside, making our way toward the chapel.

My month in the monastery ends like this—in a single moment containing both darkness and light. A few days later, when I finish my Exercises, certain of my monastic calling, I write a solitary quote from the Gospel of John on the final page of my notebook, Jesus' last conversation with Peter, the verses that for me have come to symbolize my choice:

> *I am telling you the truth:*
> *When you were young, you used to get ready*
> *And go anywhere you wanted to;*
> *But when you are old, you will stretch out*
> *Your hands and someone else will tie you up*
> *And take you where you don't want to go.*

I am still holding them both, that notebook and the small black chaplet from Frédéric's hand, when I climb down the mountain two days later to make my way home.

Part Three CRUCIFIXION

You could not be born at a better period

than the present, when we have lost everything.

—SIMONE WEIL

1.

DAMASCUS IS FREEZING.

Last night while I was sleeping, I managed to dye all of my neighbors' clothing black. It wasn't a dream—I actually ruined all of their clothing in my sleep. I should have known better. The Baron has warned me a thousand times that I might set off an explosion or poison the entire neighborhood if I kept my heater running through the night, and for once it seems that he was not exaggerating. I've decided to take this latest disaster as further confirmation from heaven that my life is truly as awful as I imagine it to be. I have become a walking, talking, ticking disaster. I don't even have to be awake to cause the world harm.

It is January, and a month has passed since I left the monastery and the Spiritual Exercises. I have been sick in my bed off of Straight Street for the last two weeks. It began with a high fever and an exhaustion that ran so deep into my bones that I could sleep for fifteen hours straight and awaken still feeling tired. Soon a terrible cough, chest pains, and a sore throat set in. A few days later, it hurt to move my arms and legs. Bruises swelled from inside my body until I felt like someone was punching my rib cage repeatedly and drawing blood each time I tried to hold a conversation. Perhaps I am dying of tuberculosis, or avian flu, or possibly pneumonia. It is only a matter of time before men wearing white paper masks will evacuate my corpse through the back door of the house before setting fire to my sheets.

Last week the doctor at the local clinic told me that I am suffering from severe fatigue, my body rebelling from the strain of too much prayer in the desert, too much work. "Spiritual Exercises" might just be an accurate name for what I weathered in November, for apparently I have run my body into the ground. *All you can do is rest*, he told me, which doesn't help at all. It is like telling an insomniac that all he can do is sleep.

My neighbors have started whispering about me. They are convinced that I have caught *Muridat-al-Huzn*, the "sickness of sadness," a chronic and severe depression not unheard of by inhabitants of the war-torn Middle East, particularly during the long and gray winter. *Hazeen*, in Arabic, suggests not only sadness, but also a longing for what you can no longer have. They have no idea how much I've lost, though. I've lost everything.

The Baron checks on me several times a day in his gentle, grandfatherly way. Every three or four hours he knocks on the door and forces me to drink bottles and bottles of 7UP, which he is convinced will cure everything from broken hearts to cancer.

"*Shrubee, shrubee*, drink, drink!" he moans, cradling the green bottle at the base of my mouth and cupping my chin. "How do you expect to get better if you never drink? And are you really only sleeping under blankets? How many times have I told you to boil water, fill empty Jack Daniel's bottles, and put them under the sheets beside you when you sleep? It is the only possible way to keep warm!"

But he's lying—there is no way to keep warm in this room. Sometime during the month of December, my house off Straight Street was transformed from a charming sunlit open space into the dark, frozen, inner core of hell. The marble tiles on my floor glazed over into rose-colored slabs of ice. The pages of my books began sticking together, yellowing and curling up at the edges so that now I can't open them. Wind seeps through the windowpanes, under the door, through the cracks in the foundation. Every morning I pour petroleum into the tank of an ancient heater Syrians call a *sobba*, my only source of warmth, watching as it slowly drips down into the black belly of the furnace, forming a puddle. When I throw in a match to light it, this puddle transforms into a lake of fire, roaring and rattling, emitting smoke and gas fumes into my bedroom. I watch it through a circular glass window for hours. It is like owning a giant snow globe of Dante's inferno.

I am too sick to leave my room, and even if I wasn't I would not know where to go. Long ago, I stopped answering my telephone or visiting the neighbors. The last place on earth I want to travel is the monastery, where God and Paolo and the accusing angels are all waiting for me. And so I have developed a routine. I wake up in the morning. I light my *sobba*. I let the Baron in and allow him to force-feed me half a liter of 7UP. Then I crawl back into bed and spend the rest of the daylight hours wincing at my own breath, staring at the ceiling, and quietly counting the minutes until I die.

Every evening before he goes to sleep, the Baron knocks on the door and reminds me to turn off my heater before bedtime to keep the pipes from clogging with smoke. I have always listened, obediently cutting off the fire and crawling into my bed at midnight, waiting with dread as the room gradually lapses into coldness. Yet last night I reached my breaking point. I couldn't bear another night of trying to sleep without any heat, shivering restlessly, and listening to the street cats screeching on the roofs outside.

So I left the heater running when I fell asleep in the evening, just once. I was planning on nodding off for a few moments and then getting out of bed to close it.

I woke up this morning to my Roman Catholic neighbor's high-pitched screaming, *"Ya hmar!* That donkey! What has she done? Oh God! It's not possible! Oh God! Oh God! Oh God!"

The Baron started knocking on the door. I peeled a corner of my curtains open and peeked into the courtyard.

A line of my neighbors' shirts hung on the clothesline outside with their arms pinned in the air in resignation, each of them stained entirely black by my smoke. They looked like the tired and vengeful ghosts of coal miners, haunting the space between our rooms.

2.

MY PROBLEMS BEGAN just after I descended that flight of three hundred and fifty stairs a month ago and attempted to pass back into ordinary life after the Spiritual Exercises. I traveled from the monastery to Damascus by taxi, watching the desert slowly revert from red stones to high weeds, then grass, then houses, and finally the bustling, familiar downtown streets of the city I knew. But when I walked up Straight Street and turned into the alley in front of my home, I found the front door standing wide open and all of the people gone. The clotheslines had been stripped of their laundry and the lights turned off. The *Ustez* and his wife were nowhere to be found near the fountain where they bickered in the mornings. No neighbors were complaining on the roof in the language of Jesus. For the first time since I could remember, the Baron was not sitting near the door in his plastic lawn chair, waiting for me. It was as though the world had given me up for dead and had simply moved on without me.

I tried to open the door to my room, but the key stuck in the lock. I tried again without success. I spent the next five minutes standing at the door, pushing the enormous key into the stubborn keyhole, worried that they had changed the locks and rented the room to someone else in my absence. I prayed, silently. Finally, after my fingers ached from pressing so tightly against the keys, I looked down at my hand and noticed a small rectangular keychain with blue Arabic handwriting: *bishop's room*. I had left the key to my Damascus bedroom back at Mar Musa, two hours away and on the top of a mountain, and I was now trying to open my bedroom with the key to my room at the monastery.

There was no one at home to appeal to for help, and so I had no choice but to break back into my room by force. I walked around to the window facing the courtyard and pulled open the glass shutters, then used the pointed edge of my key to tear through the mesh wire screen, the ragged edges cutting open the palms of my hands. When the window was an empty hole, I lifted my backpack over my head and pushed it through, the bag landing with a thump on the floor, and then climbed into my room behind it. I collapsed onto my bed, locked in on both sides, wind pouring through the open window. I felt like a thief, trying to break my way back into my life.

I passed a cold, sleepless night in Damascus, and the next evening I caught a late flight back to San Antonio, Texas, where my family was waiting to spend the Christmas holidays with me. When I arrived at the Damascus airport, the lobby was crowded with Saudi Arabians and tourists from Dubai carting mountains of suitcases, poor Syrians dragging broken plastic bags on the floor, and entire families the size of small villages waiting near the entrance, cheering whenever a loved one came into view. I felt, for the first time since I descended the mountain, an intense, painful loneliness. I had no small village to see me off, not even a village elder, no, not even the Baron. The sum of my months in Damascus was that I was as alone as when I had arrived. I boarded the plane, watching through the window as Syria descended in a haze of long, wide boulevards and streetlights beneath me. *You have chosen*, I told myself. *This is where you will live forever.*

I arrived in San Antonio eighteen hours and three flights later. When I walked into the arrivals area, an enormous banner with a yellow ribbon greeted me, gently drifting back and forth over the hallway. *San Antonio Proudly Welcomes Home Its Troops!* it proclaimed. The rest of the scene looked like that moment in *The Wizard of Oz* when Dorothy walks out of the front door of her black and white house into a world of strange and peculiarly colorful people. Crowds of men and women in starched United States Air Force uniforms chatted cheerfully to one another around the baggage claim, halfway across the world now, safe from the war. Interspersed among them were young boys in bright baseball caps and men strutting in cowboy boots, and about a thousand cell phones were ringing at once.

I always stayed with my dad and my stepmother of many years on the rare occasions I came back home—my mother found a house on the other side of town when I was sixteen years old. So it was my father who was waiting for me at the curbside of the terminal, wearing a terrible bright red shirt, the kind of shirt that men wear only in countries where modesty is not a factor, where clothes are meant to say *I am here*, instead of *Don't mind me*. He embraced me and then took a step back to inspect me. I was wearing a smoke-stained gray fleece with a cigarette burn in the sleeve and torn corduroys, my official Syrian monastic uniform. It was ninety degrees.

"Hey Daughter, are we expecting a snowstorm?" he asked.

I tore off my fleece, embarrassed, only to compound the problem by exposing a long-sleeve turtleneck torn at the seam of the neck and beneath my armpit. I could smell my own body odor, along with the faint remnants of a kebab sandwich I had eaten the night before. But to give my father credit, he managed not to look alarmed.

"You must be starving," he said. "Why don't we stop off at Taco Cabana?"

And so that was that. We drove his silver Jeep Cherokee out of the airport and around the corner, and when we reached the fast-food parking lot I stared at the giant drive-through menu with the voice coming out of it. I spoke to it, and it answered, and two minutes later a stranger mysteriously offered me a tray of food while leaning out a window. That was my homecoming—a mysterious, disembodied voice, two beef fajitas folded up in aluminum foil, and a side of jalapeños, together with a large Dr Pepper. After four months of sanctions and thirty days of eating nothing but yogurt and goat cheese, pita bread and bitter olives in the desert, I couldn't quite fathom fajitas. I unfolded the foil inch by inch, eating slowly, chewing each bite as many times as I could.

For the first ten minutes I barely spoke to my father. I was too busy chewing and staring out the car window at the strange world I had landed in: lines of pickup trucks and four-wheel-drive vehicles, strip malls and billboards, the giant forty-foot sculpture of cowboy boots standing outside of the North Star shopping mall covered with flashing Christmas tree lights. I had forgotten the world could be so full of *things*.

"How's Syria treating you?" my father finally asked me. I was notoriously bad at keeping in touch when I lived abroad, and so he had no idea that I had just spent a month in silence in the desert. As far as he was concerned, I was living in a Western-style apartment with central heating, dutifully studying Arabic.

"It's good," I told him. I didn't know what else to say. That the visions in the desert can be terrifying, but on the bright side the Kurds make a mean falafel?

"It's cold," I added hastily.

"Here it's not so bad," he said. "Close to eighty, sometimes ninety degrees every day. I still manage to go for a swim in the pool most afternoons."

I nodded, wondering if there was a swimming pool anywhere in Syria. Outside, the traffic had backed up around the shopping malls into lines of a thousand cars. Traffic lanes extended over us and beside us. My father kept honking each time we slowed down. The world could have broken open from the weight of it all.

"How about them Spurs?" he asked.

"Excuse me?"

"How about them Spurs?"

It took me a moment to realize that he was asking me about our city's basketball team.

"You get to follow them much there in Syria? Do you watch their games on the Internet?"

The games of the San Antonio Spurs were so far from what I had been following for the last month of my life that I didn't know how to respond. But that didn't seem to bother him.

"Well, of course we've been watching every single game," he assured me. "They've got a good lineup this year. That Tony Parker—young kid from France—he's really something. We got you and your sister tickets for this Thursday night if y'all want to go."

3.

THE NEXT MORNING, there were no bells—church, goat, or otherwise—ringing outside of my window, and so I slept. I slept through my alarm clock, then through breakfast and lunch. I slept through the sound of the dog running back and forth through his special plastic doggie door downstairs, the answering machine speaking aloud, the doorbell ringing. I awakened sometime in the afternoon and looked out from beneath my covers in wonder, to find myself lying in the midst of my very own bedroom, in my very own bed, and not in an austere cell in the desert, suspended over the earth.

I dragged myself to the shower, sat on the floor, and let the water run over me in great, warm torrents. It was my first normal shower in four months, and as I looked down at my arms in the light, I noticed that a layer of smog had settled onto my skin and that some of the hairs were sticking together. In ritualized fashion, I sat on the bottom of the shower for an hour, scrubbing away smoke and dead skin until my arms glowed pink. I shaved my legs for the first time since September. Finally I dried off and prepared myself for my afternoon, taking my slow time. I looked in the wide, broad mirror as I brushed my teeth. I flushed the toilet once and then again, savoring the simple turn of the handle. I carefully used and then replaced the towel on my very own metal rack on the wall. It was so far from the cold concrete room on Straight Street with the red plastic stool and the bucket of water, the spiderweb in the ceiling and the hole rotting through the door.

I returned to my bedroom, and after hesitating, I selected a short-sleeved white T-shirt and a knee-length floral skirt from my closet. It was a small gesture of acknowledgment that I was home in America; still, I felt strange and exposed as I allowed my white arms and legs to peer out from where they had been hidden from the sun for more than a hundred days. I walked outside, the sun beating down on my bare skin. Then, like a tourist in my former life, I set out for the enormous H-E-B grocery store around the corner, just to be around groceries. I nearly jumped back as the doors opened automatically at the entrance. I wandered slowly through the aisles. I examined peaches and pomegranates, avocadoes, five kinds of apples, mangoes and pineapples imported from Central America, taking them in like any pedestrian lost in the markets of Paris. I picked up triangles of Camembert and Roquefort and smelled them, gazed at counters of salami, pastrami, honey-glazed ham, Shiraz from Australia, drinkable yogurt. Cocoa Puffs. Lucky Charms. Golden Grahams. Corn-flakes. Frosted Flakes. Bran flakes. Who thought of these things—cereal with marshmallows for each of the colors of a leprechaun's rainbow?

As I was examining the row of breakfast cereals, I heard the voice of a woman in the next aisle, scolding her child. *She's speaking English!* I thought to myself with a rush of excitement. I slowly made my way to the edge of the aisle and peered around the corner, trying not to appear too obvious as I stared at this young mother in her ponytail and jogging outfit speaking to a little girl with her two feet swinging out of the shopping cart.

Then I remembered. I was now in a place where everyone spoke my language. It hit me with the force of a revelation.

4.

THE NEXT MORNING I woke up in my bed once again, and the sun was shining through the windows and lighting up the entire room. I could smell coffee brewing. I said to myself, *Today, you will tell your family that you have chosen to become a nun in the desert.*

But I didn't. I walked down the stairs to join my family for breakfast. My younger brother, on vacation from college, was reading the comics from the newspaper, and my older brother and sister were chatting over mugs of coffee. The Three Tenors were singing "O Holy Night" in the background. My father, when he saw me emerge from the staircase, opened up a white box of glazed doughnuts.

"Breakfast?" he asked me.

It didn't seem like the right time.

So I pushed my secret to the back of my mind, and at the breakfast table I tried my best to impersonate a normal human being. My sister filled me in on the latest sales at Banana Republic, while my brothers discussed *The Simpsons* between themselves. None of them had any idea of how strange it was for me to talk about television and shopping. *So this is what people talk about,* I thought, *when they are not asking why so many men and women are dying in Iraq.*

After breakfast, I walked down the street to the neighborhood Starbucks, with its green umbrellas and perfectly round tables. Behind the glass counter, blueberry muffins were displayed with cranberry muffins. There were stacks of the *New York Times.* I stood in line and listened to the men and women ahead of me ordering, speaking again in my language: *Frappuccino. Tall latte. Pumpkin maple scone.* It sounded like music. I could have stood there for hours, just listening to them.

Then my turn arrived, and I forgot that for years I had been anxious before speaking to strangers.

"Nonfat iced grande chai," I told the man, blushing. He nodded, took my money, handed me my change, and then called my order out. I loved hearing it again, repeated in his deep voice. The barista called it a third time, *Nonfat iced grande chai,* louder to overcome the sound of steamers and coffee grinders.

I claimed my drink from the counter, even though I could not have cared less about the beverage. I had just wanted to say its name. I just wanted the sheer, exotic pleasure of hearing those words roll off of my tongue and knowing that they were mine.

What had Gerard Manley Hopkins written? *The world is charged with the grandeur of God.* That night, my sister and I did go to see the San Antonio Spurs play the Orlando Magic. We bought nachos and foot-long hot dogs with credit cards and drank beer in big white Styrofoam cups. When a young woman stood at a microphone and sang the national anthem, I placed my hand over my heart. Then, the oddest thing happened: I felt a tear falling down my cheek. I was in a room full of tens of thousands of people who loved my country. For four long months, I had only heard my country associated with the dead.

Then the game began. The players ran onto the court, fluid in their long, lean, muscular bodies, and cameras flashed and thousands of people yelled. I stood on my chair to get a better look. They were like dancers. It seemed impossible that human beings could move like that. I cheered for the French point guard Tony Parker until I almost lost my voice. We swayed in rhythm with the Spurs' coyote mascot. We jumped into the air and tried to catch Spurs T-shirts launched in our direction by cannon.

Somewhere in the middle of it all, a thought slipped into my head. No doubt the desert fathers would have called it *waswas*, one of those tempting thoughts sent by the devil to lure me away. Evagrius Ponticus, the early theologian, would have called it the "noonday demon," that famous voice that reminds the monk that he might have chosen an easier, more comfortable life. But I knew that the voice was none other than my very own voice, reminding me that if I spent my life living in a monastery in the deserts of Syria, then I would probably never again attend a Spurs basketball game. And, in a way that took me by surprise, it was not the idea of leaving my family, or the English language, or even my country, but the simple fact that I would never again watch Tim Duncan make a slam dunk that made me realize just how permanent my monastic decision was. It was as if this was the only way I knew, concretely, how to process the reality that overwhelmed me: *I won't come home again.*

5.

IT WAS ST. AUGUSTINE who wrote the famous prayer in his Confessions, "Give me chastity and continence, but not yet." I could relate. I was only now conscious of how many things in my life remained to be *done*. By the time I had been back home for a week, I was clinging to my former life like a terminally ill patient given only three weeks to live. Paolo had warned me that because my body was still weak and vulnerable from the Exercises, tending to interpret any visual image at all as a message sent straight from the Almighty, it would be a bad idea if I watched too much television. But, since I knew I would not be getting cable in the desert, I allowed myself the luxury of sprawling out on the couch to watch hours upon hours of *Sex and the City* on DVD. I then sat through an entire series of *Smallville*, the television show chronicling the life of Superman during his high school years. Without Jesus to speak to, I began to compare my spiritual predicament to that of the superhero Clark Kent, who also happened to be both human and otherworldly. How did he manage it? How did he walk the fine balance between two such contradictory lives, spending days as a writer and his evenings battling demons, interceding on behalf of mankind?

I showered twice a day, and I bought clothes I could never wear in Syria, tank tops and tight-fitting jeans and short skirts, hardly the uniform of a desert novice. I told myself that I was buying them just for these few weeks, just because I could. I called the quarterback of my high school football team and asked him out to lunch, because I had wanted to do that for years and would never again have the chance. I gained several pounds in tacos. Then, in true Catholic penance, I promised myself before bed each night that the next day, the very next morning, I would announce to my family that I was going to become a nun.

Then I would wake up the next morning and start over, showering and binging on Coca-Cola, watching Superman and saying nothing to my family and at the end of the day feeling terribly guilty about my giant sin of omission. Yet something was holding me back. It was not just that I was no longer living in a simple, austere cell, walking in the desert and passing my afternoons conversing with God. Since I left the monastery, I had stopped praying at all. In fact the idea of falling on my knees and speaking to someone invisible in the air was now bizarre and even slightly repellent to me. I found it hard to believe that I had just passed a month praying ten hours a day and speaking with Jesus. I didn't know who that person was in Syria who witnessed men and angels appearing from the ground. I knew that she existed. I just did not understand how she could possibly be me.

If it had been only my spiritual life that seemed distant to me, then I could have blamed Paolo, I could have blamed the Exercises. But the entire person I was in Syria seemed unrecognizable, not in any way associated to the real me. It felt as if an impersonator in some science fiction version of my life had briefly taken over my body and brainwashed me. I avoided speaking about it in detail, not because my family did not ask me, but because I discovered that my Syrian life belonged to a world of images and associations that I could not hope for them to understand, that even *I* could not understand once removed from their context. What could I tell my father about the family on my roof speaking the language of Jesus, or of Hassan painting the same lost streets of Baghdad over and over again? What would he say if he knew that, in another city, I was known as Grandfather? What would my siblings say if I told them that I went to the mosque every single day, or that I rarely showed my elbows, that I dreamed of Iraq almost every night and passed a month of afternoons summoning up images of Jesus and the disciples and asking them questions?

And so I remained silent, and in my fourteen-hour nights in bed I sometimes awakened and asked myself who I had become, what kind of life I had been living these last years, and why I had chosen to align myself with one of the most difficult regions in the world. I had often met foreigners in the Middle East who became obsessed with conflict, who did not know how to live outside of war areas because they no longer felt alive without the rush of it. Maybe I had also convinced myself that a deep and fully examined life could only be lived in a monastery in the middle of a region at war, that it was not enough to find a place in the inhabited world among those I loved. And perhaps I was not wrong. Maybe life takes us to a certain point and we cannot go back again without betraying the life we have been given, the person we have become. And yet I was starting to hate that life. I wanted to trade recipes and buy baby clothes, to watch television on cable, not to spend my whole life praying for peace.

I had been home for a week when I woke up at five in the morning, unable to go back to sleep again. I pulled aside the covers and crawled out of bed, tiptoeing down the flight of wooden stairs toward the kitchen, only to find my father in his Superman pajamas, sprawled out on the leather couch in front of the television. He looked up at me and smiled.

"Well, hi, Daughter. Couldn't sleep?"

I nodded. "Do you always watch the television in the morning without the sound on?"

He shrugged, motioning at me to take a place beside him. "May as well. There's nothing good on at this hour."

I climbed onto the couch and curled up next to him, in an imitation of a thousand childhood Sunday mornings, and we watched as the stations moved back and forth in the dark. I was so confused. I remembered that my father had once hoped to become a priest, and that as a young student in the seminary he had waited long afternoons for a vision of the Virgin Mary to appear in a garden, hoping she might tell him what he should do with his life.

"Dad, I want to talk to you about something important," I told him.

He put down the remote, leaned over, and kissed my forehead. "I'm listening."

I tried to explain it without sounding crazy. "Last month, I went to the desert to pray . . ." I described that long, labored walk up a flight of three hundred and fifty stairs, and the monastery that hung like a pearl over the valley below. I told him about living in silence, praying in the chapel in the early morning, the way the desert seeped into my bones. I felt as though I was confessing to him. I said that I had decided to become a nun. He listened patiently, not asking questions, just staying there beside me, with the same tender patience in which he had received every far-fetched idea in my life, my childhood desires to run in the Olympics and win the Nobel Prize. When I was finished, he waited for a moment in silence. Then he reached down and pushed away the few strands of hair that had fallen down onto my face. His eyes were full of tears.

"You know, Stephanie," he said softly, "I have always told you that you have my heart."

I didn't dare look at him. It was too early in the morning to cry. He took me in his arms, and we held each other and watched the television on mute, the images flashing in front of us like silent scenes in a human life, one after another.

6.

My confession to my father was the beginning of the end for me. I didn't want to become a nun. I dreaded giving up my life. I felt like the mother in Solomon's parable about splitting the baby in two. I had given up everything because I thought I didn't have the choice. But now I wanted the baby back.

The next morning when I woke up, a voice was speaking from inside of me. Only this time, it wasn't telling me to become a nun.

I don't want to go back to Syria, it said.

When I went downstairs for breakfast, I took a long look at my family, seated around the table. They looked so normal, so human. My father was wearing his terrible red shirt. My siblings were laughing. My stepmother was setting out a plate of cinnamon rolls. Here they were, my roots, tying me to the earth. I couldn't imagine letting them go. I thought of Hassan, almost gasping: *My Baghdad doesn't exist anymore.* I thought of a Palestinian refugee cabdriver taking me home from school in Damascus and shyly asking me if I had ever been to his village in Israel, if I knew what it looked like. Of the Baron, dreaming of a house abandoned in the middle of a war and never returned to again.

I had a home. I had a family. I had never touched the simple, alarming beauty of it.

CHRISTMAS CAME AND PASSED. At the Christmas Eve Mass, I watched the priest lift the holy bread in the air and I longed for the rush of light that had sometimes accompanied that moment at the monastery, that sense of participating in holiness, in the transformation of the world by God. But the desert felt like another life, and that feeling was too far gone by now for me even to try to retrieve it.

The days moved on, one after another in succession, and the date of my flight back to Syria approached. I had promised myself that I would finish my Fulbright year, no matter how much I longed to remain in America. Yet I had one demon left to face. I missed Mark. Terribly.

I had managed to push him to the back of my mind for almost two months, to busy myself with thoughts of my cursed family, of the war in the Middle East, conversations with Jesus, and the weight of a monastic choice. Yet now I could barely go minutes without thinking about him. When I heard the phone ring, I rushed to answer, hoping that he might be calling. I couldn't watch nighttime talk shows without remembering curling up beside him in front of David Letterman. I thought of him when I ate chocolate, or drank red wine, or heard any mention of Russia. I couldn't drink a cup of tea without missing him.

I knew that our relationship contained a laundry list of problems, and that we had said so many awful things to each other in moments of anger that there was little hope of patching things up between us. Still, I wanted to hear his voice. Day after day in San Antonio, all of the feelings surged back that I had suppressed up in heaven, in the desert, when I was trying so hard to be perfect. I missed his black glasses from Russia with their peculiar shape. I missed running with him in the park. I missed grilling portobello steaks on the porch and drinking cheap wine. I missed receiving his phone messages in the middle of the afternoon. I missed wearing his bathrobe, I missed coming home at night and seeing him typing at his desk by the window, the lamp shining on his face, his profile casting a shadow over his open books.

I had mourned a thousand losses in the monastery, war and murder, suicide, the deaths in my family. But I had not let myself grieve losing him. It had seemed shallow of me to mourn a broken heart in the middle of so many greater, more dramatic losses. I had not been ready to admit to myself the one truth that no one seems willing to tell us—that no matter what the circumstances, there is no weight quite as heavy as losing someone you love. It does not matter how they disappear—if they flee the country, if they are killed, if they are run over by a bus, or if they just say *I never loved you* and shut the door. What matters most is that they are *gone*.

Ten days passed before I drank a very large glass of wine and found the courage to pick up the phone and call him. The phone rang and rang, until the ring was replaced by the familiar sound of his voice.

"Hello?"

"Hey you," I said.

"You're kidding me," he answered, and I could hear him smiling.

We talked for hours. I lay down on the floor of the hallway, curling the phone cord around my fingers, listening to him. We didn't talk about our relationship. I didn't mention my boxes of clothes still stowed in the basement. Instead we filled each other in on the stories we had missed. He told me about the afternoon he had scoured all of Boston for veal bones to use in an obscure recipe from the *New York Times*, the gas company that had forgotten to collect for an entire year and was now seeking revenge.

I told him about stumbling through Arabic, and about the cabdriver who, upon hearing that I was from Texas, worried that I was in danger of being attacked by either cowboys or Indians. We laughed until I had to cover the phone and catch my breath. For the first time in months, I allowed myself to remember that I had lost my best friend. "My God," he gasped on the other side of the line. "I haven't laughed this hard in a year."

I told him about the monastery, the way it looked like a jewel from the valley below. And I admitted, for a moment, how lonely life could be, an American in Syria, halfway across the world.

"Stephanie?" he said quietly. "You know, there's no point in saving the world if you can't be happy."

"If I can't be happy, then I might as well save the world," I snapped back. I did not realize just what I had said until I was done.

We were both in shock for a moment. "You know that I wish that I could be there to help you," he said quietly. But they were empty words, because he couldn't be here, and we both knew that. *Here*, in my life, was not where he was supposed to be anymore.

I hung up the phone and went to the bathroom. I undressed and sat on the bottom of the shower and let the hot water run over me. I remembered the last time I had seen him, the sad, awkward moment of good-bye at the airport, his promise that he would wait for me to return at Christmas.

He had been right—we didn't work together. Now that we had been apart for four months, longer even than we had managed to be happy together, I could see the truth in that. I could never have been fully myself with him, I would have had to suppress the core of who I am, the girl who searches for God on top of mountains, the girl who always looks, desperately, for a way that things might be good. But he had been wrong about one thing—I had loved him. I still loved him, despite knowing that we were completely ill equipped to make a life together. And I knew that, despite anything he said in a postelection rage, he had also loved me.

It was only logical that I had crawled up a mountain in the desert trying to find the meaning in my life again, after having my heart so thoroughly broken. But for the first time it occurred to me that I might have chosen to become a nun not just to intercede for mankind, not to save my mother's family from a curse, but because I had lost the man that

I loved, and the world was so full of him that I did not know how to live in it again without him.

A few days later, I received a broad manila envelope in the mail addressed in Mark's familiar scrawl. I opened it on my bed and pulled out a recording that I quickly put on the stereo. Old-fashioned tango music floated out, and there he was, in my mind, gliding around the kitchen with his two hands in the air, holding an imagined partner and dancing.

I reached inside again, and my fingers touched folded pieces of paper. One after another, I pulled out newspaper articles from the months during which we had not spoken to each other. There was an article on religion from the *New York Times,* a recipe, a few cartoons, and a single poem by one of my favorite poets, cut out from a recent edition of *The New Yorker*. He had underlined sentences and scribbled beside them— *Thought you might like this* or *Reminded me of you*—in watery blue ink. I remembered how often I used to crawl out of bed in Cambridge to find such small gestures left by him on the breakfast table on busy days.

It was only after I read them that I thought to glance at the dates posted on the upper corners: the first and second weeks of November. It seemed impossible. In the moment in which I had felt most abandoned in the desert, someone in the world had been quietly saving newspaper articles for me. As though at any moment, I would walk through the kitchen door and find myself home again.

I sat on the bed and I wept, not only for all of my losses, but for all of those treasures I had not even known that I had possessed. I could not help but wonder how much of my life had always been a secret, even to myself—how much had been far more beautiful than I had allowed myself to believe it might be. So this was the poetry Hassan had told me about, the poetry that exists even in the war, though we cannot see it. I understood it now. I understood my neighbors. I understood how a single recipe, cut out and left on the table, is enough to make the world good again.

I crawled into bed. My flight back to Damascus was leaving in three days, and I wanted nothing more than to stay in America. But God had become the romantic relationship that I had fled a country to sever, and I had promised myself I was through with those days. I would not run away, not this time. I had to return and face God, at least sit across from him at the table and tell him I had changed my mind. I owed him that much.

As for Mark, we had not been able to love each other, but for the first time in my life, I was certain that I was at last, finally, ready to love. I drifted off to the memory of tango music, dreaming of the life I would begin after Damascus, of all that it might still contain for me.

I woke up the next morning with a raging fever, my chest sore and my body aching, barely able to breathe. That was two weeks ago.

7.

DAMASCUS GROWS COLDER AS JANUARY WEARS ON. I pass my days lying in bed and staring at the red flame inside of my *sobba*, working up the courage to return to the monastery. I know that I cannot avoid it forever, but I'm terrified. I am afraid of Paolo and afraid of God. I'm afraid of whatever or whoever has brought on this sickness. More than anything I am afraid of meeting my former self again in the desert. I don't want to revert back to the girl I was in November, speaking to angels and offering up my life. I'm scared that if I see her I might touch her for a moment, might be seduced by her and the choices she made. I am afraid that I might accidentally become her.

In the meantime, I turn twenty-eight years old. I lose fifteen pounds. I lie in bed and memorize the footsteps of my neighbors, climbing up and down the stairs of my house. I listen to the faint strains of Mexican soap operas sliding from beneath the Baron's door and imagine a passionate drama playing out between a girl named Maria and a boy name Felipe and all of the tragic circumstances that keep them apart. And I dream of my room back home, and my family, and the big open sky, and short skirts that cling to the back of my knees, and grass on the front lawn, and being in love again.

For lack of better reading material, I decide to reread the information package I was sent by the Fulbright program before setting out for my year in Syria, the set of instructions for how to survive a life abroad. I review subject headings I had written down in a spiral notebook during my September orientation: *How to Change Dollars to Syrian Pounds, How to Access the Embassy Gym, Avoiding Health Problems.*

It strikes me that no one ever teaches us the most difficult things in life, the lessons we might actually find useful. I have no notes on preventing loneliness. There are no quick answers for how to cope with walking down the streets of Damascus, a citizen of an enemy country, burdened by the weight of war and refugees and a conflict escalating every day.

There are no notes on what to do when you miss your family.

There are no notes on surviving a broken heart.

There are certainly no lessons on how to proceed after weeks of hallucinations, when you have promised your entire life to God in the desert but then decide that you want to back out of the deal.

There are, however, directions to the nearest doctor's office.

This morning I pulled from my shelf the writings of St. Anthony, the famous Egyptian hermit and founder of desert monasticism, to see what he might tell me about my problems readjusting to life. I don't know what I was expecting, but I found almost nothing about navigating the troubled earth. Instead, when I combed through his writings, I kept finding more and more advice on how to leave the world behind. "Hate the world and all that is in it," he said to his followers. "Hate all peace that comes from the flesh. Renounce this life, that you may be alive to God."

But I don't want to leave the world behind anymore. I want to go back to it again.

I want to wake up in the morning and feel at home in my own body. I want to wake up in my own room, in my own language.

Where is the spiritual guide who will teach me how to climb out of bed and sit down for breakfast, to just be human again?

8.

IT IS LATE JANUARY when I finally crawl out of bed, brush my hair, and change into clean clothes. I summon up all of the courage I have and pack my small black backpack, then once again make my way to the crowded bus station with its rows of rickety, decades-old buses. A crowd of jumpy men race out to meet me: *Aleppo? Deir Ezur? Homs? Madame! Madame! Where do you want to go?* I push past them all until I hear the voice, calling out from beside a minibus in the corner: *Nebek! Nebek! Nebek!* It is my very own call to prayer.

A few minutes later we are traveling north. I watch out the window as the earth rolls away into desert hills and the blue sky intensifies. We pass tiny roadside villages, nothing more than a smattering of houses and a single minaret slicing the air. After two hours we turn onto the lonely, narrow desert road, and the smooth pavement changes to pebbles crackling beneath the wheels of the minibus. I am the only person left on board, and in front of me there is just endless open space and clouds of dust swimming before the dashboard. At last we stop at the foot of the mountain.

The driver shakes his head as he hands me my bag. "It's a long way up," he says. He has no idea how long. I place my hand over my heart to say good-bye.

I start walking. Above me, the light is catching on the red stones, making them seem to glow from within. *My God, this place is beautiful.* The stones haven't changed at all, completely aloof as they are to all of us human beings. After fifteen hundred years on that cliff it must not matter to them what I choose. They are older than all of my choices, than all of us. Right now they seem older than the earth. I can no longer conceive of becoming a nun, and yet a voice from somewhere within me is saying, *I'm home again.*

I am weak as I ascend the stairs, this climb up the mountain the first sustained effort I have attempted since I became sick. But the air at last feels crisp and clean in my lungs, and I can breathe again. Slowly, I settle into a rhythm, placing one foot in front of the other, and I try to imagine that I am ritually lifting myself above the last month of my life, leaving it behind altogether.

Paolo is waiting for me in the courtyard wearing his gray wool cassock, rubbing his hands together and blowing on them. He embraces me with fatherly devotion. "Look at you, you've lost so much weight," he laments, putting his hand on my forehead. "They don't feed you enough in America."

He has no way of knowing that I gained five pounds in America, that Syria is solely responsible for the deterioration in my body that has left me looking like I was just scraped off the streets. Still, we don't need to articulate that something has gone terribly wrong since the Spiritual Exercises. I was supposed to have returned here weeks ago.

"You look good," I tell him, even though he also looks ill, the circles under his eyes magnified beneath his enormous glasses, making him appear like a caricature of human exhaustion. We climb the narrow flight of stairs together up to his office and close the door behind us, and with the click of the latch we are alone, and I no longer need to be brave. I am simply a girl in front of my confessor, the man who had seen me to hell and back again, my own personal Virgil.

"You're tired, Stephanie," he says.

"I'm sick, Abuna."

He sighs. "For how long have you been sick? Why didn't you tell us?"

How long have I been sick? I can't remember what life was like before this sickness.

"I'm not sure, Abuna. Three weeks? Four weeks?"

His eyes widen. "What is it that hurts?"

My heart hurts, I want to tell him. "Everything hurts. My arms hurt and my legs, my back, my whole body. It hurts to breathe." I laugh softly, trying to hold back my tears. "The neighbors say that I've caught *Muridat-al-Huzn*, the sickness of sadness."

He smiles faintly at my Arabic. "You know, you worked so hard during the Spiritual Exercises, you shouldn't be surprised that you're tired. It will just take time."

My heart falls inside my chest. *It will just take time.* Of course he thinks that I will still become a nun, that once this illness passes I will pack up my bags to begin a novitiate in the monastery. Why wouldn't he? Two months ago I had been so sure.

I take a deep breath. "Paolo, it's all gone now."

There is no other way to put it. It's all gone—my relationship with God, my religious calling, and my belief that I can discern the meaning of my life with clarity. *She's gone. She's gone. That girl who gave up her heart in the desert no longer exists.*

Shhhh, he whispers.

If I were a braver person, I would just tell him the truth: that one day during the Spiritual Exercises, I had climbed a mountain in the rain, shouting my life out to God. I had called out the prayer from the Psalms—*Create in me a pure heart. Give me back my life*—and God had listened, had given me everything back again, just at the moment when I had agreed to give everything away. I would tell him that the curse I once imagined

I could undo with my promise doesn't need my promise, and that I want my life back now. I want to be released from my vow.

"You feel trapped, don't you?" Paolo asks me, quietly. "Trapped in your choice?"

I close my eyes tightly. "There is no choice anymore, Abuna. It was there and then it was gone."

9.

THE MONASTERY COURTYARD IS ABANDONED, and the only sound is the faint ringing of bells in the distance as goats clamber along the nearby hills. Everything else is quiet. I don't think I've ever seen this place so quiet in my life.

At the entrance to the chapel I remove my shoes before pulling back the heavy sheepskin blanket that covers the door. The familiar smell of smoke and wool and incense meets me. I enter without a sound, afraid to penetrate the silence that seems to have settled over the earth, and find a space to rest among the frescoes. With each breath, the silence settles into my bones, a balm rubbing its way deep into my exhausted limbs. On the wall above me, Samson busies himself wrestling with a lion, his body lifting off the ground so that the two bodies merge into one, lion and man. Behind me Elijah is sailing into the heavens in his chariot of flames. Everyone seems to be flying, on the path to somewhere else. Only we humans are bound so firmly down to the earth.

What was it that Rilke had written? *If only we too could discover a pure, contained, human place.*

A beam of light shines through the small arched window above the altar, illuminating the faces on the far wall. As the day continues the light will travel, lighting up different faces and leaving others to sleep. It is never the same church from one moment to the next.

I had forgotten this silence. I close my eyes and attempt to walk through it, a series of long white corridors extending out over the earth toward eternity. My arms and legs start to remember themselves. But nothing will remove the knot of pain that has locked itself into my chest.

It was not true, what I had said to Paolo. My calling did not simply disappear. I had held on to it, at least the faintest kernel of it, despite the divide of thousands of miles, and even when I no longer felt the desire to pray. I had held it in my heart as one holds the memory of a lover who leaves to fight a war, and even though you cannot remember his face, or his voice, or what it felt to speak to him alone, you know someplace in your heart that the love must have been real.

I had held on to it. It was not until I had seen my mother that the calling had truly vanished.

I had been dreading seeing her that Christmas. Even after I descended the steps of the mountain, I could never completely shake the vision of my mother, small and frightened, trembling in hell. There she was, shivering at the bottom of a very cold room, calling my name. It haunted me. I dreamed of that vision at night.

It propelled me forward. Each time I saw her in agony, I felt a physical pain that made me want to leap to the bottom of that chasm and carry her out in my arms. I had never wanted anything quite so much. For all of my doubts, for all of my longings to hold on to my life, I would still give it up entirely if I could save her and her family.

I wasn't at all ready for the woman who came to meet me one December afternoon in a coffee shop in San Antonio. My mother was slightly late, and she arrived wearing jeans and an oversized red sweater, with a necklace of Christmas tree lights around her neck. She ran up to embrace me. "Stephanie Celeste!" she crowed. "I'm so happy to see you!" Then she smiled a real smile, a smile I don't remember having seen before, and hugged me with such vigor that I thought the air would be pressed right out of me.

That was when I knew that something had gone terribly wrong on the mountain.

We spoke for hours. She told me about her new house, with wooden floors and a front porch with a swing. She described a recent voyage to Spain, when she had spent weeks walking on remote paths that ran near the sea. She talked about the Thanksgiving feast she had cooked for her entire extended family, and the students she taught in her classes, and the way she often thought of me across the world and hoped I'd come home again.

Then I knew. She wasn't the woman I had imagined trembling in hell. I had offered up my life to save someone who didn't exist.

A week later, I was at the Cantu family's annual Christmas party. I had been running away from them for years, scared of them and their curse. Yet they looked familiar to me, despite the distance. I had seen them all in a vision, only a month before, lying side by side in the mountains on that first night of the Exercises, almost dying. They had enough strength left in their arms simply to hold out their hands, to ask the angels for their pieces of bread.

Yet now, they looked just like people. My aunt Geri, who had traveled all over the world and could ask for directions in ten languages, showed up in an Indian sari, followed by my aunt May, an artist who cooked three-tiered wedding cakes, and my ponytailed uncle Carlos. Wallace, the husband of my aunt Loretta, who had been killed by that bus, made me a drink. In the wings I met violin-playing uncles and aunts with legendary singing voices, and a cousin who had just returned from digging up Mayan cities in Mexico.

They weren't dying. I suppose no one would have blamed them if they were, if they had gone over the edge and never come back again. But that's not what had happened, after all.

"When is it going to end?" my cousin had once asked me, fifteen years before, sobbing at a funeral.

"I don't know," I said to her, because I didn't know if it would ever end, if that was too much to ask for.

But it *had* ended, somehow, during those years when I had been absent. If it had not ended, then it had at least become muted, bearable. Otherwise they could not have been there, in a kitchen in my hometown, passing cups of coffee back and forth to one another. Both were true. They were somehow on that mountain, calling, and yet still on the earth, alive. What I had decided on the mountain hadn't changed that. They had done that on their own.

And the dead were dead. There was no bringing them back, not to this world. My grandmother and my grandfather and my aunt were dead, and there was nothing that I could do. No sacrifice on the mountain could save them.

It was then that I knew that I had been wrong to give up my life. No one was asking for my intercession. They didn't need me. But I needed them, now. I needed to stay on the earth, to know for the very first time that happiness there was possible.

I had wanted so much to save someone's life. But it turned out that the only life that I could hope to save was my own.

10.

AN HOUR PASSES BEFORE I HEAR A DOOR CLICK OPEN, summoning me back to the chapel and the world. *Frédéric.* I recognize the sound of his footsteps, pressing against the ground as though they are part of it, barely tapping. He pulls up a cushion and sits beside me on the carpeted floor, the bottom of his gray monastic robe gathering in a pool around him. His loose blond curls hang beneath his black skullcap, and his beard has grown patchy. I can't remember the last time I faced a man who was not my confessor or a neighbor plying me with bottles of 7Up. I'm relieved to see him again.

"It was good, America?" he asks me.

"Yes, it was good. It was strange."

He smiles, just barely, at the corners of his mouth, and I return his smile despite myself.

"Of course. Going home again is always strange." He pauses for a moment before adding, quietly, "I'm glad you came back. We've been waiting for you."

Hearing this expressed so directly sends a pang to my heart. We sit side by side in the church. His feet remain bare despite the winter outside, making him appear even more like an antelope or some desert creature, not just a human being like the rest of us. He calmly passes one prayer bead after another through his hands, and I know that he has already guessed that I have changed my mind about a monastic vocation. It is written all over me.

I sit for a while and watch him siphon off the minutes with the beads in his hands. He asks nothing of me, and slowly I recognize the inevitable, that I will tell this man everything, the way someone confesses to a stranger sitting beside him on an airplane. I have no one else in Syria to talk to, perhaps even no one else in the world I know who can understand the place I've just come from. I suspect that he knows this very well, and this is why he has come.

"Frédéric?" I ask softly, and he nods, his eyes meeting mine, encouraging me. "I'm scared."

"I know," he answers.

I feel better now that this terrible truth has been released into the air. He nods gently. "Tell me what happened to you."

I don't even know where to begin. So much has happened. "Do you remember what you once told me about the Exercises?"

It had been in October, just after Michael had left Damascus. One afternoon after classes, I had left Damascus abruptly and fled to the monastery to ask Paolo if he would allow me to do the Spiritual Exercises. Yet when I had climbed my way up that long flight of stairs, it was Frédéric who had met me at the top of the mountain. *Be prepared*, he had told me when I mentioned the Exercises. *You're going to live your whole life over again. You'll remember things that you didn't even know that you had forgotten.* And it had happened, just as he warned that it would.

"In the beginning, every day I went out there on the mountain and I prayed. I tried to remain focused on the Exercises. But then slowly I started to remember my whole life. I remembered my childhood. I think I even remembered things that happened before I was born. I felt the world tearing open from the inside. And for a long time it was so real, it was more real than anything I had ever lived anywhere else. The whole world became electric—almost like it was on fire."

He nods again, not at all startled. For the first time I understand that on those evenings when I watched him returning from the mountains, he was seeing the same things I was.

"Then, after two weeks, I received a calling. Well, at least I thought it was a calling. But now I am pretty sure that I just went nuts."

"Went what?"

"Nuts. Crazy."

He smiles kindly. "I'm sure you didn't go crazy, Stéphanie."

I remember those afternoons watching Jesus cursing the fig tree and healing the blind, those few days when another world revealed itself to me that was not of my own making.

The Bread of Angels

"But I did. When I was in the mountains, everything felt so clear. It was like the world finally made sense to me, in a way that made me want to live like that forever. But then I went home to my family, and that was the world that I belonged in. Everything from the desert was gone—just like that—as though nothing had happened." For a moment I remember my family sitting around the breakfast table, how ordinary they looked, and yet how the sight of them had startled me as deeply as anything I had witnessed in the sky. "No, that's not true. I went home and everything was *different*. My father was wearing this red shirt, and I just *saw* him sitting at a table with his red shirt. It was so strange. My dad has been wearing red shirts for as long as I can remember. But then I saw it—my dad in his red shirt, and I didn't want to be a nun anymore. I know this sounds stupid."

"It doesn't sound stupid, Stéphanie."

But it does. And I have not even told him the rest of it: seeing my mother smile for the first time in years, speaking with Mark and laughing with my siblings, or even the way the small, ordinary objects of everyday life had taken on a peculiar beauty—Christmas tree lights and sweatpants and bad country music on the radio. I had come to the desert to try to heal the world in its brokenness—and yet I had returned home only to discover that I loved the messiness of the world.

Frédéric looks at me, acknowledging my gray fleece, full of cigarette burns and smelling like petroleum, my tangled and unbrushed hair, my bloodshot, swollen eyes ringed with black circles.

"Everyone falls apart after the Spiritual Exercises, Stéphanie," he tells me quietly. "Dima's not doing very well either."

"That's easy for you to say, Frédéric."

"That's not true. All of us have fallen at one time or another. I also fell after I finished the Spiritual Exercises five years ago."

He is so calm, so perpetually shining, that I can scarcely imagine him falling after anything. "What happened to you?"

"I was depressed. I grew out my beard. I stopped eating. I couldn't even recognize myself. Everything took effort."

I am strangely relieved to be told that I am not crazy. "What was hard for you?"

"It's hard that everything seems so trivial after the Exercises. I think it's not a good idea for people to leave the desert so suddenly—the body needs to learn how to transition from one experience to another. You can't expect it to be easy, praying for eight hours a day and then trying to be normal again. It takes time."

But it wasn't that I had experienced culture shock. It was as though life had pulled me to every extreme and that all at once I had been given a chance to live everything, not just the spiritual life, with the depth of a vocation. "Do you think I received a calling on the mountain?"

He surveys me for a moment. "I don't know, Stéphanie. I wasn't there. Only you can answer that question."

"I did experience a calling," I say quietly. "I just don't understand yet what I was being called *to*." I remember what the poet Richard Wilbur had written, that *love calls us to the things of this world*. It seems more and more that this was the calling I had received on the mountain—a voice that called me away from the deep precipice over which I was leaning and slowly back to the earth.

Frédéric lets his prayer beads fall loose in his hands. "The Spiritual Exercises only begin in the desert. Your choice doesn't mean anything until it becomes incarnate, until you take it back into the world." He pauses to think for a moment. "Have you ever read the book of Job?"

I had often thought about the book of Job those last weeks in bed, the story of a man who gives his life to God and receives everything in return, only to have it taken away from him: his sheep, his land, the family that he loves. For me the story contained not only my life, but the stories of so many I knew who had woken up one day to find that they had lost everything, that for some unknown reason they had been cursed by God.

Frédéric leans his head back against the wall. "I've read the book of Job over and over again. And finally I've decided that it can't really be a story about a man who is tested by God and loses his sheep and then loses his children and then loses his fields, and then at the end of the story is rewarded for his patience by getting back another set of sheep and new fields and new children. That doesn't make any sense to me—you can't compensate for losing one thing just by replacing it with something else." He stops for a moment, considering. "It must then be a story about a man who has become so tired of his life that he can no longer love his sheep, he can no longer walk his land, he can no longer see his children as though they are his own. And so they become dead to him. In this way they are completely dead to him. And he must suffer to the point of dying before he knows how to get them back."

I imagine that moment, Job's body blistered and worn, his mind nearly gone, and the pure recognition on his face as he enters through a door frame and looks up to see the ones he loves in a room, as though they had never left him. He runs up to embrace them, like a soldier wounded and returning from battle, the dream every refugee must have of coming home.

It is time for both of us to go. We stand up, and Frédéric hesitates at the door. He turns for a moment and looks at me.

"Stéphanie, you know, I never really thought that you should become a nun."

His words sting terribly. "Why?"

"You don't believe in resurrection," he answers, his voice soft and barely audible. He does not say it cruelly. He sounds sad.

"What do you mean by that?"

"It's simple, Stéphanie," he says, looking in my eyes. "You don't love your life."

He leaves the church silently and closes the door.

11.

FOR DAYS AFTER I leave the monastery I try to shake Frédéric's words. *You don't believe in resurrection.* I have always been good at faking it— at smiling and laughing at people's jokes, at waxing on about the possibilities in life. Still, I can't help but feel that Frédéric has managed to nail the part of myself that I have tried to keep hidden. I was, after all, the girl who told my father when I was five years old that I feared he had only twenty-five years left to live. I was the student who in the second grade asked for smoke detectors for Christmas when the rest of my class asked for Cabbage Patch Kids. I have spent a lifetime waiting for the world to come crashing down on me. And, to be perfectly fair, I am not entirely delusional. I have managed to escape near death five times already, like the magician nailed down in a wooden box and then placed into a tank of water who always manages to emerge at the last minute, still alive.

Yet it's been a long time now since I've brushed against death. For years, I could still convince myself that I was cursed, that I was living out the same battle as everyone else in my family, biding my time until I eventually died tragically. But now I can no longer delude myself. The curse is finished now. I have no idea how, or why, but I am absolutely certain of it. Now I am like someone born into a country mired in a decades-long civil war, on a day when both sides unexpectedly declare a truce. I have to learn to live again in the world.

Only I don't know how. I've never tried to navigate a world without complications. I don't know the rules. But I've been an apprentice to death for too long. I want so much to at least try to be happy, to remember what it feels like to be light for more than a few hours at a time.

I was thumbing through *The Lives of the Desert Fathers* this morning. I think I've finally found some guidance for life here in the world.

A brother asked Abba Sisoes: I have fallen. What should I do?
Get up again, he answered.

12.

February

MY BODY STILL ACHES, and so I've been taking it one step at a time. During my first few days back from the monastery, it was enough to climb out of bed and join the Baron for coffee. Then I began to answer phone calls again, to put on different clothes in the morning, to brush my hair. Finally I worked up the courage to walk to the main street of Bab Touma to buy *shawarma*, meat stuffed in warm pita bread, for lunch.

"You're still here?" the man asked me as he sawed off slices of meat with a long electric knife. It gave me the feeling of being Lazarus, risen from the dead.

What is increasingly becoming clear to me with each passing day is that, much to my surprise, I am beginning to speak Arabic. This may be the only miracle I have salvaged from my time in the desert—that a month of not speaking and of hearing only Arabic have somehow made the language stick in my brain. True, many of the words I picked up—*lepers* and *disciples* and *Pharisees*—won't do me much good in the market (though the *lamb* from *Lamb of God* has already proven useful in ordering lunch). But I can hear Arabic, and what's more, I can remember it.

Recently, I have begun walking through the streets of Damascus, passing my prayer beads through my hands and practicing walking meditation. I try just to listen to the world around me, the way I listened in the desert for ghosts and angels to appear. I can hear the call to prayer, floating over the rooftops—*God is great! God is great!* As I walk down the winding lanes near my house, I listen to the hammers of carpenters, pounding against nails, and chain saws blowing sawdust in the air. I can hear a woman shouting before lowering a basket by a rope from her window down to the street. The fruit seller is calling, *One kilo for ten lire! One kilo for ten!* A coin dropping into a beggar's tin cup rings like a cymbal. A boy passing on his bicycle tinkles his bell and calls out, *Habibi! Habibi!* My love! My love!

I can hear wind, funneling through a tiny alley, speaking in a low voice. The wooden shutters of houses beat back and forth against old Ottoman walls. I can hear keys, fastened on the loops of men's belts, jingling when they walk.

I spend a few days like this, just listening. Then, very slowly, I begin receiving words.

It all starts with the Straw Man. One day, I set out to buy a juice from the jolly, slightly potbellied man who works at the corner store just across the street from my house, and it dawns on me that in all of my years of studying Arabic I never learned the word for "straw." I point to the small can of straws beside the cash register as he hands me my mango juice. "Can I have a . . . what is this thing called anyway?"

He laughs, handing me a straw. "A *mussasa*. Or a *shalamona*. You choose."

So that was *straw* in Arabic. I love it. It is such a useless word, a luxury. I could go my whole life without needing this word, like a diamond ring.

Now I pass by every day and buy a can of juice from him, just so I can ask him, "Do you have a *mussasa*?" He winks at me.

Then the Tin Man came into my life. Earlier this week, I woke up and began to make a sandwich, only to realize not only that I did not have a knife, but that I do not know the word for "knife" in Arabic. I ran outside, to the Straw Man, my ally on the street, anxious for him to help me. I began to saw at my hand furiously with my finger, until I noticed that a look of alarm had crossed him face.

"Are you hurt?" he asked.

"No, no, I just need one of these things," I said, pointing to my hand.

He sighed in relief. *"Sikkine,"* he said. Go ask the man with the cart outside.

I ran to the cart, but by then I had forgotten the word again. I began to repeat the charade of sawing off my hand to the man with a cart.

He pulled a knife out, concealed beneath mountains of toothbrushes, hairpins, batteries, extension cords, mirrors, and decks of playing cards.

"Sikkine," he said firmly. "Say it after me."

I parroted his word obediently. Now, when I pass the Tin Man in the street, he calls out to me, "How is your *sikkine*?"

Today a woman ordering at a juice stall gave me *carrot*, a Greek Catholic priest gave me *forgiveness*, and a frustrated neighbor unwittingly taught me a handful of vulgar expletives, together with the rhetorical question, *So, what do you expect me to do?* I love them all. I feel like a lost wanderer scooped up from the side of the road, given directions and a glass of water to drink.

I can't fathom how I missed it, during all of these months living in Damascus, chugging through Arabic classes. The Arabic language is so poetic. My neighbors don't just give me words—they have started giving me phrases that don't make any sense, pure music strung out into words. When I buy something from the store, the storekeeper thanks me by saying, `Ala Rasi!` On my head! He then touches his hand to his head in a gesture that shows me he would do anything in the entire world for me. Sometimes instead of saying, "You're welcome," he calls out, *"Tikram eyoonik!"* Which means, I think, "May your eye be honored."

I am growing accustomed to their over-the-top, syrupy endearments. Men call their wives *My moon* or *My stars*. Friends call each other *Ya elbee*, My heart. When a day, or a landscape, or a dish of food is beautiful, it is said to be *bi-jinan*—which implies something like "This is so incredible that it is driving me crazy!" Even the standard greeting of Good morning, or *Sabah al-kheir*, is answered by the phrase *Sabah al-noor*, which means "Morning of light!" Though sometimes my neighbors like to mix it up, and when I call out *"Sabah al-kheir!"* they'll smile and respond, *"Sabah al-ward!"* "Morning of roses!"

It is so very far from the language I have studied up until now. I need this. When I am struggling for a word and I sift through my trove of possibilities—*guns, bombs, politics, explosion, sin, adultery, cross*—it is such a relief to finally come upon something as simple as *afternoon*.

Yesterday, I saw a woman walking through the neighborhood with a newborn infant swaddled in her arms. *"Al-hamdulillah al-salaami!"* the neighbors called out.

At first I didn't understand, but then I remembered. "Thank God for your peace!" they were saying. It is the greeting you give someone who has finally arrived safely after a very long journey.

THE BARON IS DOUBLY THRILLED THESE DAYS, not only that I am slowly healing from my mysterious illness, but that I am finally learning to speak Arabic like a normal human being. He likes to greet me in the courtyard every morning with a barrage of Syrian endearments: *Ya habibti, elbee, eyoonie!* My love! My heart! My eye! I have a feeling that it reminds him of his past as a smooth-talking shoe salesman in Lebanon. I might get used to speaking this way.

The fact that I'm willing to try to speak like a local and not like a foreign diplomat imitating Shakespeare has also begun to endear me to my neighbors. In fact, they seem to have forgotten both my nationality and my bewildering sickness of sadness and now seem positively eager to talk to me. I could have never guessed that so few streets could contain so much scandal and intrigue. The *Ustez* informs me about the neighborhood girl who might be a lesbian, or another who has a Muslim father and a Christian mother and so has lost her identity. The florist tells me one hundred jokes about the stupid people of the city of Homs, Syria's version of Polish jokes. He tells me every herb I should use for sadness or heartburn or if I hope to find a lover. I overhear a Christian old woman complaining that the Christians gave the Muslims the idea for the head-scarf in the first place, which is pretty obvious when you look at the Virgin Mary adorned by her veil. I have a feeling that it's no accident that oral history originated somewhere in the Middle East. The Syrians are talkers.

These days I often sit in the nearby pastry shop of a Palestinian named Ahmed, who spends his afternoons spooning out *knafeh*, a thick, cheesy Arabic pastry dripping with orange syrup. He resembles a character out of a novel, with shining black eyes, a mustache with no beard, and a pale blue shirt with his name, *Ahmed*, sewn in English over the pocket. He has designed a trapdoor in the ceiling above his shop, where he conceals himself when there aren't any customers, so often his shop looks empty. If someone calls out, "Ahmed!" then the trapdoor falls open and he hangs himself out upside down from the ceiling, waves, and then climbs down below to resume his duties.

Ahmed, whose family originally comes from Nablus in the West Bank, is one of the hundreds of thousands of Palestinian refugees whose relatives fled to Syria, most of them in 1948, and are still unable to return home. Like everyone else in Syria, he knows that Nablus is the legendary home of *knafeh Nablusi*, the most delicious *knafeh* in the world. But because no one in Syria is allowed to travel there, he holds the status of the honorary ambassador of *knafeh*. When I taste his sweets, I always like to imagine that I am biting into some far-off exiled place.

Now, each afternoon, if I happen to pass by Ahmed's shop and he isn't hidden behind his famous trapdoor, then he spoons me free servings of dripping *knafeh*, makes me a sweet cup of Arabic coffee, and pulls up a stool in his shop for me to sit on.

"Stephanie," he says, "you know I have a great dream."

I feign suspense. "What is your dream?"

"When I have saved enough money from my shop, then you are going to take me with you to America."

I sip my coffee innocently, trying not to smile, imagining him handing out syrupy orange pastries to my neighbors.

"And when I have reached America, then I will open a sweet shop just like this one, right across from the White House. I will serve the most delicious *knafeh* and Arabic sweets anyone has ever tasted in America. And when something goes wrong between America and Syria, and the president is tempted to bomb us, then I will send someone over to fetch the president and invite him over to tea."

I laugh and then take an extra large bite of *knafeh* to show my approval.

"And when Mr. President tastes the incredible sweetness of the *knafeh*, together with some slightly sugared mint tea, suddenly he will be forced to reconsider. How could I? he will ask himself. How could I bomb a place with sweets that taste like that?"

Now, whenever I pass him on the street, he asks me, "When are we going to America?"

"Don't worry," I assure him. "I'm leaving room for you in my suitcase."

Every morning and afternoon, after I pass Ahmed's sweet shop, I stop at the neighborhood juice stand a few stores down, where laughing Kurdish teenagers pour me overflowing cups of sweet banana milk, decorating the rims with strawberries and banana slices until no place remains for me to put my mouth. "You're from America?" they exclaim. "You know, we call your president the Brother of Freedom. He's going to get us our own country!"

Every afternoon, a good-looking young man named Fahd invites me into his bakery for tea, pulling up a chair among the fresh bread stuffed with spinach and spicy red sauce. He may be the most gentle soul in the world, which is why I find it strange that Hezbollah stickers are pasted all over the oven. Yesterday, Fahd showed me a tattoo on his arm, which read F+H, proof of an infatuation from the year before that had ended in heartbreak, when H married someone else.

"Come in, come in—we've had the teakettle waiting for you all day long!" he tells me every time he sees me. I know very well that the teakettle is always in the oven, waiting for any guest who might drop by, and yet I'm flattered anyway.

My new friends are not limited to shopkeepers. I am in hot demand with the retired crowd as well, and in addition to my nightly visits with the Baron, Maurice, a Syrian Catholic in his seventies who lives down the street, has begun inviting me over for after-dinner drinks. He is one of those Christians in the Middle East who never stopped lamenting the end of the French Mandate, when he was the cream of society just for being Catholic. He pours me stiff gin and tonics and wistfully describes the

French missionaries who taught the Syrian Christian children about the geography of France but neglected to teach them their own geography. After showing off his dusty French wine collection, his picture of Charles de Gaulle, and a Bible in Latin, he stands in front of me at attention, half drunk, and recites the major rivers of France:

Seine! Rhône! Rhine! Loire! Garonne!

And for a moment, he is a child again in his school uniform.

I have a new favorite language partner. His name is Mohammed, and he is a devout Muslim who owns a carpet shop on a quiet alley deep inside the Old City. I've been trying to stop by to see him every afternoon, and I usually find him sitting in a torn plastic lawn chair in front of his shop, tirelessly repairing carpets by hand. He looks just like Groucho Marx, with deep, dark eyes framed by bushy eyebrows, a shock of brown hair, and a mustache.

"Ahhh, Stephanie! *Yalla, ta'al, ta'al,* Come in, come in," he greets me. Then, like everyone else, he hands me a glass of tea and a cigarette.

Mohammed is religious the way most Syrians I know are religious. He prays in the mosque on Friday and keeps the five daily Muslim prayers during Ramadan. In all other ways he lives as a mystic who always has a cigarette in his mouth and a pair of prayer beads moving through his fingers. He lives his own, informal version of Islam and has no problem speaking with a woman alone. In fact, I suspect that he rather looks forward to it.

Today, after I settle into drinking my glass of very sweet Arabic tea, the bottom a small lake of sugar crystals, Mohammed takes a carpet from the wall, hidden among the piles of blues and reds and deep forest greens, Bedouin saddles and bits of prayer rugs, to teach me my daily lesson.

"Now, a carpet is a story, and your job is to learn how to read it," he tells me, his voice deep and serious. "Take this carpet, for example. You have a region in Afghanistan that takes refugees from all directions. They take a long, long time to arrive, years perhaps. They stop along the way and learn to weave carpets in local traditions, in order to support their journey. When they finally sew this single carpet, they bring with them all of the traditions they know.

"Now look, Stephanie. Look at this single carpet, and here you will see Iran. Here is Pakistan. Here are countries across Central Asia, and just the smallest bit of China. Look hard enough, and you will find the story of a people coming together, and all of the cities they had to flee along the way.

"Now for me, this whole business gets messy. When a carpet breaks, I have to be able to fix it. For a moment I have to put myself inside of that man and sew like someone from Pakistan or Uzbekistan or Iran, so that you cannot see the line where they end and I begin. When I mend a carpet, I have to forget myself."

"Thank you, Great Professor," I tease him, smiling. I think of Mohammed as a Muslim monk who happens to have a job and a serious smoking habit. I have rarely met anyone who gives so much thought to spirituality, or to every aspect of life, for that matter. He possesses remarkable patience, and I suspect that only a man who has spent all of those years slowly and carefully repairing carpets would be able to sustain hearing me day after day, butchering the Arabic language when I speak.

Mohammed's shop is almost always empty when I come by, some sad ghost town of a carpet shop, which is why he has so much free time to philosophize. I keep telling him that he needs to raise his prices—that he is the only carpet salesman I have ever met who allows himself to get suckered by customers, but he refuses. "I take what I need," he always insists. "God will provide the rest."

Since the cold spell, there haven't been any customers at all. Today I ask him, "How is business, anyway?"

"Al-hamdulillah," he sighs. "Thank God."

"But you don't have any business, Mohammed. Why thank God?"

"You have to thank God for everything, good or bad. He knows what is best for us."

He quietly rolls a cigarette back and forth between his fingers, before looking up at me. "Did I ever tell you the story of the *jihad al-akbar*, the greater jihad of the soul?"

"No, you didn't, Mohammed."

"When the prophet Mohammed, peace be upon him, was returning from battle, he stopped on the top of a hill before entering the city. He turned to his companions and he said, 'Now we return from the lesser jihad to the greater jihad.' " He pauses, inhaling from his cigarette. "Do you know what that means, Stephanie? The lesser jihad, the jihad of holy war, is simply to fight in a military battle. But the greater jihad is to work all day repairing carpets without any new business. It is to feed your family. The greater jihad, Stephanie, is just to live."

13.

I HAVE NOT PRAYED IN SIX WEEKS now—by which I mean that I have not meditated or tried to fall down on my knees, I have not spoken to any Woody Allen Jesus, or summoned up angels from the ground. Other than my single, difficult trip to the monastery, I have not been to church. My only way of praying is by passing a set of green jade prayer beads the Baron gave me through my hands while I am walking, my way of reminding myself to breathe, to listen, to pay attention.

Still, something inside of me is slowly healing. I can sleep through the night again.

I sometimes wonder if it is not only my life, but also my vision of the world that is healing, if my neighbors are slowly altering it with their conversations and glasses of tea. I can't help but shudder at how I pictured the Middle East during the Spiritual Exercises, all cities in flames, Beirut studded with bullet holes, refugees fleeing from their homes in the middle of the night, Baghdad burning, and that field of wounded bodies, reaching out for their pieces of bread.

That *is* the Middle East. But it is also a caricature of the Middle East, missing all of those human elements that make it possible to wake up in the morning, to go on living here. For years, I convinced myself that I was lucky to escape before things truly collapsed. Now I wonder if it isn't more difficult to watch such falling apart from a distance. CNN carries stories of the bombings, their news cameras filming crowds lifting caskets through the streets and shooting off machine guns in the air, young men with suicide belts strapped to their waists. I had forgotten long ago that a Palestinian refugee could also be a man hanging upside down from his shop, serving desserts so sweet that they make my teeth hurt, or that a Hezbollah supporter could be a shy baker who blushes every time he hands the nuns from the nearby convent their change. I had forgotten that the Kurds, many without citizenship and also dreaming of their homeland, could be teenage workers joking behind the juice counter in their own language.

These days, God comes back gently hidden in the Arabic language I am learning how to speak. When someone asks me in Arabic, *How are you?* I answer, *Thanks be to God.* When a neighbor returns from a journey, I say, *Thank God for your peace.* I hear the phrase *Inshallah, If God wills it*, a thousand times every day, for Syrians don't like to speak about the future with any certainty. Even to say good-bye, one calls out, *Allah maik, God be with you*, which I find touching. It reminds me of the Spanish phrase I heard so often from my mother's family when I was a child: *Vaya con dios, Go with God.*

I walk with my prayer beads through the streets of my neighborhood, whispering the Prayer of the Heart beneath my breath as I wave to my neighbors and pass advertisements for Magic Cola and Syriatel mobile phones, trying in my own awkward way to live in the world and still pray without ceasing. And I think that maybe the desert isn't the only place where we have to clean our hearts before we can take in the visions around us. This Damascus of sidewalk saints and philosophers always existed, after all, this world where people open their doors and invite me in, for all of the years I have traveled in and out of the region. I just didn't know how to see it until now.

Today, I walk across town to the National Museum to visit Rania. I've been passing by often since I crawled out of bed, Rania being my only girlfriend entirely in the Arabic language. We share a rare friendship for having survived something extraordinary together, and because of our month lived side by side in the desert we might be bound together for life. I have many friends in the world, but they are friends I meet for coffee or after-dinner drinks. I have never huddled in the snow next to them, speaking of visions. I have never shared with them a month in silence, trying to discern my destiny. It makes me feel even closer to Rania that we can speak only Arabic together, this sacred language in my life. I get to talk to her using sentences I have never uttered to anyone else in the world, ever.

"My love," she calls out to me when she sees me. "My love," I answer, kissing her cheeks—not because we are melodramatic, but because Syrians really talk this way.

We have also been bound together by the difficulties of life after the

Exercises, supporting each other in our slow crawl back to normality. Rania, who is already in her mid-thirties, fell even harder than I did after the Exercises. She is in the unenviable position of being a single woman in Syrian Catholic society, and the fact that she is not married or a nun means she is living in between the prescribed norms of the society, not praying or bearing children. She still lives with her parents and had been counting on her ability to make a choice during her second week of the Exercises so that she could change her life. In the end she descended the mountain still undecided, more confused about her life than ever.

"I don't feel a calling to be a nun," she told me, frustrated. "And I'm not in love with anyone, and no one is in love with me."

"Don't be ridiculous," I answered. "You won't let anyone fall in love with you."

The problem with Rania is that she is one of those rare women who is absolutely oblivious to her own beauty. She has short brown hair with blond strands that she often pulls back away from her face, revealing delicate hazel eyes and rosy cheeks punctuated by two deep dimples. She possesses a radiant smile. She is also perhaps the most sophisticated Syrian I know, and the French words that often creep into her Arabic not only hint that she is Christian, but in her case also that she is fairly fluent in French.

Today I find her hunched in her basement office at the museum, completely natural in a loose white T-shirt, jeans, and canvas tennis shoes, her hair framing her face. In front of her, a series of photographs are spread out over her desk.

"Come look," she says. "I wanted to show you how to restore an icon."

I find a place beside her, peering over her shoulder at the odd, unfamiliar face in the photographs. In the first image, a man in an ancient Greek icon lies buried beneath soot and candle smoke, unrecognizable after more than a century of having his face slowly worn away. In the second photograph, the icon has been cleaned enough to allow me to discern the vague outlines of a body. It is St. George, a common sight all over the Middle East, here attempting to ride his horse through smoke as black as night. Slowly, he gallops out of the dark, until three photographs later, the world is intact again and imbued with light, and St. George is healed and slaying the dragon, restored and surrounded by a sky of deep gold.

"You did *this*, Rania?"

"Yes."

I can't believe it. I had known that she restored icons, but I had not exactly grasped what that meant. She is a magician.

"I just don't get it. You spend your days literally bringing saints and angels back from the dead, and you were on the mountain asking for a calling?"

She shakes her head, in her typical *you have not lived what I live* frustration. "You don't understand Syria, Stephanie. It's not like America. This isn't considered a vocation here."

Yet I can't imagine deriding a brilliant cellist or a world-class sculptor for not having found a calling, much less for never getting married. Why hasn't anyone told her that working on Byzantine icons might be the deepest form of prayer one could hope to discover, like being born with a miraculous gift to heal? In fact, the original icon painters insisted that they "wrote" icons instead of painting them, breathing and whispering a prayer before every single brushstroke, their hands guided by God. Icon painters were often considered saints, for no one could write an icon unless he had purified his own heart first.

"Now Rania, *habibti*, you know that I love Syria. You know how much I adore the people living here. But, with all respect, when I see this work, I'm sorry, but I wish that you were living in Europe somewhere—because if someone in France saw this, they wouldn't care if you weren't a nun or married. They would call you a genius."

"Do you think so?"

"I know so. They would tell you that you are one of the lucky people in the world who has discovered a calling."

She examines the final icon again, looking at the restored face of St. George with familiar affection, and then smiles at me. I *see* her now, so calm and self-assured, completely unlike the defeated girl I knew in the desert, pacing back and forth in the valley on winter afternoons. I remember one morning, when she had been too frightened to climb up the mountain, I had taken her hand to lead her there. *I'm scared*, she had whispered. *Don't be scared*, I whispered back. *You should never be afraid of anything*.

Though now I think she had no business climbing that mountain.

She was looking for something that was already waiting for her here on the ground.

14.

I'VE ALWAYS BEEN JEALOUS OF PEOPLE skilled with their hands. I never even learned to hold my pencil correctly, much less blow glass or build my own chair or restore hundred-year-old icons. Now I live in a neighborhood of artisans, furniture makers, coppersmiths, boys who carve swords from camel bones, bakers. Most of these skills have been passed down from father to son, one generation after the other, so that more than one neighbor has told me something like "Sword carving is in my blood" without a hint of irony or jest. The more I watch men bending over their workbenches in total concentration, the more I can't escape the notion that what they are engaging in is a form of prayer.

Today I ask Mohammed the carpet seller, "Do you remember the story you told me, of the *jihad al-akbar*?"

"Yes, the jihad of the soul."

"I've been thinking about it a lot. I was wondering if you could teach me a little more about what this jihad means."

"Let me tell you a story instead," he says. Syrians like to answer questions by telling a story—which makes me laugh, because it is so much like my Woody Allen Jesus, stuck in his parables, going off on tangents about lost sheep and mustard seeds (the fact that half of my neighbors are carpenters only encourages me). "There was once a very simple, poor man, whose job it was to wash the hands and feet of the faithful as they came to the mosque to pray," Mohammed starts. "Every day, he stood at the door of the mosque, making sure he washed the feet of the sheikh when he entered. Now, one day, the sheikh was about to walk inside when he was suddenly distracted by a very beautiful girl who happened to pass by, and his eyes wandered. The poor man immediately stood up and poured the water directly over the sheikh's head!"

He chuckles to himself. But, like most parables in Arabic, this one is lost on me. "I don't get it, Mohammed."

"The poor man washing feet was a much better Muslim than the sheikh—he was focused on serving God, not on some girl with a short skirt."

He smiles and then stops to inhale from his cigarette. "Stephanie, if you want to find prayer, you don't need to go looking far. Just look to the *fallaheen*, the people of the countryside, or the street sweepers and the men in the marketplace, trying their best to take care of their kids. That's where you'll find the jihad of the soul."

He reaches to the top of a pile of carpets and pulls down a beautiful carpet from Iran I had often admired, with a very detailed geometric design. "Look at this carpet, for instance." He turns it over and shows me the tiny knots, tied one next to another. "This can tell you something about life. You could just as easily use another carpet. It would still cover the floor. But a carpet like this one takes months to finish. Others with even smaller knots take years. You have to have a lot of patience to tie every single knot in place, which is why such a carpet is so precious. That is jihad."

I sit drinking my tea, mulling over his words. Then he reaches into his desk and pulls out two enormous tomes, each one at least six inches thick.

"I bought you a present."

"A present? What for?"

"What for? For Valentine's Day," he says, trying to hide his smile.

"Very funny, Mohammed." Tomorrow is Valentine's Day, and he has been teasing me all week for being the lone American in Damascus still without a valentine. He can tease me only because his situation is even grimmer than mine, as his family is pressuring him to marry a particularly unattractive cousin.

"I'm just kidding. I thought I would buy you a gift to celebrate you finally getting over your sickness of sadness. Here."

He hands over two Arabic dictionaries, each one several pounds, like the Arabic version of the Oxford English Dictionary. I open the translucent onionskin pages delicately. Inside, hundreds of intricate drawings describe every kind of plant, flying machines, forest creatures, and ships with their sails extended, each example lovingly labeled with its unique

Arabic word. They are magnificent. They must have cost Mohammed an entire week's salary, money I know he doesn't have.

"Your Arabic is good enough now," he says with affection. "If you ever feel lonely or sad again, you can open them up—and you'll have the names of everything in the world, right there waiting for you."

I remember the story from Genesis, when God asks Adam to name all the birds and the beasts, and in doing so briefly bestows on him the power of God himself. In the Old Testament, what someone was called was always deeply tied to who they are, their deepest essence. Words *were* creation, which was how God created the world with his own speech: he named the world, and then each thing responded in turn by existing.

God said: Let there be light. And there was light.

I fall asleep that night with a dictionary in my bed, murmuring new words to myself until my eyelids slowly fold down into the dark.

15.

I SLEPT DEEPLY. Then the next day, an enormous car bomb explodes in Beirut, and Rafik Hariri is dead.

Of course, the day began normally. I had always been warned that it would. I woke up in the morning and drank my single glass of strong Arabic coffee with the Baron. When I went to catch a taxi on Straight Street, I saw bouquets of roses spilling from buckets outside the flower shop. Menus were set up in front of restaurants, and plush stuffed animals were on display in the store windows. A man rolling up the metal frame of his storefront whistled a tune softly to himself.

It was Valentine's Day in Damascus, a holiday that Syrians, with their affection for terms of endearment such as *my sun, my moon, my stars, my eyes*, their devotion to soap operas, and their fondness for syrupy music in which every third word is "my love" could not help but celebrate. This was a country, after all, where I had seen macho-looking bus drivers hang plush hearts from their dashboards. Where a very devout Muslim girl had gushed to me of the president, "He's just so handsome!" This was the country where Nizar Qabbani, the famous twentieth-century Arab poet, had written hundreds of love poems celebrating the women of Damascus (and Damascus itself, the woman he adored most). Where Ibn Arabi, the famous medieval Islamic mystic who once wrote, "I am the slave of passion and the slave of the beloved," was buried.

I made my way across town to gather my mail at the American Cultural Center, subconsciously, I suppose, hoping that some long-lost secret admirer had tracked me down from across the world and decided to send me a valentine. I was just retrieving my envelopes when all of the phones began ringing at once, the television set switched on, and I found myself staring at live images of a charred car in flames. The windows of the car were blown out and the roof was collapsed in. At first I couldn't tell what happened. The picture was all fire and white smoke and blackness, bodies too burned to recognize being pulled from the vehicles.

Then the voice in Arabic in the background announced, "Rafik Hariri, the former prime minister of Lebanon, has just been killed." But that wasn't possible. I stood there, staring at the television, waiting for the announcer to say it again.

At the front desk the secretary's face was locked in mute horror. She couldn't take her eyes off the television. "It's just like the 1980s," she whispered, not so much to me but to the walls. "What will happen next?" I didn't want to think about the answer. The 1980s had been an entire decade lost in Lebanon to civil war.

I returned home to find the Baron in front of his television set, his eyes glassy and a single tear staining his cheek. When he saw me he wiped his face with a handkerchief and then thrust it into his pocket in frustration.

"Hey, Stefanito, they're animals, they are . . . ," he trailed off, forcing a smile. "They'll make another civil war."

I put my hand on his shoulder, remembering that his two children still lived in the Armenian Quarter just outside of Beirut. "Let's drink coffee," I suggested, and he nodded, slowly getting up to make it, studying the dark liquid until it reached boiling before he removed it from the flame, stirred it, and then set it to boil a second time.

We sat drinking the coffee silently, as if that act alone could hold the world in place.

I wonder if this is what my parents felt like when Kennedy was assassinated. Rafik Hariri is supposed to be an untouchable, a larger-than-life personality so tied to the story of the modern Middle East that I can't get my head around the fact that he is dead. A billionaire Sunni Muslim with strong ties to both Saudi Arabia and Europe, Hariri took power in Lebanon following the civil war, intent on building a country out of the ruins and devastation of the conflict. He served as prime minister from 1992 to 1998 and again from 2000 until his recent resignation, investing his own money in rebuilding downtown Beirut, and in the process becoming an international symbol of Lebanon's ability to miraculously come back to life after fifteen years of sectarian violence. By regional standards he was certainly the most important public figure to emerge from Lebanon since the war, possessing a rare ability to appeal across sectarian lines. Yet he also had his enemies—chiefly the Syrian government, which he resented for keeping thousands of Syrian troops and secret police in Lebanon, constantly interfering in Lebanese political affairs, and fixing elections in what by international standards amounted to a foreign occupation. Just months before, he had finally resigned from his post in frustration after Syria insisted on extending the term of the pro-Syrian Lebanese president, guaranteeing that Syria would continue to manipulate matters of state from the back room.

During my time living in Beirut, I had watched the spirits of my friends and colleagues slowly rising as their city was rebuilt, as each new month passed without violence. I had watched tourists cautiously trickle back into the city that had once been called the Paris of the Middle East, full of outdoor cafés, seaside resorts, bars, and discotheques. And now Hariri is dead, and the fine sectarian balance of postwar Lebanon is in danger of once again collapsing. I know where he died so well that I can close my eyes and transport myself in space to that charred, burning car. I can picture it perfectly, ten minutes from my old home, on a strip of road beside the sea, smelling of salt. Nearby, sailboats come to moor, Mercedes line up outside of the Phoenicia hotel across the street, and a street vendor sells steaming corn on the cob from a pushcart. I often used to stand there in the early evening to watch the sun falling over the distant Lebanese mountains, catching on the windows of houses, so that the sky became a hundred small, shining lights. It was my favorite place in Beirut.

Now, in Damascus, there is the initial gasp that Beirut might once again be lost, the romantic capital that Syrians fawn over and flock to whenever they can afford it, relaxing at restaurants and buying the American blue jeans and electronics that are under sanctions in their own country, breathing. For this, there is an outpouring of grief. The darker realization settles in more slowly. Syria will be blamed for his death.

By late afternoon, Lebanese are gathered outside of Hariri's home in Beirut, chanting, *Syria out! Syria out!* The next day, America removes its ambassador from Damascus in protest, coming just short of directly blaming the Syrian government for Hariri's death. I wake up an American in Damascus, a "scholar-ambassador" tied to an embassy without a real ambassador and now hailing from an official enemy country.

And I'm scared.

16.

WE'VE BEEN WAITING DAYS TO HEAR if there will be retaliation, but then another morning passes and nothing happens. I'm learning how waiting can turn people mad; it might be worse than actual war. At least war is tangible. At least it involves real events, objects, human beings living and dying. My neighbors have been left only with their minds, everyone imagining what *might* happen. The mind, I'm learning, contains its own wars.

Every day Straight Street crumbles a bit more. It is a sad, slow falling apart, and it reminds me of watching my mother grieving after her father was killed, the way she would forget things in the kitchen, leave pots of beans on the stove until they burned so badly that the bottom of the pot seared off. Here, everyone is trying so hard to be brave, but fear breaks through the surface. I first notice it under their eyes. Merchants continue on with their daily habits of carving wood, selling jewelry, and baking pastries, and yet very distinct black circles begin rimming their eyes. Then neighbors who always wore impeccable ironed shirts begin to appear with their collars wrinkled, folding up at the edges. Storekeepers fumble with their change, handing out the wrong coins. Keys refuse to catch in door locks. Everything in the world seems just slightly off balance.

It's not only Straight Street. The entire city is deteriorating, silently, just beneath the surface of ordinary life. I keep checking the stores, expecting my neighbors to stock up on canned goods, but the stores are empty of shoppers. I wonder if this is perhaps because such blatant planning would amount to a betrayal, an admittance of defeat before anything has gone wrong. No one has bombed us yet, after all. Still, some aren't waiting. Today I passed by the diplomatic quarter, and I saw lines for visas snaking around the buildings and onto the sidewalks as Syrians with any connections at all try to escape before retaliation from Lebanon or America. In the meantime the streets downtown are flooding with new refugees, Syrians who worked in Lebanon for years fleeing home again, frightened and bitter after being spat on in Beirut or refused rides in taxis. "Those Lebanese are Jews, they are," a woman down the street muttered to me in disgust today, just after her brother returned from his job in Lebanon. "They'll shake your hand with one hand and use the other to stab you in the back."

As for me, I'm lost. I can't quite fathom why I'm still here, but as no one has asked me to leave I stay put. By now I'm fairly certain that I am being followed. I hear my voice, echoing twice, on all of my phone calls, cluing me that someone is probably listening. I can't log on to my e-mail account without confirming the password several times—which can only mean that someone has been trying to hack into my accounts. I don't feel alone when I walk down the streets, and I sense that my neighbors are increasingly afraid to talk to me, worried that I might be a spy, or worse, that by simply liking me they might be labeled collaborators.

When I do get out, I walk down the street holding imaginary conversations with the secret police, fielding their questions, practicing my answers in Arabic. I keep mental schedules of the places I have been so that I can tell them if they ask. This morning, when I returned home from a cautious walk through the city, the Baron was making a great spectacle of pacing back and forth in front of my door, looking worried.

"What's wrong, Grandfather?" I asked him.

"Where were you?" He threw his arms in the air in frustration. "I've been looking for you everywhere! Condoleezza Rice came searching for you!"

I sighed in relief. I thought there had perhaps been an explosion. "Very funny."

"Do you get it? Condi?"

"I get it, Grandpa."

"Condi," he spat onto the ground. "That little prostitute. That Satan."

With no proof of who was responsible for the killing, rumors fly thick and fast. Taxi drivers warn me that America was behind it and will now invade Syria, filling the skies with Apache helicopters and the streets with tanks, killing even more innocent women and children, seizing this opportunity to finally weed out the last bastion of Baathism in the Middle East. Journalists worry that internal forces will be pushed into action, either leftist political dissidents or the Muslim Brotherhood, forcing a coup that could eventually lead Syria to an Iraq-style civil war or to the creation of an Islamic state, a hellish thought for my Christian neighbors. So far, I have heard agreement only on two things: one, that the Syrian regime is innocent, the victim of a conspiracy, and two, that nothing good can possibly emerge from any of this. Though I have no idea if the Syrian government *is* innocent, there is some comfort in my neighbors believing that it must be. We might be bombed from the outside, but as long as the local population supports the government, at least we don't have to worry as much about a coup.

The only person I can imagine who might still be sane is Mohammed, who can repair a torn rug sewn by several hands and has the presence of mind to thank God even when he is almost starving. I find him sitting alone in the back of his store, next to a space heater with thin orange rims giving a faint heat. He is restless and sleep deprived, and for the first time, he is not repairing a carpet or smoking a cigarette, so that his hands are idle and nervous. In the back of his shop, a portrait of Bashar al-Assad is staring down at us in a suit and tie, smiling confidently. Mohammed has always admired him, calling him a "strong, smart man," one of the few leaders in the Middle East who hadn't sold himself and his people out to foreign leaders, one who maintained his principles.

But today he doesn't look confident. He forgets to offer me a cigarette or tea, and so I pour a glass myself and then grab a cigarette from the pack he has left on the table. I am practically chain-smoking these days.

"How are you, Mohammed?"

"Thanks be to God, Stephanie," he sighs. "Thanks be to God."

He keeps staring up at his television showing thousands of Lebanese marching in the streets of downtown Beirut against Syria. The sight of Christians, Muslims, and Druze all marching together has been particularly surreal, and more than one person has mentioned to me sarcastically that after fifteen years of hating one another, the one thing that could finally unite the Lebanese is hating Syria.

"Mohammed?"

"*Shoo?*"

"Who do you think killed Rafik Hariri anyway?"

I prepare myself for the inevitable answer: the Americans, the Israelis, Al Qaeda, the Saudis, or even the rumor that Rafik Hariri staged his own death and is sunning on a beach in South America. Instead he examines the street beyond the window. I am not sure what he is looking for. Then, very slowly, it dawns on me that he is making sure that no street sweeper or window washer is casually walking by, listening.

Finally, he looks at me wearily. "I think that we did, Stephanie."

"What?" I can't believe what I am hearing.

He quietly nods his head. He looks heartbroken, like he has just caught his girl in bed with another man.

This is when I know the Syrians are waiting for the government to fall.

17.

I'VE PROMISED MYSELF that I won't flee the country, in part because, if relations between America and Syria remain this icy, this might be my last chance ever to spend time here. So I escape into books, the world in which I have found solace throughout my entire life. I have a grant to study the Muslim Jesus, after all, and since my Arabic is improving it is high time that I get started on my research. Yes, books are the safest solution. They don't listen to my phone calls or worry that I work for the CIA. If they become too scary, I can simply shut them and hide them under the bed.

Unfortunately, I have hit upon a bit of a snag in my plan, for the only book I truly want to read now requires a guide. After years of studying Islam in English, I feel ready to read the Quran in Arabic, but I know I can't do it alone. The Quran in Arabic is an uncharted country and hardly a book one picks up and reads at random. It is a difficult journey, and you simply don't start walking unless you have someone beside you to show you the way.

This is how I find myself halfway across the city this morning, sitting on a minibus crammed with very religious Muslims, the women covered except for their faces. A man rises and gives me the seat next to his wife, so that as a single woman I will run no risk of touching him. The Quran plays on a tape recorder. Outside the window, mosques seem to sprout out of almost every corner, along with bookstores selling prayer books and cookbooks based on the food of the prophet Mohammed, hair salons with black crepe covering the windows so that Muslim women can show their hair inside, Internet cafés with separate entrances for men and women. Damascus is really a series of very small cities folded together. I often forget that I live in only one of them—the Christian one, at that.

After a full half hour I arrive at the apartment of the female sheikh who has agreed to take me on as her student. The city descends beneath me from the window of the elevator as I rise to the fourth floor. Then I knock on a door until a shy young boy with his hair in a bowl cut opens it for me. He must be only five.

"I'm here to see your mom," I tell him.

He nods and then turns and shouts at the top of his lungs, "Mom!" He giggles hysterically.

I slip off my shoes, as is the custom in an Islamic house, replacing them with the pink house shoes soled with loose wooden bottoms waiting at the door, so that now I clank gently against the ground when I walk. Then she is in front of me, kissing my cheeks.

"*Ahlan wa sahlan,*" she tells me, her voice light and warm.

"Thank you very much for having me," I respond in very formal Arabic.

"*Ma'shallah*, you speak Arabic so well!" she responds, putting her hands to her cheeks.

And, instantly, I love her.

My sheikha doesn't look anything like I imagined a female sheikh might look, not that I have much experience with sheikhs of any persuasion. I had secretly worried that she would be the image of the feared Catholic-school nun, wrinkled in her habit and brandishing a ruler in her hands. But this Sheikha's loose brown curls drop to her shoulders, as she does not wear the headscarf in the privacy of her home and with another woman. Her big brown eyes light up each time she speaks. She is wearing a long, elegant gray robe with fur-lined sleeves and a collar (making her a rather chic Sheikha), and I can glimpse the edge of highlights in her hair, which for some reason I never even thought a Muslim leader *could* have. There is nothing severe about her. She rushes to the kitchen to prepare me tea, which she serves in thin, delicate teacups like those my grandmother used to serve me hot chocolate when I was a child.

"Can I help you?" I ask, feeling slightly ridiculous, sitting on her plush sofa like a queen while she is running back and forth to serve me.

"Shhh, you rest now," she scolds. "*Ahlan wa sahlan*, How do you take your tea?"

It is all rather odd. I am drinking tea with a female sheikh, like Alice in Wonderland. Just when I think life can't be more bizarre, God throws this in to surprise me.

I suppose that it might be unusual for a prominent Muslim leader to invite a young Christian woman into her home under any circumstances, but with the current political tensions it is particularly remarkable. I am, after all, tied to the enemy. In the last week, many of the Fulbright scholars have lost their local sponsors, as Syrians become increasingly afraid of being labeled as collaborators. Yet if the Sheikha has any reservations, she reveals nothing. She watches me finishing my tea, and then a few minutes later she leaves the room and returns, handing me a dark red leather-bound Quran, the chapters threaded with colored lettering through the Arabic words, written right to left. The pages resemble tiny tapestries.

"It's yours," she tells me. "It is my gift to you." I have been a collector of books since childhood, and this is the most beautiful book I have ever owned in my life.

She opens her Quran to the first page, the *Fatiha*. "Let's begin at the beginning."

The opening of the Quran parts the air as one would hear the first, faint notes from a violin in a symphony. The lines she recites are breathy and effortless and altogether lovely. I have never heard *words* sound like that—the end of each line holding in space, filling the empty air around it, almost tangible. She memorized the verses so long ago that they escape from her mouth effortlessly. *This is Arabic*, I think to myself. *This is the Arabic language as I dreamed it might sound, pushed to its limits, water filling a vase.*

"Now you try," she encourages me, and I nod. I struggle reading the Arabic, fumbling over the vowels, until we begin chanting, call-and-response, her voice calling and my voice reaching out after it, as my mother taught me to sing when I was a child:

Bismallah al-Rahman Al-Raheem . . .
In the name of God, the merciful and compassionate . . .

There are hundreds of female sheikhs in Syria, women who can teach other women in the mosque and who visit women in their homes to provide solace and advice in a society where a man, even a sheikh, should not be left alone with a woman. My Sheikha is somewhat famous, as far as female sheikhs are concerned. She descends from an extremely prominent family of religious scholars, so that she was raised learning the Quran and Islamic law from the time she was old enough to speak. She memorized the Quran in her teens, as well as thousands of sayings of the prophet Mohammed. She is an authority on Islamic law and founded one of the most prestigious women's madrassas—religious schools—in Damascus more than twenty years ago. She is also the mother of three. Oh, and I forgot to mention: she believes that non-Muslims can achieve salvation. Which is also why I am sitting here without a headscarf, carrying all of my Catholic-school, rosary-reciting Christian past, and our two voices are calling out a common prayer, blending together and floating through her living room.

In time, the reading becomes easier, and I find myself falling into a rhythm that feels like singing, though Muslims would be quick to call this *tajwid*—not song, but recitation. While it is my first time reciting the Quran, there is something familiar about this moment, this calling out in Arabic, this language rising in my chest, only I can't pin down exactly what. Then, slowly, I understand. I understand when I keep saying his name, *Allah*, over and over, which in Arabic is simply the name of God, for both Muslims and Christians. Just as in the monastery I sang, *Allahu nooree wu halasee*. The Lord is my light and my salvation, so do not be afraid.

I am praying. It has been months now since I felt the simple rising in my heart, this direct communion with God, not since those winter days in the desert. But I am once again praying in Arabic, my monastic language, and even though I am struck by the oddity of being led in prayer by a female sheikh, I am relieved that my prayer life is not lost entirely.

After an hour, she guides my hand through the second chapter of the Quran and then leaves it to rest on a verse.

"This is one of the most beautiful stories in Islam," she tells me. "It is the story of how God created Adam, peace be upon him, out of clay. I know that in Christianity you think of Adam as a sinner, but for us he is the first prophet, even if he sinned in front of God."

"How can he be a prophet if he sinned?" I ask her.

"Prophets are human, Istifanee, and God is merciful and forgiving. If the prophets weren't human, then we would never be able to follow them. We would think that what they do is impossible for the rest of us."

I remember that Adam's name in Hebrew means simply "earth," "soil." As if man was built from all of the heaviness of the ground, the hard reality of earth, making who we are and the road we must travel one and the same.

"After God created the world he gave Adam the names, allowing him to see the essence of the world and all that was contained inside of it," she tells me. "He then asked the angels to bow down to him."

I imagine this for a moment, the angels bowing down in front of man, their wings folding softly over their backs, their foreheads briefly touching the ground.

"All of the angels bowed down in front of Adam, except for the one named Iblis," she says, closing her Quran and looking at me. "Iblis asked God, 'Why should I bow down if I am made of fire and Adam is only made of clay?' "

I smile at the question, so human to my ears.

"Iblis could not understand why God would ask him to bow down to a human, when he had been made an angel."

"Well, why would he?"

The Bread of Angels

She meets my eyes, kindly. "He could not comprehend the miracle, that despite our weaknesses, God has made mankind higher than the angels."

18.

IT DOES NOT TAKE ME long to fall in love with the Quran. I stop at the Islamic market on my way home from my first lesson and buy the entire Quran on tape, and I spend the afternoon listening and running my fingers over the lovely threaded lines of my new book, trying to whisper along. This is the first time I have ever read a religious text in its original language, and I am surprised by the difference it makes. Very often, even if I don't understand the text, I can sense the meaning in the *feeling* of the words. It reminds me of studying a difficult piece of music. Like unchaining a sentence and letting it fly into the air. In Islam, the language of the Quran is considered to be a miracle. I have met men from Pakistan who memorized the entire Quran when they were boys without understanding a word of it, just so that they could possess that sound.

The truth is, since the Spiritual Exercises I've been afraid to go too deeply into the Bible, afraid that I might get thrown again over the edge of a psychological abyss. But I'm not afraid of the Quran. It is not a linear narrative but pieces of stories, woven together, sometimes nothing but music holding them in place. The same story appears over and over in different contexts, the meaning each time changing slightly, shifting, so that the entire book becomes a process of understanding and reunderstanding what happened in the past, and even what can happen in the future. Every time I think I have completed a story, it appears again, challenging the previous belief. Every time I understand what a word means, it repeats itself in a slightly different context. Reading the Quran is a lesson in personal humility. They say that no word ever means the same thing twice. So I can do nothing but finally let go, surrender to a story greater than my own understanding, letting it be.

Letting go. It feels like such a relief.

Somewhere, alone in my room, in this letting go, is where I feel a small bird stirring within my heart, a feeling I might reasonably call happiness. I have not earned it or discovered it. It has simply been given to me, without asking for anything in return.

"Hello, God," I whisper, smiling to the empty space of my room. "It's so nice to see you again." I think that somewhere in the universe, God winks at me.

SOME MORNINGS, when I can't bear the thought of studying alone in my room, I visit the women's mosque across town where the Sheikha lectures on Islam. I sit in a room covered in carpets and crowded from wall to wall with women dressed in long coats that fall to their ankles, slowly passing prayer beads through their hands. It feels so refreshing to find myself in a room full of women. I've spent so much time with Ahmed and Mohammed and the Baron that I've often wondered where all of the women *are* in this country who aren't nuns or potential nuns. I just haven't known where to look for them.

The Sheikha looks slightly intimidating up there at the lectern, her hair covered in a navy scarf fastened firmly beneath her chin, her clothing hidden by a navy coat buttoned all the way down to the ground. But her voice is as light as ever, and she teaches us the stories of the Quran, about Noah floating away in his Arabic Ark, Joseph abandoned by his brothers at the bottom of the well, Abraham searching for God in the heavens. Hearing these tidbits feels like knowing a close girlfriend for twenty years and then suddenly learning something totally unexpected about her, like that she knows how to fly or is a Cordon Bleu chef. I have been acquainted with most of the characters in the Quran—Abraham, Isaac, Jacob, Mary, Jesus, John the Baptist, Moses—since I was a child listening to Bible stories. But I have always known them as holy people, members of some other species. The Quran makes them human.

My favorite parts of the Quran, though, are when, in the midst of all of this glorious language, a small and completely ordinary detail is slipped in. For example, I read that John the Baptist was kind to his parents. In the chapter called The Cave, which tells the story of a group of men who fell asleep in a cave and woke up hundreds of years later, the text mentions that a dog followed them on the way and fell asleep beside them. In the story of Moses, a mysterious guide named Khidr appears to teach him the mysteries of the universe. But he ends up telling Moses in very human frustration, *You won't have the patience to understand.* It is nice to hear from a prophet the same kind of scolding my mother would give me when I asked her about grown-up conversations I'd overheard as a child.

I never call the Sheikha by her first name, which seems much too informal for someone who possesses so much knowledge. And she calls me Istifanee, which in Arabic means "he selected me." She tells me that it is from the same verb that the angel Gabriel uses in the Quran to tell Mary what has happened to her. *God has chosen you, chosen you from all of the women of the world.*

So it is as Istifanee that I sit across from her during our lessons, trying to understand these new stories that have been placed in my life. Sometimes it only takes a single word to change the meaning entirely. Last week, for instance, I was reading the story of Adam and Eve expelled from paradise, and I noticed that before they left, "God turned to them." I looked that up in my dictionary.

"God *turned* to them?" I asked the Sheikha later at our lesson. "You mean that he forgave them?"

She laughed. "That's what it says."

"So there is no original sin?"

"No, in Islam, everyone is born without sin."

"You mean there is no curse?"

She eyed me with confusion. "How could someone be born with a curse? God is compassionate. We can only be responsible for our own choices."

What a difference a word makes. God turns for a moment without us even seeing him, and the entire universe for generations becomes lighter in response.

19.

THE MOOD IN DAMASCUS continues to shift, and increasingly Syrians are defying the government, openly voicing their frustrations to anyone who will listen. In a country so dominated by the secret police, this carries the air of the impossible, like a mute man suddenly, out of nowhere, starting to speak. One is not supposed to be able to criticize the government without instantly disappearing in a puff of smoke. Yet now it is happening every day, and it is a bit unnerving. Shopkeepers complain that the president has not come out in public to defend them. Journalists line up to interview political dissidents on the record. I hear intellectuals in cafés advocating war and whispering of a coup. I had no idea how much people had been suppressing until now.

I try to keep to myself, and still every day I maintain my evening appointment with the Baron in front of his beat-up, rickety television. All of the programs have been canceled in Lebanon for forty days of official mourning, so that we are left to stare at montage after montage of the martyr Rafik Hariri beamed to us by satellite, interspersed with footage of tens of thousands of Lebanese citizens protesting against Syria and waving Lebanese flags.

"Hariri, Hariri, Hariri," the Baron moans in agony. "No more soap operas. No more dancing. Just Hariri. My God, how long do we have to mourn him?"

I have monitored the Baron's slow decline since regular programming halted, cutting him off from his lifeline of Lebanese women in short skirts and high heels, shaking their hips in music videos and competing on game shows. It rather resembles my post-Mark descent into depression. Initially the Baron simply stopped taking his afternoon walks, opting to remain at home and stare at the repetitive television shows. Then he quit bothering to change into his clothes from Milano at all. I knew things were bad when yesterday I caught him resorting to the Hezbollah television station, the only station left with non-Hariri programming. When the female newscaster appeared on-screen with her entire body covered in black clothing and her hair hidden beneath a scarf, he groaned.

"Why?" he asked the television. "Why?"

Now, when I enter the courtyard at noon, I find him already reeking of whiskey and cigarettes, wearing green sweatpants and plastic house sandals, stirring a pot of noodles on a portable stove. He looks like a train wreck.

"How's life, Grandpa?" I ask him cheerfully. He shoots me a sarcastic glance.

"Like shit, Stefanito," he answers. "Life is just like shit."

20.

I'VE BEEN STUDYING with the Sheikha for several weeks. So far we've been progressing through the text slowly, like two gardeners nimbly carving our way through the forest, stopping at each blade of grass. At this rate, we'll finish reading the Quran in Arabic in another ten years.

"I know that you only have a few months left in Damascus," she mentions somewhat coyly today during our lesson. "Do you have any requests for what we might focus on this week?"

Yes, yes, and yes. Ever since the Spiritual Exercises, when Mary appeared to me out of the stones of the desert, I've wanted to know about the Virgin Mary in Islam.

"Maryam al-Adra," I tell her.

She smiles. "I thought that you might suggest that."

She reaches over the table, guiding my hand gently until it falls on Maryam, the nineteenth chapter in the Quran, named after the Virgin Mary.

"Even the prophet Jesus, peace be upon him, does not have a chapter named after him. Mary is extremely precious to us. There is a debate in Islam as to whether or not Mary herself is a prophet. In fact there is a hadith of the prophet Mohammed, peace be upon him, which says that Mary will be the first of us to enter paradise at the end of the world."

She begins reciting the story by heart and I echo her, the two of us summoning Mary into the room to sit between us.

Bismallah al-Rahman al-Raheem

Once, there lived a woman from the family of Imran who was unable to bear children. One afternoon, she went off to pray alone. She asked God, "Oh, you who hear and know all things, if you will give me a child, then I will offer that child for the rest of his life to your service." She became pregnant, and when the time came for her to give birth, she discovered that she had delivered a girl. *"Oh God!"* she said. *"I have delivered a girl and not a boy!"*

"I know what you have delivered," God responded, *"and I shall name her Mary and protect her and her descendants from Satan."*

Mary grew in purity and beauty. She dedicated her life to praying in the temple, and she knew no man. God watched over her, and took care of her, and gave her fruits out of season.

One day, when Mary was alone in a place in the east, God sent an angel to her in the form of a man.

Mary was frightened. "I seek refuge in the Compassionate," she called out.

The angel answered, "I am a messenger from God, sent to announce the gift of a holy son. Oh Mary! God has blessed you with a Word from him named the Messiah Jesus, son of Mary."

Mary responded, "How can I give birth to a child, when I have known no man?"

The angel answered, "That is how it is, for God creates what he wills, he can simply say Be! And it will be."

Mary became pregnant. So she left the city for a faraway place and waited. Her labor pains hit her so strongly that she collapsed beneath a palm tree and cried out, "Why did I not die before this, that I would have been forgotten and out of sight?"

But he called out from beneath her, "Be not afraid! For God has sent from beneath you a source of water. So shake the tree trunk, and he will make new dates fall on you from the tree. Eat, and drink, that your eye can rejoice, and if you see any man, do not speak to him."

So Mary gave birth to Jesus.

WHEN SHE FİNİSHES RECİTİNG THE VERSES, we both sit there silently, listening to the last words hanging in the air. "It's beautiful," I finally say.

"It's one of the chapters Muslims memorize the most often. For us, our mother Mary, peace be upon her, is the model of female piety. She is also a rebel in her society who risked losing everything in order to follow her destiny. She never married, and no one would have believed her if she told them about her meeting with the angel. Still, she had faith, even when she did not understand what was being asked of her life. That is what allows her to leave everything and to walk off alone, without food or water, waiting to give birth to a child."

Months ago, just before I fled Damascus to spend a month in the monastery, a young Muslim had told me solemnly, "You are taking the journey of the Virgin Mary in Islam, who goes off alone for many days, to take a fast from speaking, and to wait."

21.

NOW I AM ALONE IN MY ROOM, the curtains drawn so that my Christian neighbors won't gawk at me studying the Quran. I read Mary's story again, with all of the depth and attention I had given to the Gospel of Matthew during the Spiritual Exercises, pausing and meditating on every word. I close my eyes, taking deep breaths, waiting. Now I am in two places at once: in my bedroom in Damascus and high on that mountaintop in the desert, waiting for Mary to appear.

"Come back," I whisper.

I wait in the silence. Then, she is here. So young, with her pale, moon-shaped face, her hair tucked quietly beneath a white scarf, her frightened eyes looking out at me. She is just a girl, thirteen, maybe fourteen, too young to face angels in her room. She is my age when my grandfather was murdered, the first truly awful year of my life.

She walks out into the desert in silence, the long path extending in front of her, drawn forward by the memory of the voice of an angel. Her stomach cramps with hunger, each step an effort, her feet making small imprints in the dust. Around her there is nothing—just scrub bush, the odd yellow flowers collecting bees, and the wide desert hills extending all the way past the horizon. The vast and unending silence, unfolding in front of her feet, and the intense desert sun, casting its terrible white light.

She had told no one that she was leaving. They would not have let her go alone. She senses that this is one journey in her life in which she must be solitary, that no one else can take her forward, save for that voice speaking to her heart. In her belly, she feels another life, stirring. She will keep walking until a voice tells her that the journey is over, that she can rest.

She walks for hours, stopping only when she sees the date tree alongside the path, with its broad leaves making small gray patterns on the rocks. She doesn't stop for the shade, but because she is on the edge of falling and needs something to hold on to.

She falls too soon, stumbling over a stone and then collapsing onto the path, seeing the entire world lost in that falling: her mother, her home, that quiet room of hers that had once held the body of an angel. Any hope of one day falling in love. Rose bushes, and the familiar voices of other people, walking in the street at night. In that moment, they are gone forever.

Then the baby begins pushing at her insides, and there is no one's hand to hold on to.

"Why did I not die before this?" She is weeping now. "Why not be invisible and out of sight?" When really she is thinking about another life, the life she might have been given, not here, alone in this place, hungry, thirsty, and waiting.

A voice comes. She turns, listening. It belongs to no one, but she hears it as the sum of all who have ever called to her in her life.

It whispers from beneath her, "Be not afraid." She looks down to see a stream of water, slowly moving through her hands.

I READ MARY'S STORY so many times that I begin to memorize it: Mary, collapsing beneath that tree, wishing that she had never been born. I examine each word, then each letter, beginning with the mysterious Arabic letters that open the chapter on Mary, *Kahf, Ha Ye Ain Sod*, one letter after another, like sounds knocking on a door and begging it to open. It all seems so familiar to me. I could almost believe that I was born with this story written inside of me and am now only waiting to understand the words.

Most Muslims believe that the Quran is eternal, that it always existed but was only revealed over time. Just as they believe that our lives are *maktoob*, written, but it takes a lifetime to understand them. This does not mean that we have no say in our lives—for the famous Islamic saying insists that prayer can change destiny, that we small humans can enter into an exchange with God. Yet it means that in prayer, as in destiny, we are wading through divine material greater than ourselves.

The Sheikha has memorized every single word of the Quran, so that I sometimes feel that she contains it. Often when she discovers a new meaning of a word in the Quran, I have a sense that her entire interior self is slightly shifting, like a plate moving beneath the ocean of her being. For her, reading is not just about who she is, but is also about who she will become. I know that as I am a Christian she has elevated me above her students, because I am also her teacher, just as she is mine. I know different ways of seeing words. We are each teaching the other a new way of reading.

Every time I confront two different versions of a story, in the end I ask myself, What is the story that I want to contain? For the early monks believed that there is no such thing as a story—we each meet the text, and who we are and the text together create a unique event. We change for it and it changes for us, the act of reading becoming an essential way of transforming ourselves. We can only bring to the text what is inside of ourselves—even if the story is a story of death, if we contain life, we will find life.

For me, the Virgin Mary of the Quran does not replace the Annunciation story of Mary from the Gospels but narrates the voyage within Mary's own heart. There is, after all, nothing easy about saying yes to an angel. It changes everything. I had never been convinced that life for Mary continued on, undisturbed, until she arrived at Bethlehem. The Quran tells us something else, that she was so frightened and lonely that she left everything behind to walk in the desert, until she collapsed, wanting to die. That is the story I have lived. That long, excruciating battle back to life. That journey through the desert that is entirely solitary, no matter how many other people I encounter on the path. That moment when everything felt so lost that I sank onto the ground of my own heart, wishing that I had never been born. Yes, that is what had been missing from the story I have known until now—the recognition of falling down, the moment when everything is lost forever.

Then, after this small death, the child arrives. I can see her, holding the child to her breast, skin against skin, keeping the infant against her body to remind her that this moment is real. Amazed that such an incredible gift could come now, so soon after falling down. The Virgin Mary in Islam, who is by any other name a desert contemplative, a young hermit who never marries, who gives her entire life to prayer and God. Who collapses beneath that tree, before she receives the bread of angels.

22.

March

TODAY IT IS MARY'S VOICE finally leading me back to Mar Musa, that quiet *Yes* she whispered to the angel, the promise of her fidelity, calling her into the desert alone. I pack my Arabic Bible and a change of clothes, and after a long ride out into the desert, I reach the valley beneath the monastery, that vast expanse of bare red stone. This time the stairs don't feel so daunting—I am almost grateful for them, for the chance to slowly climb above the troubled earth.

I begin ascending, one step after another, no longer laboring under the effort as I once did. It feels strange to come back again. I have dreaded it. I am one who runs away. Yet now I am climbing back to God. It isn't easy to keep this long-postponed date in the desert, to sit across from an empty space and admit to God with all candor: *Clearly something went a bit haywire between us, but I still love you, and I am fairly certain that you still love me. I know I'm not the easiest person to live with, but I would really like to try to work it out.*

I arrive at the summit after half an hour to find Frédéric scrambling back and forth with his small pot of tea, trying to welcome the swarms of Christians seeking relief from the political crisis. When he sees me, he sighs in relief, loping over and kissing my two cheeks.

"Hey Stéphanie," he says, softly, and it makes me shy to hear my name, the way he says it, so very French. He looks oddly happy to see me.

"Where's Paolo?" I ask.

"He's in Europe for the month."

"So you've been in charge here since the crisis?"

"That's right."

I can't imagine. The country is literally falling apart at the seams.

"I know. It's a little bit crazy. Are you staying for a few days?"

"I think so."

"I'm glad."

It feels just like coming home again, to this house in the sky with its familiar tables and chairs, the kitchen with its cupboards full of plates and spoons, the monastic bell siphoning off the day and holding everything in place. I am just settling in, climbing the stairs to gather my bedsheets for the evening, when the phone rings.

One of the workers runs out to meet me. "Stephanie?"

"Yes?"

"The phone is for you."

That is decidedly odd. Why would someone call me here? "Who is it?"

"It's the secret police. They want to talk to you."

I can't believe it. After all of this time in Damascus without a follow-up visit, Mr. X has tracked me down, and here, in the middle of the desert of all places. With the rest of the country collapsing into chaos, why do they possibly care that I am here?

"What do they want?" I scream. Right there in the middle of the monastery.

"They just want to talk to you."

"How do they even know that I am here?"

The worker shrugs, somewhat helpless. "They just know."

"And why do they want to talk to me?"

"They want to know what you are doing here."

I grab on to the side of the stair railing, lean back, and I yell, "Tell them I came to the monastery to PRAY! Did they ever think of that? To PRAY! Is that so hard to believe?"

The worker looks at me with astonished eyes. He then rushes off, explaining to Mr. X that I am slightly high-strung but mean the country no harm. But for the rest of the afternoon, each time the workers pass me, they open their eyes into wide saucers and shout like lunatics: "I just want to pray!" And then they burst into laughter.

But it's true. I just want to pray. Now that I have shouted that fact from the rooftops of a monastery for all of the visitors and goats and angels to hear, I am quite certain. I am ready to truly pray again, at last, and I'll be damned if I'll let anyone, even Mr. X himself, attempt to stop me, short of dragging me down from the mountain by force.

I set up my books and fold my clothes in my room and walk out to the desert for the first real time since the Spiritual Exercises, finding the narrow indent in the mountain and climbing, my feet catching in the almost invisible path until I slowly lift myself high above everything—above the valley floor, the monastery, and, most of all, the life I have left behind. I have no illusions anymore that I can change the world completely—that some prayer I whisper today will mend the brokenness of the city in which I live, that I can make the dead walk again. I just want silence. I want God to come into that silence. I want an invisible hand to reach through the air and hold me for a while.

I wait and let all of the noise of my life in Damascus swell to the surface, the faces of each of my neighbors with their red, bruised eyes. I watch the face of the political dissident who had confided to me earlier that week, *I am just waiting to be in a car accident. Maybe they will kill me, just like that.* The journalist who told me in a restaurant, *Sometimes there is no alternative to war. War is better than standing still forever.* The crazed cabdriver who sped through traffic and shouted, *Your country can bomb my country for all I care. There's nothing left for me here!* They wash over me, and instead of explaining them away I sit with all of them, on the top of that mountain, with them and the dozens of others I know who are not like them, who just want to keep waking up in the world that they know.

"Hello, my loved ones," I whisper. I stay with them a long time, until they fade into the horizon.

I return to the monastery to find Dima alone in the courtyard, drinking a glass of tea. She is wearing her long monastic robes, the black scarf of a formal novice hanging loosely on her shoulders. It is striking to see her. I remember distinctly when I first met her that I could not get my head around the fact that she wanted to be a nun. She was just so full of joy. She didn't look like she could sit through a rosary, much less the stations of the cross. Sin and redemption didn't seem to be subjects she would obsess over. And this tiny monastery in the mountains didn't feel large enough to contain her. She danced and clapped and twirled to the music at the end of the Mass, caught smokes with the workers in the afternoon between chores, and wore sweatpants whenever she was not confined to the robes of the novitiate. While Frédéric fasted, she delighted in Arabic pastries brought by the guests. As she was from the city of Homs, the butt of Syrian jokes, she often joined in the fun by telling jokes about her hometown to the visitors. I could barely look at her without imagining dozens of nuns singing in *Sound of Music* unison: *How do you solve a problem like Dima?*

The Spiritual Exercises were no exception. During our month of silence, Dima couldn't help but talk a little bit every day. She knocked on my door to bring me cookies and tea. She bounced in and out of the valley in the afternoons. But then, like the rest of us, she slowly fell apart in the aftermath. I had found it grueling to see her exhausted and confused by post-Ignatius depression, confined to her room for long periods after I had returned from Christmas, circles under her eyes. It had seemed particularly unfair.

Yet something has changed since I saw her last. Now her face is smooth and serious, with a fresh self-awareness I have often seen in mothers of newborn children.

She hugs me tightly. "My sister," she calls me.

"*Ya ayoonie*, my eye," I call her back. "How has it been here?"

"You can't imagine. It's been full every day."

"That must be difficult."

She shrugs. "What can we do? We're all helpless. All I can do is pray and pray."

She looks exhausted but oddly confident. I reflect on what she has just told me: *All I can do is pray and pray.* It doesn't sound like nothing. It sounds like resisting.

"Are you better now, Dima?"

"I'm better. It was difficult for a long time, but I think I've passed to the other side now. I'm at peace with my choice."

For the first time, I don't see her as a young girl. I suppose that this is how crisis transforms us. She has chosen to be a nun, to try to intercede on our behalf, but even I am surprised to see her choice made so visible. Seeing her here, I can't help but be grateful. I know that she has been watching over me from the mountain these last weeks, praying for me, for all of us. I never thought that such a small gesture could give me comfort. But it does.

"I missed you, Stephanie," she tells me.

"I missed you too, Dima. I missed the monastery."

"And I missed your laughter."

I laugh, and then she nods. "You see?"

We sit together, side by side on our small wooden stools, and as I place my head on her shoulder for a moment I hope that I haven't lost her completely, that this business of saving others won't snatch her away from being the dear, boisterous, and slightly rebellious woman I love.

"Stephanie?" she finally asks me.

"Yes, Dima?"

"How do you keep a man from Homs busy?"

"How?" I answer, barely able to conceal my smile.

"You put him in a circular room and ask him to find the corner."

I laugh in relief.

23.

THE NEXT MORNING FRÉDÉRIC ASKED ME, "So, Stéphanie, do you want to wash the dishes with me?"

"You're washing the dishes?" I teased him. "I thought you got all of the guests to wash the dishes so that you could go off and meditate."

"*Ikteer* funny, *inti*," he said. "You're very funny."

"I haven't washed dishes in months, Frédéric. You'll have to remind me how."

Mountains of dishes awaited us in the monastery kitchen, more dishes than I had ever seen in one place. Here there was no avoiding the task. When a monk asks you to wash dishes, you wash. *Ora et labora*, the Benedictine creed says: work and prayer, the two pillars of monastic life.

We settled in the kitchen, Frédéric filling giant aluminum vats with boiling soapy water, two vats of clean water beside them for rinsing.

"So, does washing dishes with you mean that I have to chant the Prayer of the Heart and breathe every time I scrub away the eggs?" I asked, laughing.

He pretended to be scandalized. "Don't joke about that. When I was in the monastery in Athos, every night the monks gathered to peel potatoes, and one of them was assigned to recite over and over, *Kyrie eleison, Kyrie eleison*, Lord have mercy, in rhythm to the peeling." He mocked a face of exaggerated piety and pretended to peel an imaginary potato in the air with a rhythm like someone fingering a rosary. "Then the abbot would point to another, ancient monk, who would rasp, *Christe eleison, Christe eleison*, Christ have mercy, and all of the potato peeling would slow down."

I laughed. "I guess they're pretty serious about their vow to pray without ceasing."

He started working his way through the piles of breakfast plates before he asked, "So, do you know any songs by the Beatles?"

Now this was my kind of novice monk.

We spent the rest of the morning scrubbing dishes clean and singing, me in my mediocre voice, Frédéric in his luminous, monastic tenor. "Hey Jude" became "Get Back," Lucy flew out in her sky with diamonds, we walked the long and winding road. Finally, of course, because we were in a monastery after all, we belted out "Let It Be" in homage to Mother Mary, Frédéric inventing half of the words and singing in his French accent: "When I find myself in rhines and runnels, Mother Mary runs to me . . ." I was covered in soapsuds and my clothes were sopping wet, at some points he managed to nail about one word in every five, but I didn't care, because for a single moment the war was completely gone, because nothing was real, and we were just two people in a room singing "Strawberry Fields," forever.

Frédéric's favorite of the four Beatles, by the way, is John. That suits him. It is also his favorite Gospel, after all.

After we finally finished what felt like twenty thousand plates, I took a last walk high into the mountains, finding that narrow path I once navigated in the dark, climbing above the world. The demons weren't coming to meet me. Just silence. The most silence I had felt in my heart for a very long time.

I didn't stop to meditate. I just walked for several hours, and as I moved forward I called up the names of all of those I love. I called up the Sheikha, so lovely in her room, teaching me to sing the names of God. I called up the Baron, hitting me on the head and crying in front of the television set. I called up Mohammed, slowly piecing together those threads so long broken that they seemed beyond repair. I called up Hassan, whom I had not been to see for such a long time now, with his deep, pained brown eyes, trying to let go of a homeland he may never have again. I called up all of the people in the streets who had given me words, language, stories, quiet vowels that have somehow served to heal me in these last difficult months. I called up Rania, trying to bring back angels from the dead, and Dima, wrestling with God in her room each evening. I called up the faces of those I saw in a room last night, praying for peace.

Then I prayed that God, whoever or whatever he was, would not abandon them.

Evening fell, and the light descended over the desert hills, slowly covering them with darkness. Beneath me, I watched as Frédéric made his way down the mountain from the opposite path, his body casting a shadow walking over the stones, the prayer beads dangling from his hands. He paused, leaning over, to speak to a bird.

"Cuckoo," he said, and then the rest of his words were lost on me.

And now I am walking back to the monastery. I love this view from the mountain path of the monastery visible between two mountains, the enormous sky extending on every side of it. The world appears divided in two, between land and sky, with the monastery perched just between them. A bridge connects one side of the valley to the other. From here, when someone walks over that bridge, it looks just like he is walking through heaven.

When I reach the courtyard, Frédéric is already there, staring out over the valley below with that ever-present glass of tea in his hands. He pours me a glass, and I sit down beside him.

"Frédéric," I finally ask him, quietly, "I was wondering if we could talk about something."

"*Tfaddali,*" he says, grinning, using one of my favorite Arabic words. It is what someone says when he invites you inside his home, or gives you a place ahead of him in line, or allows you to speak. It says, *I am making space for you in my life. Come in.*

I had not expected to speak to Frédéric about serious matters again, not since our last conversation in the church. Still, in these past few days at the monastery, I've noticed that Frédéric is far more *human* than

I imagined a novice monk might be. He fumbles over his Arabic prayers in the mornings, just as I do, so that half of the time we know that he is praying, but we can't understand what he is asking God *for*. When he speaks English, he often says "never" instead of "ever," mentioning the strangest thing he has *never* seen in his life, just as he has a sweet habit of adding *h* to the front of his English words, saying "harms" instead of "arms," "hair" instead of "air." There is nothing at all affected about the moments he escapes from conversation to chat beneath the table with a kitten he named Muzika, or the way he speaks with affection about his favorite goat (number 44), or the bees he keeps for honey. I suspect that he feels more at home with animals than humans.

Maybe Frédéric is a saint. Yet in my eyes he is above all a poet, searching for his life on a mountaintop. I might lack the courage to speak to a saint, but a poet I can manage.

"Do you remember when you told me that you never thought that I should become a nun, because I don't believe in resurrection?" I ask him.

He lifts his eyes in surprise. "I said that?"

"Yes, you said that."

He whistles softly and waves his hands, as though recovering from touching something hot. "Sorry. That's hard, isn't it?"

I find it difficult to believe that he has completely forgotten something that I have been obsessing over for the last month. "I was just wondering—I've thought about it so much since you said it. I guess I was hoping that you might explain what you meant."

He pulls his string of amber prayer beads from the pocket of his robe, begins moving them from one finger to the next.

"Frédéric?"

He continues passing his prayer beads. I have come to the conclusion that this is the monastic form of a stall tactic. "When I came back from Mount Athos, I used to see you walking in the mountains," he says, carefully choosing his words. "I didn't know you well, but you looked so serious and sad, like you were living within the mind of suffering. Like you were trying so hard to carry some cross that you had chosen. I felt sorry for you. It looked like your heart was stuck in suffering and not in life."

It's true. He had seen me just after I had lived the Crucifixion, just after I had given my life to God in the desert on my mother's birthday. "But you told me that you thought that I could never become a nun. I'm not sure what one has to do with the other."

He smiles. "I don't know whether or not you have a calling to be a nun or not, Stéphanie. All I know is that whatever choice you made during the Exercises was one made out of suffering, and I can't believe in a choice made that way. A monastic choice should be made in the fruit of resurrection, in the belief in life, not death."

He is right, of course, but he should try his opinion on the priests and nuns who schooled me, encouraging Lenten fasts and personal guilt. In addition to the normal rations of Catholic guilt, I was a Mexican Catholic, which means we had Passion plays and plenty of statues of Jesus covered with thorns, his bleeding heart exposed. I had always been taught, though perhaps not explicitly, that suffering was at the heart of being Catholic—which was perhaps why I had abandoned my faith so entirely when I left the Exercises. I didn't want to suffer anymore, not at the moment when I had finally discovered that I might be happy.

Frédéric seems to be reading my face, somehow taking in my thoughts without my needing to speak them aloud. "On Mount Athos, I was living and praying in the monasteries of the Orthodox Church, and I felt a kind of mysticism that I had never experienced in my life as a Catholic. The Orthodox monks in many ways insist on the Resurrection much more than we do. Their emphasis is on the rising, and not so much on the Crucifixion, which is why Easter is the most important holiday in the Eastern Christian world, why you rarely see a cross inside of an Orthodox Church. Many monks in Athos even wear black, to show that they have already died to this world and are alive in the Resurrection of Christ."

I'm confused. "If faith is about the Resurrection, what happens to the Crucifixion then?"

"The Crucifixion exists, Stéphanie. Resurrection doesn't say that the Crucifixion didn't happen. It simply says that it is not the only thing that happened, that life still exists somewhere on the other side of suffering. We run the risk of getting so stuck in the Crucifixion that we forget about life. The Crucifixion is the *way* toward resurrection, simply part of the journey. The Resurrection appears here, in this moment when things seem dead, when we have reached our human limits, when it feels as though there is no love. Resurrection is not an event in the past but a concrete reality, something we look for every day. It is to be completely poor and to receive God in that space as life."

It is true then, what historians say of the frescoes of the Syrian Church, that here we never find an image of the cross without the symbols of resurrection hanging over it, so that death is never without new life, already sprouting at its heart, growing out of it. In the Eastern Church they even call Holy Saturday, the day in which Jesus is dead in the tomb, *Sebit al-Noor*, the Saturday of Light. Even in that moment, when everything is lost, light is hidden in the midst of it all.

We look out over the mountains, slowing turning red in the evening, and the single strip of desert road that runs in front of them. "Do you know what I have always thought is strange, Stéphanie?" he asks. "Did you ever notice, when the priest holds up the bread, he says, 'Lord, I am not worthy to receive you, but only say the word and I shall be healed.' Isn't that bizarre? We ask him to say a word, but no one ever tells us what that word *is*."

Maybe each of us has our own word. Like the name we are given at Creation, which tells us who we will become. Like the Quran, where no word ever means the same thing twice.

In the evening, I find a place in the chapel among the warmth of bodies huddled in every corner, in a room so dark it gives me the sense that we have fled somewhere beneath the earth to seek shelter. It is not easy to sit still, to breathe in this room full of people carrying the conflict. Even after all of these months in Syria, my instinct is to run away. But I stay.

During the Exercises, when I would meditate, I would often find myself carried away, lifted above myself to an empty space in the air. Now I resist. When I close my eyes and feel the familiar soaring emotion in my heart, I gently root my feet to the earth and settle back into that room. I don't want to be carried off to another place. I want to stay here, with these people. Praying with them, I no longer feel like a stranger.

There are dozens of Christians in the chapel for meditation, the air heavy with a weight I only gradually recognize as fear. I quietly sit behind my candle and examine their faces, one by one, praying in the dark. I know many of them by now. In the streets of Damascus, everyone tries to look brave. Like me, they come to the desert to allow themselves to be weak. Beside me a woman is crying. Several young men are hanging their heads in defeat. A young girl is kneeling beneath an altar, lighting candles, with a face so innocent that it cuts me to the heart. The war has never looked quite so stark as it does in this room of human faces with their eyes closed tightly, begging to be spared.

And in that instant I love them. Paolo had been right—in the moment of suffering, humans take on a transcendent power and beauty. I love this room full of people, just as I love the country that just months before I had been so eager to flee. I don't know why it has taken the threat of everything vanishing for me to understand. In the Bible, the moment in which Abraham is asked to give up his son is the first time that love is mentioned by name: *Take now thy son, thy only son Isaac, whom thou lovest.* Love is given a name in the moment of sacrifice, at the moment in which we face the terrifying possibility of loss. Suffering is the moment when love appears.

The hour finishes, and in the corner Frédéric picks up his guitar to play a song before the Mass. I close my eyes, and as I hear the first notes of "Blackbird" floating through the room, out from his corner and into the heart of that thousand-year-old chapel, I look over at him and smile, at this small, unspoken message meant only for me, *"All your life/You have only waited for this moment to arise."*

24.

THEN THE CONFLICT IS OVER, inexplicably, almost as quickly as it had begun. I left the monastery and traveled to Beirut for two days, crossing the empty border, and I visited the site of the bombing. I stood near the crater in the ground and gave witness to the surrounding buildings with their scarred facades, the gaping holes where there once were windows. I saw with my own eyes the students demonstrating in the streets for democracy, ecstatic in their baseball caps and Western clothing, waving their Lebanese flags in the air. I felt the Cedar Revolution, this rebellion against the Syrian regime, further proof that the government would fall at any moment.

But then I returned to Syria, and the next morning when I woke up to take my morning stroll through the neighborhood, I glanced up to see a brand-new enormous poster of Syrian president Bashar al-Assad looming over me, his fist in the air. "Whenever we are united as a country and a people, then there is nothing to be afraid of," it read in Arabic script over the background of a Syrian flag. "We're all with you, Bashar al-Assad."

I knew that Syrians were *not* all with Bashar. I had heard that expressed explicitly many times in the previous weeks. Which is why I found it odd that everyone in the neighborhood continued to promenade back and forth beneath his face, not paying him any notice. That afternoon more posters began surfacing, on car windows, in almost every shop. Teenagers gathered at cafés wearing T-shirts with Syrian flags. Where was this coming from?

The next day the Syrian president finally addressed the nation in a televised speech, declaring confidently that everything was under control and that Syrians need not fear coup or invasion. Soon after, hundreds of thousands of Hezbollah supporters marched through downtown Beirut, supporting Syria and shocking the so-called international experts who had predicted that a flood of Western-style democracy was headed toward the Middle East, the Cedar Revolution on the verge of triumph. Hassan Nasrallah, the spiritual leader of Hezbollah, called to the exultant crowd, "I want to tell America, do not interfere in our internal affairs. Tell your ambassador to relax in his embassy, and leave us alone." Then he yelled, "Death to Israel!" and the crowd shouted, "Death to Israel!" in response.

My neighbors were ecstatic. Merchants played the speech of Hassan Nasrallah over and over again, so that from street to street I was greeted by that image of the leader in his beard and turban, shouting and holding his fist in the air. When I returned home, the Baron was shaking his fist in proud imitation.

"Did you see Nasrallah?" he asked, beaming. "He's strong, isn't he?"

I never expected to see an Armenian Christian with a passion for Italian heels cheering on a radical Shiite.

The next day I walked downtown to watch tens of thousands of Syrians march in the streets of Damascus, my friends and neighbors among them, to demonstrate their support of the Syrian government. They raised signs in the air and shouted, "With our souls and with our blood, we sacrifice for you, O Bashar!" The streets pulsed with schools of young Muslim girls in headscarves marching together, crowds of boys chanting in unison, civil servants, groups holding Communist flags, and other groups holding Hezbollah flags. Above all else, thousands upon thousands of Syrian flags and giant posters of Bashar al-Assad swam in the distance, the president smiling in a suit jacket and tie beneath the words "All of us are with Assad."

I found a place in the crowd near the Umayyad Square and watched as those thousands passed by me, proud and waving, like Americans asked to march in a parade on the Fourth of July. After weeks of the we-might-be-bombed-at-any-moment sentiment in the air, the mood was ecstatic. The march was doubling as a protest against the American government, and though perhaps this should have frightened me it seemed only surreal, those teenage boys holding up signs that read "No to Bosh" and "Boosh, get out." A young doe-eyed teenager carrying a Syrian flag removed himself from the crowd and paused in front of me.

"Where are you from?" he asked.

"I'm from America."

"From America? Welcome!" he gushed, enthusiastically shaking my hand. Then he merged again into the crowd and continued demonstrating against America.

I watched them flooding through the streets, merging together, until they amassed in a great circle around a statue of former president Hafez al-Assad, climbed up on top of his body, and draped it with their flags.

I remembered Mohammed and the many cabdrivers, shopkeepers, and neighbors who had angrily criticized the government in the weeks before. We would now sweep that quietly under the carpet and not speak of it again; I understood that much. Now those same people were in the streets, cheering on their leader. The cynical would tell me that they were forced to be there, but when I looked at those faces they didn't look forced at all. They looked proud.

I caught a cab home, and as we sat stuck in traffic the driver turned to me.

"Where are you from?"

"I'm from America," I answered.

"Really? So what do you think of Syria?" I had been asked this question so many times, but after watching a demonstration against my country it rubbed me differently.

"It's beautiful," I told him, finally. "There's this tight social life like I have never experienced in a country before. They're the kindest people I have ever met, the Syrians. But the problem is that there's just no freedom. You can't even read a newspaper and believe anything that it says."

He laughed. "That's true. It's all lies, lies, lies. But, anyway, what do I need a newspaper for if I can't walk across the street to buy it without getting shot? Syria is the safest country in the world. I can walk home in the middle of the night with a bag full of money and nothing will happen to me." He shook his head. "I have my family, and I have my work, so what else do I need? George Bush wants to take over the whole world."

I thought about that question for a long time: *What else do I need?* Perhaps war and revolution only sound romantic in the ears of those unfamiliar with death, with those of us content to put Live Free or Die bumper stickers on our cars as we drive through safe suburban neighborhoods. I could understand how my neighbors could have changed their minds so quickly, marching in the streets in favor of a government I knew they neither always loved nor supported, but which had come to mean stability in a region where simply surviving was a triumph and where no other power existed to take its place. Perhaps there is something brave, noble even, in the collective insistence on staying alive, on having the patience to believe that change might come slowly, from within. Still, I don't know what to feel. I am uncomfortable with my own sense of relief, relief that my neighbors were spared invasion or coup or war, even if this comes at the expense of my friends in Beirut, who had glimpsed for a moment a better, freer life. I am confused that I could feel anything other than anger at a man like Hassan Nasrallah holding his fist in the air. None of this is as easy as it looks from a distance. I know that from now on, I won't judge so quickly what people will do to protect themselves and their families. If I criticized my neighbors, it was only because I had one thing none of them possessed—a passport that allowed me to leave.

As we drove through the streets, I looked out the window at life continuing on as normal, the women walking with their children in tow, the cars lined up in traffic, the men selling cigarettes on the corner. Maybe this is a resurrection I can believe in. I had never considered what a miracle an everyday morning could be—a walk down the street, uninterrupted, to pick up the newspaper, a mother walking her little girl to school—when you are surrounded on three sides by countries falling apart.

25.

THEN, AFTER THE LONGEST WINTER IN MY LIFE, I wake up and light is flooding through my front window, and it is finally spring. The neighbors are removing their carpets and washing their floors with buckets of soapy water, the merchants are hanging cages with tiny singing canaries outside their shops, and green furry almonds and peaches come into season. I drain the petroleum out of my heater with triumph and open my windows to finally let the air in.

I climb from my bed, pull on my clothes, and wait for the Baron's knock on the window. I drink my coffee. Then I walk into the streets, waving hello to the man with the knives. "How is your knife?" he asks me. I buy a drink from the man who taught me the word for "straw." I wave to the pizza guys, and the *knafeh* man hanging upside down, and Mohammed mending his carpets, I salute the woodworkers pressing mother of pearl into the backs of chairs. When I slide into the counter of the juice stand, the young Kurdish vendor asks me, "The usual?" I nod and laugh out loud, because I have been waiting to be asked that all of my life.

It's all still here. None of it has vanished. There are no American tanks in the streets. No helicopters dropping bombs from overhead. No one has fled to a safer place. Everything remains. Everyone is still alive.

"*Shoo fi? Ma fi?*" a shopkeeper asks me as I walk by. "What is there? Is there anything?"

"*Ma fi, shoo fi,*" I answer, grinning. "There's nothing. What is there?"

I pass by the florist. "*Sabah al-kheir*, Morning of goodness," he calls out.

"*Sabah al ward!* Morning of roses!" I answer, smiling.

"How's life today?"

"Like paradise," I tell him. "Like paradise."

26.

BUT THAT IS NOT THE ENTIRE STORY. Or perhaps I should say that it is the entire story, but only the version of the story that I lived. That March, the Sheikha finally taught me about the Muslim Jesus. She said that he was a human being, just like the rest of us. He performed miracles and raised the dead, just as the Gospels said he did. He lived the Passion leading up to his death, and was betrayed by one of his own. But at the last moment, when he was supposed to be killed, God put someone in his place, and he did not die. It was not Jesus on the cross at Golgotha on Good Friday. It was a copy of him.

"But who was it?" I pressed. "Who died that day?"

"The scholars say many things," she answered me. "Some say that it was Judas, the one who betrayed him. Some say that it was no one, just a shadow. We don't know."

A curious sensation was rising in my stomach, relief mixed with confusion. So in another story, Jesus didn't die. He was raised up alive to heaven at the last moment, just when he was expecting to be killed. Part of me wanted to preserve the story in my memory, like that.

And part of me was haunted by the vision of a man on a cross who looked so familiar, and yet whom I could not identify, whose name I did not know.

Who is he? I kept asking myself. *Who really died that day?*

I cannot stop asking myself that question, even now.

27.

IT IS ONLY AFTER THE CONFLICT has passed that I find the courage to seek out Hassan again. I have not spoken to him for many months, have invented excuses to avoid his shop on the way home and memorized alternate paths from the Old City so that I would not run into him. Long ago he had stopped being simply a man to me and had come to embody in my thoughts the war in Iraq in its entirety, the daily news of bombings and cars exploding in marketplaces. I was afraid of him.

Yet in these last months the war in Iraq has become more real to me, more tangible, no longer a distant horror on the news or a story that a single person can contain within him. I have met many other Iraqis like Hassan, stranded in Damascus, as this city continues to be a desperate refuge between places. There is my friend Ghaith, an Iraqi photographer who had been the only survivor of an American air strike several months before and who now wears a deep, jagged shrapnel scar on his face. I had often watched him walking through the marketplace dazed, taking photographs of beams of light falling through holes in the roof. "I'm sorry," he once apologized to me when I lost him in a crowd. "It's just that there is this terrible white light in Baghdad, overexposing everything. Here, I feel like I'm discovering light for the first time." In Baghdad, he photographed the dead, and in his photos I see the light he speaks of behind the corpses, covering them, making it hard to look at any one photo for long without needing to look away. Though he does not believe in God, Ghaith says that just before they die, the dead often reach into the air, trying to touch someone invisible. He wonders who it is.

There is the Iraqi translator for the American military whom I met at a party, who fled Iraq after eight of his colleagues were assassinated for being collaborators and who was now waiting fitfully as the American embassy continued to deny him sanctuary abroad. There are priests and parishioners who left Iraq after a series of church bombings, their migration dismantling one of the oldest Christian communities in the world. Each one of them reminds me of the fabled messengers in the book of Job, who stumble into the room to give news of the dead and then finish by saying, in farewell, "I am the only one who has escaped to tell you."

Like everyone here, I have spent many hours trying to understand why some of us are taken and others of us are left to live. I've made my uncomfortable peace, in part because I don't think that the dead would want us to spend our time left walking on earth absorbed in such questions. But they would want us to notice. To at least give thanks. For the simple miracle that my childhood prayer, *Give us this day, our daily bread*, has been answered.

I have missed Hassan in these months. The image of him hunched over on his stool, in his heavy leather jacket and with his dark, black eyes, has haunted me. Every time I considered coming to visit him I was embarrassed by how long I had stayed away. Yet now I feel ready. I have heard from other shopkeepers that he has abandoned his closet-sized shop with Ali beside the mosque to establish his own small gallery—no longer content to reproduce the "tourist art" that marked the first months of his exile. So today I go looking for him in the Old City, passing the stands of pomegranate juice and the rows of antique stores and bakeries selling fresh chocolate croissants, until there he is, sitting in front of me in a tiny stall, still larger than life. This time he is boxed in by color, dozens of canvases of strange geometric patterns and cubes of light hanging on every inch of the walls around him and stacked on the floor. He has propped a blue canvas to sit beside him like a person, sad and quietly beautiful.

"*Shlonitch*, Stephanie!" he calls out, dropping his paintbrush abruptly to fetch a chair. "I missed you. How are you?"

"I'm beautiful," I say, wishing I had other words to give him. "I'm beautiful."

I don't bother to explain why I have been absent, and he doesn't ask. I take a seat on the small straw chair he has placed next to his own and examine the colors and patterns surrounding me on all sides. They are fierce and abstract, bearing no resemblance to the scenes of city life that he had painted when I first met him.

"You've been busy."

"I haven't been sleeping," he answers. He smiles, but his eyes look more raw and worn out than I've ever seen them, the black rims beneath them almost the same color as his dark leather jacket. "These days I sometimes wake up at three in the morning to paint."

I sit there silently for a moment, thinking of the hellish news we hear of his city every day now. "How is your family?" I ask.

"They're fine," he says. "Thank God they're still okay."

When I met Hassan, he was still in his first, awkward months of exile.

Yet he, too, has changed. Before he would have rushed to explain his paintings, to read me poetry, to express a theory on the violence rocking his city. But today he is humbled, I think, by life. I look up at the shapes on the walls, how dark and wild they are. He is finally painting the city that he loves as he lived in it, and even in its abstractness it is far more recognizable than the endlessly repeated alleys and laundry of his previous paintings, the women without faces. He is truly painting Baghdad, a city falling apart.

I stand up to examine the canvases more closely, but my eyes keep settling back on that singular blue painting propped up on the easel nearby, like a third person sitting in the room, mute and yet taking the space of everything.

"Something's happened," I whisper.

"Yes," he says. "Something's happened."

A week before, Hassan had awakened in the middle of the night, his dreams possessed by a bright, strange vision of blue. He understood immediately that a close friend of his, an Iraqi artist, had just been killed in a bombing. Now he was being given his friend's last vision to be recorded on canvas. Hassan had stayed up all night, copying it down, the luminous boxes and subtle changes in color.

So this is what the dead see when they are dying.

The news arrived by telephone a few days later. It was true. His friend was dead. His body had been shattered, his briefcase of paints erupting onto the sidewalk.

I look up at Hassan, lost in his thoughts, and I feel a sudden tenderness for him. He no longer seems frightening to me. He looks more like a mythical hero. Like a man who has spent all night wrestling a pearl from a demon's hands.

We sit side by side for a long time, watching pedestrians pass in the street in front of us. Finally, Hassan touches my shoulder and points to a picture I had overlooked, hanging in the top left-hand corner of his shop. He smiles at me.

"Do you know what that picture is?"

I get up and walk over to it, surprised that I hadn't noticed the painting until now. Among the canvases cloaked with cubes of blue and black, all of those dreams of the dead, here a round shape shines in the center of a yellow background like the sun, sparks of orange and gold light emanating from its center. I look closer. No, it is not the sun. It is the face of a woman, just beginning to smile, the line of her mouth gently turning up. She is somewhere between human and star. In her ears, two earrings hang loosely, small pearl beads at their ends.

I touch my ears self-consciously and feel the same earrings with my fingertips.

"It's you," he says, but it couldn't be. She's radiant.

"That's you, as I see you."

My eyes fill up with tears. He removes the painting from the wall and hands it to me. I turn it over and read the inscription on the back, in Arabic: *To Stephanie.*

"Every day people come in here and want to buy it," he says. "But I tell them that they can't have it. It already belongs to someone."

I cradle it gently in my arms. Then I carry my canvas home through the streets of Damascus, this unexpected gift of my own face emerging in the ruins, and here of all places, shining and alive.

Part Four RESURRECTION

If you want to witness the resurrection, then be it.

For this is the condition for witnessing anything.

—RUMI

1.

TODAY IS A LOVELY, breezy day in March, and Frédéric is knocking on the window of my room in the house off Straight Street, waving to me with this small fluttering of his hand like I have seen him make to wave to birds. I hardly recognize him. He has abandoned his monastic frock in favor of ordinary human clothes, a tan-striped button-down linen shirt, a brown leather bomber jacket, and khaki trousers, the perfect combination of St. Francis earth tones and French style. It is a look we often referred to as "monastic chic" in divinity school.

I run to answer the door, but it is like a scene in a bad movie where a mother sees her child walking in front of a dinosaur from a distance and rushes to save him, only to see him snatched away before her very eyes. Before I can manage to push open the double doors, the Baron gets to him.

"*Bonjour! Tu parles Francese? Italiano? Portugueso?*"

"Speak to me in Arabic," Frédéric pleads, visibly overwhelmed by this sudden assault.

The Baron looks horribly disappointed. "Really? Because *Je Parle Francese. Italiano. Portugueso. Armeniano. Turki.*"

Oh dear. I may have lost him for the entire day.

I have traveled out to the monastery every week this month, leaving after my Saturday lessons with the Sheikha to make my way back into the wild, wide-open desert, slowly trying to piece together a spiritual life that makes sense to me. I've come to know everyone at the monastery over time—the workers, the novices, bizarre pilgrims who refuse to speak and write all of their sentences on pieces of paper, Sufis and saints and beautiful young children who light candles in wooden boxes before icons of the Virgin. Yet it is Frédéric I'm closest to, and every time I climb that mountain, he is waiting for me at the top of the stairs with a steaming glass of tea cupped between his hands.

I grew up enough of a Catholic to know a thing or two about the magnetic appeal young men in the clergy can have for women. I seem to recall giggling with my sister in the back of St. Anthony's Church when I was barely a teenager, both of us infatuated with a certain young priest with blue eyes who looked remarkably like Rob Lowe in the film *Oxford Blues*. Yet Frédéric manages to remain oblivious to his pop-icon status, and that endears him to me. I have watched lines of young women climb up the mountain to swoon over him, and yet when he appears from his afternoon chores of keeping bees he just waves his bee-swollen hands, rattling on about the queen in her hive, Hafif the donkey, his guilt over an apparent addiction to sugar, or any number of equally bizarre topics, his blond curls flying in the air and his eyes shining. Really, the man lives in his own world.

Still, I have discovered that this bee-keeping, "Yellow Submarine" singing, very French mystic is perhaps my favorite company on earth, someone I would enjoy passing time with even if we weren't both in the middle of Syria, because we seem to understand each other intuitively. We take walks in the mountains and chat about the desert fathers, and during the morning prayer we always sit next to each other, trying our best not to burst into laughter as we read the Psalms in Arabic, because we keep making really terrible mistakes, which is embarrassing in the midst of a solemn prayer crying out to God about walking through the valley of the shadow of death. Sometimes during the Mass, he will lean over and whisper in my ear, "What does that word *mean*?" and I just shrug, because I have no idea either. I haven't a clue.

Frédéric never eats dinner. He fasts every Monday and so does not eat at all. I once caught him playing Pink Floyd on the guitar in the church, when he thought no one was listening, strumming an opening number from *The Wall*. Among his favorite all-time recordings are the vespers of a Russian Orthodox monastery in Finland and Jacques Brel, the chain-smoking, passionate French singing troubadour.

I do believe that he has become my best friend.

Now, unfortunately, my best friend is marooned on the Baron's sofa, surprised and a bit dazed, like a trapped squirrel unsure of what wire cage has just collapsed on his tail. The Baron is busy fixing coffee for all of us.

"Hi, Frédéric. This is my neighbor, the Baron."

"Yes, we've met." His eyes sparkle with amusement.

The Baron glances back, both slightly annoyed that he is no longer the center of Frédéric's attention and that we are now speaking English, which is one of the few languages he doesn't know. "So, are you from America like Stefanito here?" he asks in Arabic.

Frédéric flinches, momentarily taken aback not only at the fact that he could possibly be mistaken for an American, but also at the unlikely insertion of my Italian name. "No, I'm from France."

The Baron's jaw drops. Sound the alarms—there is a real, live Frenchman in the house.

"Are you from Paris?" the Baron asks, his cheeks flushed. He asks this in a way that reveals that he is hopeful, madly hopeful.

"No, I'm from the Alps."

"You mean, near *Italy*?"

"Yes, just an hour from Torino."

The Baron stumbles over himself, coming just short of burning the coffee. "I used to travel to Milano. Do you know Milano? I bought the most beautiful shoes in Milano. Leather. Nothing but leather. I stayed in a hotel owned by a gorgeous woman, and the first time I met her I brought her pistachios from Aleppo." He looks at Frédéric and raises his eyes, expecting him to intuit that pistachios from Aleppo are both a delicacy and an aphrodisiac. " 'What are these?' she asked me. So I said, 'You don't have *fustuq halabi* in Milano?' I couldn't believe it. Can you imagine—no *fustuq halabi*? You should have seen her." He moves his hand to illustrate her curves. "Anyway . . . after that, every time I came to Milano, I brought with me a bag of pistachios from Aleppo, and she was waiting for me. If you know what I mean."

It is not a particularly subtle point. Luckily, before he can launch into the opening of his story about how he also seduced a KLM stewardess by laying out a buffet of pistachios, chocolate, and whiskey and playing Tom Jones on his portable cassette player at thirty thousand feet, Frédéric very delicately asks whether he might use the bathroom. The Baron leaves his reverie long enough to motion him across the courtyard to the closet we call our toilet.

Frédéric has barely disappeared around the corner before the Baron reaches over to pinch my cheek and whistles under his breath.

"He's beautiful."

I'm horrified. "He's a monk."

He swats his hand in the air, dismissing me with his characteristic *if you want to ruin your life by getting bogged down with details, then that is your problem* expression. It has become a particular favorite of his.

We sit for a few moments uncomfortably, finishing off our coffee, until Frédéric appears across the courtyard, apparently having figured out that you can flush a toilet simply by pouring a bucket of water down it. I am self-conscious and eager to leave, the combination of my crumbling room and my seventy-three-year-old protector making me edgy.

The Baron, however, is trying maniacally to wave him back into his bedroom.

"*Marhaba*, Padre! You are most welcome!" he shouts. I motion that we should make our exit.

"I'm not a priest, I'm a novice monk," Frédéric objects, and I am already out of my seat and halfway to the door.

"No problem, Padre." The Baron shoots him a conspiratorial smile and a wink. "Take care of her."

A N D   H E   D O E S . Frédéric spends the afternoon escorting me through Damascus, guiding me down hidden lanes that I have somehow always managed to overlook, pointing out pastries coated in honey and cafés with cold beverages served right out of glass bottles, alleys so long abandoned that the houses with their detailed wooden frames and broken windows could collapse upon us at any moment. Nothing is lost on him. He makes faces at every child who passes, wiggling his fingers in the air, he whispers to cats and blushes as complete strangers who recognize him from the monastery cross the streets to kiss his hands.

"Walking with you is a little bit like walking with a movie star," I observe. We have just seen an older man whom Frédéric did not recognize dart across traffic to press his lips and then his forehead against Frédéric's hand.

He laughs, shrugging. "It's true. In the Middle East, they treat their monks like movie stars. What can I do?"

It doesn't help that Frédéric has also been a real movie star, recently featured milking his goats and pontificating on monasticism in a short film shot at Mar Musa. Still, today he is just a man, on loan for a few hours, and I can't quite get over the ordinariness of our day together, the wonderful ordinariness, which feels so liberating after the monastery, where life can sometimes feel so existential. We stop to drink sweet Arabic *sahlep* and eat seasoned bread, to smoke apple tobacco from a glass pipe, and we talk about everything else but God.

"I feel like I don't even know you, and you know everything about me," I confess.

"What do you want to know?"

"I want to know what your life was like, before you joined a monastery."

"It's a very long story."

"Well, I think we have all day."

So he begins his story: "When I was a child in Brittany, I climbed out the window with only a chocolate sandwich to travel around the world . . ." For the rest of the afternoon he regales me with his adventures, dressing up as Zorro when he was a child and drawing *Z*'s all over his walls, turning in poems instead of class assignments to the despair of his teachers, and finally abandoning school altogether to wander the face of the earth. He describes the mosques of Iran and the villages of Pakistan, his years in and out of India and his voyages across Turkey, until finally he comes to the afternoon when he wanders to a desert monastery in Syria and his life is changed forever.

"I was touched so deeply when I arrived at Mar Musa," he confesses. "I met Christ there." Normally, I would be annoyed if someone made a statement like that. Yet Frédéric says it with this complete, innocent enthusiasm, so that I imagine the meeting must have been like when I met the poet Seamus Heaney in Cambridge and shyly handed him a bouquet of orchids. "Jésus!" I can hear Frédéric saying in his French accent, leaning forward and kissing Jesus lightly on both cheeks. "I've heard so much about you. Am I interrupting anything?"

The afternoon wears on, and in time I narrate my own travels, through China and Europe and the Middle East, the deserts of the Taklamakan near Central Asia, sailing on the Nile. I describe the month I walked across Spain with only a small yellow backpack, and my own arrival at the monastery for the first time five years earlier, where something in the desert called out to my heart. It is a long, exhausting day, the hours flying by us unnoticed, until finally the sun begins setting in the distance and we collapse on a curb in the crowded market of Salihiya, a Muslim quarter where no one will recognize him. He asks for my passport, compares the stamps with his own, discovering countries and other lives when we just missed each other—by a few weeks in New York, a few months in Egypt, and the space of a few days in Turkey. I remember the first time I ever spoke to him, when he looked up at me in surprise and asked, *Haven't we met?*

Now, he leans over and taps a man on the shoulder, quietly and politely asking for a cigarette, and I watch as this novice monk in human clothes rolls tobacco into paper and then lights the end, inhaling slowly, blowing out smoke into the street. The world passes by us, the two of us almost invisible among green-painted wagons of peanut sellers and fruit stalls brimming with lemons and clementines, a giant yellow sign for Lipton tea scrawled out in Arabic, lines of taxis waiting for passengers, and the view of Qassioun Mountain behind us.

"Frédéric?" I ask.

"Yes, Stéphanie?" He looks at me, and for a moment I feel so close to this man, a stranger in this country, who after all of these years of wandering has found himself sitting beside me, here, on this street.

"Are you ever lonely here?"

He glances down and quietly puts out his cigarette on the pavement. "Of course I'm lonely."

"Me, too."

And that is how we become partners in loneliness.

2.

TWO WEEKS LATER IT IS GOOD FRIDAY, and I am climbing the stairs to the monastery with my arms overflowing with bouquets of Easter lilies in full bloom, my offering to the church. I like the idea of placing them in a vase of water in a church standing in the heart of the desert, the petals bringing life into that dry place. In ancient paintings the angel Gabriel is seen handing the Virgin Mary this white flower when he appears to her with the news that she will conceive a son. I love that image of Mary, the angel, and the blossom of life blooming in the space between them.

Holy Week has always been the most sacred week in the year for Christians in the Middle East, this rising again seen as even more important than Christmas. Every year hundreds of Christians flock to the monasteries and the churches, beginning their celebrations on Palm Sunday and continuing a vigil for the next seven days. For weeks I've been looking forward to seeing the entire drama acted out here in the desert, my way of completing the journey I set out on in November. I never lived the week of the Resurrection during the Spiritual Exercises, but I think that I'm ready now.

By the time I arrive in the courtyard the monastery is so crowded with visitors that they spill into the chapel and all of the adjacent rooms. Though we are meant to be anticipating the Crucifixion, there is a chatter of voices as aunts and cousins embrace one another and young children race through the courtyard. Dima smiles at me when she sees me and hands me a slender white candle. Soon the entire courtyard is full of lit candles held in the air, as the sun slowly descends behind the mountains and the sky grows dim.

Then there is silence. We walk in a single line out of the front of the monastery, each of us ducking one after another through the door of humility, until we emerge in a long necklace of lights snaking through the desert valley. In the front of the procession, Frédéric wears a long white robe and holds in the air a wooden statue of Jesus crucified. We walk his Passion, following the cross through the turns of the valley, the enormous sky a deep gray now and the clouds looming overhead. When we reach the ancient monks' cemetery deep in the valley, we stop. A young man pushes to the front of the crowd and reads from the Gospel of John in Arabic. Beside him a boy I know, who now, suddenly, looks like a man, delicately removes the body of Jesus from the cross and lifts it against the side of the cliff. Then we hear nails pounding against stone. In the candlelight

I can see faint outlines of the body of Jesus, hanging with his arms outstretched, draped with a red cloth, dying. We wait to hear the last words of his life: *I am thirsty*. Then the quiet gasp: *It is finished*.

Yet it is not finished. I know that much now. The monks remove his body, drape it in a white cloth, and carry it back to the chapel in silence so that we can bury him.

That evening in the chapel, I stand back and watch one of the most touching vigils of my entire life. One by one, people approach the body. Teenaged girls shyly caress his arms. A mother leans down and guides her son's tiny hand across his chest. Men kneel, rub his hands with oil, and kiss his feet. Many people are crying. For each of us, the body contains something different—the memories of a country that almost collapsed this winter, those we have loved and lost, uncertainty about the future. In that moment, we place all of our suffering into a body, into this man, this truly human man. We anoint him with oil, place flowers on his arms and legs, and kiss his hands. We leave the body in its tomb. And then we go to sleep.

We sleep, and we dream, and then we live another day in the tomb and we dream again. *Sebit al-Noor*, the Saturday of Light. A few months ago, I feared death so much that I could not even bear confronting this day during the Spiritual Exercises. Yet now it has become for me the most beautiful day of all, the day in which everything is lost forever, and yet we live it, all the way from morning to evening, believing that a miracle will come, if we only believe.

It is the end of the month of March, that month that took my grandparents and my aunt and that I grew up hearing was my family's month of curses. If my mother could be here, I know that she would want me to place all of those burdens into the ground. I do, I bury them all, my grandfather and my grandmother and my aunt. I bury them beside my own years battling death, and the visions I had witnessed in the desert those November afternoons. I take the nightmares of Hassan and I try my best to bury those also, together with the cities the Baron has left behind. I close my eyes, and I allow my Woody Allen Jesus to contain all that has already been taken. Then I bathe him, dress him in a clean blue suit, kiss him on the forehead, and put him in the earth, let him go, and whisper, finally, *Rest, rest*.

3.

ON EASTER SUNDAY, the bells begin ringing shortly before four in the morning. The sun has not yet risen, but the mountains are already beginning to find their shape, anticipating it. I rush down the stairs to the chapel in the faint light. The church is already alive with the scraps of hundreds of voices, the faces of saints emerging as though they are trying to arouse their tired bodies from sleep. The Mass begins in clouds of incense and smoke and the clouds of our breath. We read the story of the Resurrection in Arabic. I sit nearby as Paolo gives the homily, speaking softly about the importance of knowing that Jesus rose into a human body that once again walked the earth, a body as weak and as broken as ours.

When Paolo finishes speaking, he turns to where I am sitting. "Stephanie, I'm tired," he says. "I wonder if you wouldn't mind translating that into English for our foreign guests."

I shiver. Paolo and I have not been communicating very well lately, and he has taken to speaking to me through the Mass. "Stephanie, pray for peace," he will tell me after Communion on a day when I feel particularly sad or overwhelmed. Sometimes, when we have not spoken much for a long time, he will simply say at the prayer in the morning, "Stephanie, light the candles," which is a way of saying, *I know you're here, and that coming back hasn't been easy. But may your day be blessed.*

And now he is finally confronting me, asking me to declare the Resurrection. I know that none of this is about translation. He wants me to confirm, for him and for myself, that I am well again. That it was true what he told me months ago: "I don't think that God brought you all the way to the desert to leave you stranded in hell."

He nods at me. To my surprise, the words come easily. I don't summarize all that Paolo said. Instead, I tell the story of a man who died in a human body and was buried in the earth, having lost everything. He stayed there, for a period, in the dark. Then he came back to life again.

It is not symbolic, I say. It really happens.

Then all at once the sun rises, flooding light through the window behind the altar, illuminating the frescoes. Paolo declares the Resurrection. We are enveloped in hundreds of voices singing at once. Dima puts out her arms and twirls in circles like a dervish. Frédéric taps me on the shoulder. "Look," he whispers in my ear, and we stand side by side as a beam of light lands on the face of an angel blowing a trumpet on the frescoed wall of paradise.

When I emerge from the small chapel and into the light of the wide-open courtyard, Paolo is waiting nearby.

"I can't believe you made me do that," I say, breaking into a smile. "*Al-Masih an Qum*, Christ is risen!" I tell him shyly, giving him the traditional Arabic Easter greeting.

He opens his arms wide. "*Huq an-Qum!* Truly he is risen!" He lifts me up in his arms and swings me around in the air. I can feel my body in his arms, rising.

4.

EVERY DAY SINCE I have returned to the monastery this Holy Week, I have taken a long walk alone into the desert, rediscovering those wild places I used to hide in during the Spiritual Exercises. I have sat there, silently, and prayed. Every day, without fail, that same electric feeling I experienced during Incarnation has returned, the world breaking open, and heaven and earth becoming one.

These moments give me the courage to keep coming back, to keep wrestling with whatever it is I am meant to discover about my life out here. I think I'm getting better at listening for the answer, at not trying so hard to force my own agenda on the universe. Unfortunately, lately I've discovered that even in prayer I can be a bit of a control freak, the spiritual equivalent of that annoying date who begins the night with, "I thought that we could eat at an Italian place around the corner and then catch a movie. Is that okay with you?" Too often in my prayers, I'm just looking for a sign-off on decisions I've already made. Which is, of course, not a prayer life at all, or a relationship. It is a projection.

But the Quran has taught me to be more patient, not just with God but also with everything and everyone in my life, including myself. I love what Muslims say about the Quran, that it *descended*, in Arabic, that it was revealed, which in some way means that we have to wait around to receive it. I used to trust that feeling when I wrote poetry, and I've decided that I want a life like that. I want something bigger than me to be slowly made apparent, which I guess my Catholic-school nuns would say means I'm now open to discovering grace.

Frédéric has been great in all of this searching, acting not so much a guide as a companion on the journey. He doesn't try to force me into any boxes or ask me to be someone I'm not comfortable with. He never objects that I spend more time in the mosque than in the church and that along with the Quran I've also taken to reading Buddhist texts in the mornings before I get out of bed. He, after all, made his way to the monastery via the Hindu temples and Buddhist monasteries of India, and so such a wayward spiritual journey makes sense to him. Recently I heard him speaking to some very skeptical young European tourists who asked him how he, of all people, could believe in Christianity (he looked so very normal, after all). He shrugged good-naturedly. "I think that the thirst for something greater than us is human, not Christian," he said. "I searched for the meaning of my life for many years, but eventually I always hit a wall. But then I felt something on the other side of that wall, the"—he put out his two hands and made the vaguely Italian gesture that universally means "What is that word?"—"I guess I call that space God. But people can call it whatever they want."

Today Frédéric and I are taking one of our many walks together. We meet in front of the tiny, heavy door to the monastery and set out on the narrow path into the desert, under the vast blue sky. A hermit, in this case a jolly and rather balding British autoworker, has taken residence in a nearby cave, and I wonder if he is watching us, two tiny dots against the mountains. We descend into the canyon, our steps falling in line with each other, climbing up and down red stones, until we arrive at a path worn faintly into the riverbed that I have never noticed. I look up and see a hidden cave open to the light, two flat stones set up as chairs inside it.

"She's my secret home in the desert," Frédéric confides. "Her name is Madeleine. When I finish restoring her, I hope that I can come to live here."

So this is the woman of his life. Frédéric's Madeleine is an ancient hermit's cave the size of a small room and first inhabited many centuries before. The ashes of medieval hermit fires are still hidden beneath the earth among the remnants of a simple, ancient kitchen. The sound of birds singing filters in through the opening, and we can see the outlines of almond trees blossoming white and pink.

We take our seats on the two flat, round stones, and he offers me a mandarin hidden in one of the pockets of his robe. I sit and watch him undo the rind in a single loop and then split the fruit into pieces.

"Tell me about your retreat," I say. He has recently gotten back from a solitary seven-day retreat of silence and fasting in the desert, which explains why he looks so different than he had two weeks ago in Damascus.

"It was hard," he says. "I hiked up to the hermit's cave of Mar Maroun to live in silence." He points out into the mountains until I see the distant, open hole of a cave, barely visible and high up on the opposing mountain. "Every day I had a small routine—I woke up in the morning, I prayed, and then I read from the Psalms. I carved a cross from these pieces of wood I discovered, struck by lightning." He reaches into his pocket and shows me a few slabs of hard black wood. "Then, in the afternoon I went for a walk in the desert. I came back at night and played some music, and then I went to bed."

"What about the Quran?" Before he had left, Frédéric asked me if I could recommend a few verses from the Quran to read. I had sent him the verses on Mary, as well as a few beautiful chapters from the very end of the Quran.

"That's what's so odd," he said. "Every time I've ever been on a retreat, I went with a question. But this time I didn't have a question. I just sat there listening. I spent a week alone on the mountain, waiting. For the first few days, it wasn't hard to fast. But then after three or four more days, I felt so weak that when I went to take my walk in the afternoon, I had to concentrate just to put one foot in front of the other.

"Then, on the fifth day, I completely collapsed in the cave. I didn't have any energy left, and I felt like I was taking a step toward death. I just lay there for a while. Then I took out the Quranic verses you sent me and read them aloud. Here." He pulls out a small notebook from his pocket and begins to read his own handwriting:

N'avons-Nous point ouvert ta poitrine
Et déposé loin de toi le faix
qui accablait ton dos . . . ?
En vérité, à côté de l'adversité est la félicité!
Oui, à côté de l'adversité est la félicité!

Even without knowing French, I recognize that he is reading Inshirah, the verses Muslims recite in times of deep difficulty.

Have We not opened your breast
And removed from you your burden
Which weighed down your back . . . ?
Truly, with every difficulty there is relief,
With every difficulty there is relief.

"It was like the words were expressing exactly what was in my heart. When I was finished, I just sat there, at the bottom of the cave and in the dark. Then suddenly I was completely, I don't know, filled up. I wasn't weak anymore."

I smile. "Do you know what, Frédéric? I asked a Muslim woman from the mosque what you should read on your retreat. I told her that you would be praying and fasting for a week. All she said was, 'Your friend is imitating the practice of the angels, who do not eat, and do not sleep, and spend their lives worshipping God.' "

He grins, and for a moment I remember with clarity what the desert fathers said about monks—that they could participate in the lives of the angels.

"How did you know that you had a calling?" I finally ask him.

He laughs. "I'm not even sure if I know what that means, to have a calling. I have always possessed . . . what I would call a spiritual thirst. But I was never clear how that desire would take shape. I've always thought that the question of a religious vocation is something natural for each religious person to face. But it only needs to be a question. In my mind, the novitiate is as a relationship of love before marriage. You stay as long as you feel that it is your place, and then if you are not happy, you leave. And to leave is not a failure—it is an answer from God that he desires something else from you. I've been here for three years now, and that night in the retreat last week was the first time I really felt certain that this is where I'm meant to be."

These last days of walking in the mountains, I've been filled to the brim with a feeling that I'd thought I had imagined—the world becoming electric, again and again. I'd convinced myself long ago that what happened to me during the Exercises was a dream. But now I'm beginning to wonder if it meant something after all. How does anyone know when he has truly been called? I remember the words of Jesus during the Exercises:

I was just walking by, and my heart called him.

Frédéric looks across the cave at me. "Listen, Stéphanie, I know that you're still trying to understand your choice. It's easy enough to tell that by watching you. I just want to say that you shouldn't try to know everything already. It's all right to make mistakes, as long as you can remember that God is faithful to you in your mistakes. I was always clear that I came to the monastery simply asking a question for time and God to answer. I always said that I carried the desire to become a monk, and if God wanted something else from me then . . . he would open that door and guide me there." He stops for a moment and looks out at the hermits' caves and the lines of goat trails lacing the mountain opposite us. "But this much I can tell you—the monastery is a place we come to learn how to love. That is the only thing I have known for sure of my time here—that we come here simply to be novices in love."

We speak for a while longer, and then I watch him climb down the cliff and walk alone back to the monastery. I stay by myself and watch him disappear and then the sun slowly set after him. I stand up in the cave, think again, and then sit down again on the floor of Madeleine, holding my face in my hands.

The truth is, I had hated God, not to mention St. Ignatius, after the Exercises. I had thought of them as aggressive parents who force their children to be doctors when all they want to be is ballerinas. I had blamed the Exercises for trapping me in a monastic choice—and they had, though this was no one's fault but my own. As long as the world had been

The Bread of Angels

crucifixion, then I had no choice but to abandon everything and intercede, to throw myself in front of the car to save the baby. I had made the only choice I was capable of making up there on the mountain, given the world as I had come to understand it. But now I am beginning to think that I wasn't as much wrong about my choice as I was wrong about the world.

I kneel down on the hard earth of the cave and close my eyes and make one last appeal for an answer.

"I want a vocation in love," I pray. "Teach me how."

5.

April

THREE DAYS LATER I take my first plane ride since Christmas, watching from the window as Damascus disappears and we rise over the turquoise sliver of the sea. I land in Morocco, to a different continent and a different Arabic altogether, full of unfamiliar sounds and expressions not resembling any Arabic I have ever heard in my life. Fez is brimming with the smell of leather shoes and spices, and men dressed in long, dyed robes with hoods over their heads duck in and out of the narrow lanes. After so many months in Syria, I thought that I had seen most of what was exotic about the East, and yet Fez, with its Moorish architecture and the nearby feeling of the Sahara in the air, catches me by surprise.

I take a train to Casablanca and then switch over to a bus that climbs slowly into the green and lush mountains, finally groaning to a halt in the quiet village of Chefchaouen. It is breathtaking. The houses are nestled among forests and streams of running water, the facades whitewashed and then detailed in different shades of blue. I find a room in a quiet *pension* and then I spend my evening walking through the blue streets, dreaming I am gliding upon a colonnaded sea.

I am like some hybrid form of human in Morocco. Though after all of the political intrigue and tension of Damascus I was eager for a break, after eight months of living in the house off Straight Street, I can't make myself talk to the foreign tourists from Spain and Italy, feeling more a stranger around them than any of the Arab locals who at least slightly resemble the shopkeepers I converse with every day. Yet my Arabic in no way resembles the local dialect of the Moroccans, which is so far from standard Arabic that almost no one else in the Arab world understands it. As a result, I speak to everyone in the Syrian dialect, they answer me in formal Quranic Arabic, and Moroccans simply assume that I am a Syrian on vacation for a few weeks, escaping the political crisis with Lebanon.

"You know, we don't get many Syrians traveling in these parts," the man at the newspaper stand tells me, smiling in approval when he hears my accent. "We see plenty of Spaniards, French people, and Americans, yet never Syrians. How has life been since Hariri was killed?"

"Al-hamdulillah," I respond automatically, "Thanks be to God," because we have to thank God when things have been difficult, after all.

I spend the day wandering the markets, speaking with shopkeepers instead of buying souvenirs. Their tea is so sweet that it stings my teeth. After joining some Moroccans for dinner in the evening I make my way back to the *pension*, fishing the key from my pocket and unlocking the blue painted door. I take a shower and then sit alone on the floor of my room mildly confused by an attack of sudden homesickness. The strange thing is, it's not home I miss. I miss Syria.

So I take out my computer, and I spend the next hour scanning through photographs, one by one, taking in the images of this bizarre and surprising year of my life. I begin with a picture I took of Mark on my last day in Cambridge, him standing at the door, ready to drive me to the airport, wearing his black-framed Russian glasses. For the first time, it doesn't hurt me to look at that photograph. It is the only photograph I ever took of him, in all of our months together, the first time I had ever used the camera I purchased for my year abroad, so that he is slightly out of focus. Later, when I had attempted to sharpen the image, everything else in the photo except for him had sharpened instead, the peeling door frame and tar-colored front door taking on an exaggerated, almost ghastly quality. Now I can't help but notice how ugly that house is, the outside painted an unfortunate combination of purple and gray. It was not at all the quaint, cozy brownstone I had been conjuring up in my mind for months. The Baron was right. Perhaps the house off Straight Street, with its corroding wooden frames and cold marble tiles, is the most beautiful house I've ever lived in after all.

The Bread of Angels

Then I come upon those photographs I had taken at the Umayyad Mosque when I first arrived in Syria, women with their gowns caught in the light, those children spreading their arms out like birds. There are Syrian Christians dancing the *dabke* in the streets on the Day of the Cross, their arms draped around one another's shoulders and feet kicking in the air. I inspect my neighbors carrying an icon of the Virgin Mary past my front door and light catching on the stones of Palmyra, perhaps the loveliest ancient Roman city in the world. I sit beside the Euphrates River, and the abandoned Byzantine cities in the north. I watch the Baron, cutting his fingernails at his front door, his slip-on house shoes contrasting against the pale tiles of our courtyard. I examine Mohammed, laying out his carpets like gowns of color and light, and Muslims bowing down to pray. I look at the view of the monastery from the desert path, the stones cradled between two mountains and the clouds casting their shapes below.

Finally, after an hour of sifting through photographs, I arrive at the pictures from the previous week at Mar Musa. In the first photograph, a procession of local Christians snakes through the valley, carrying the body of Jesus. In the next, the faces of saints stare down from the walls of the church. Musicians play drums and tambourines in the courtyard on Easter morning.

Then I stop.

There are two photographs of Frédéric. In the first, he is smiling and looking to the side, a sly gleam in his eyes. Laugh lines frame the corners of his mouth. His hair is tousled all over his head. I remember taking that photograph, watching him trying to suppress his grin. The moment I finished, he had burst into laughter.

Then I turn to the second photograph. This one is altogether different. Here, he is looking straight at me. But then again, he is not just looking at me. He is looking through me. He is looking at me like a man has never looked at me before.

Then I know. Of course I know. How many times had I seen him early in the morning and felt something move in my heart? How many times had we walked together through the desert, each one of us confessing those private fears we had never dared express to anyone else? How many times had he been waiting for me, at the top of a flight of three hundred and fifty stairs, with a glass of tea in his hands?

It is just like that moment in the Spiritual Exercises when you know your experience is true, because the voice is telling you the single sentence you are least prepared to hear, and so you must believe it.

Stephanie, it says. *You are in love*.

6.

A WEEK LATER, I climb the steps to the monastery, my hair long and loose on my shoulders, my skin brown from hours of walking beneath the Moroccan sun. I might actually be sick. My stomach is turning, and though I have walked these steps dozens of times they feel different. I am walking to him now, walking in response to that calling in my heart, to his words on the phone: *Come soon*. I am not coming to pray, or to wait in the desert for apparitions. I am coming to see the face of a man. And of course beneath my excitement I cannot help feeling, *This is wrong, this is wrong*. Everything about this is wrong. Even though it doesn't feel wrong at all. It feels like a key, finally sliding into a lock and turning.

I arrived from Morocco four days ago, and it was only a matter of hours before Frédéric phoned me, saying my name in his soft French-accented English, both of us laughing in a mixture of nerves and pure relief. We sat on our two sides of the phone line, in awkward silence, neither of us quite knowing what to say. I knew instinctively that he had felt the same rising in his heart, while he was alone in his room in the monastery, that I had experienced in a small hotel room in rural Morocco. It was not a feeling we had created. It had been given to both of us.

Finally he asked, "When are you coming to the monastery?"

I didn't know.

"Come soon," he urged. "Come soon."

I promised that I would.

I attempt to arrive in the courtyard like on any other visit to the monastery, depositing my bag against the walls and retreating to the kitchen to pour myself a glass of water. I pull up a seat next to the railing, overlooking the cliff below, and watch the clouds moving and changing shapes over the mountains on the horizon. Then I look up and see him standing in his normal clothes, watching me from the banister of the upper floors. Really, this man should be illegal. He is just beautiful.

"Stéphanie," he says, and I have never heard my name called like that before. He descends the stairs in his typical, loping way, comes to me, and kisses me on both of my cheeks. I know that this is normal for a Frenchman, but I am slightly weak at the knees from the mere fact of his face so close to mine, the brief feeling of his rough beard brushing against my skin.

I have practiced this moment in my head repeatedly, strategizing how I can approach this situation with at least some amount of virtue. I dig into my backpack, pulling out a thick hand-sewn leather belt I purchased for him in Fez. It still smells of tanning oil, a monastic belt to replace the one he wore so thin that the seams are now tearing apart. I am rather proud of it. It sends the very obvious message, *I have gone slightly insane, but despite the fact that I can't stop thinking of you of course I still want you to remain a monk, which is why I am contributing to your monastic wardrobe. That is the only decent thing to do, after all.*

"I brought something for you."

He tries it around his waist, fingering the metal of the buckle. Then he looks at me apologetically. "I have a, what's it called? A *hassasiyye*."

"A what? You mean you have an allergy?"

"Yes. I have a, what it is it? An *allergy* to most metals. Do you think that you could take this to someone in Damascus and get the buckle replaced?"

"Of course." I take the belt back again and stuff it in my bag. Clearly he is not going to make this whole situation easy. He is going to make me carry his monastic belt back down the stairs, back to Damascus, through the neighborhood in search of someone to get it fixed, and back again up these stairs. I will have to carry that weight on my back—he's a monk, he's a monk, he's a monk.

And this is all, cruelly appropriate, because he is, indeed, a monk.

Frédéric stays with me for a few moments and then returns to his chores. I find a room and arrange my things, then try to make myself useful, folding the rows of white sheets that have been left in the monastery courtyard to dry. This is a desert monastery, after all, and this is what religious people do—pray and work. St. Benedict neglected to write a special clause about falling in love with the clergy.

In the afternoon, when I have finished folding sheets and chopping vegetables and he has finished scrubbing bathrooms, we find a few solitary moments to speak together in the farthest end of the church, beneath the frescoes of women saints. I press my back up against a pillar. It is so hot outside in the exposed desert that most of the visitors have retired to their rooms to rest. Frédéric is just nearby, his legs out, crossed at the ankles, as close to me as he ever has been in his life.

We sit in silence. Better to say nothing at all. I have spoken so easily to him for months now, and yet I have finally arrived at the one emotion that is so taboo I cannot give name to it.

Finally, I look up at him. "I can feel you when I'm traveling," I say quietly. "I can feel you when I'm far away."

"I know, Stéphanie." He glances at me shyly and then fumbles in his pocket before fishing out his amber prayer beads. "I can feel you, too." He appears less worried than surprised, dazed even. "I wasn't even thinking of this with you."

"Thanks."

He blushes. "No, I always thought you were beautiful. But I was somewhere else. God gave me an answer to my calling in the mountain, he gave me an answer to my vocation."

I remember our conversation after Easter, about his seven-day retreat in the desert. *It was the first time I really felt certain that this is where I'm meant to be*, he had said.

"It's a mystery, my relation with you," he tells me softly. "Do you remember the first time I met you? I'm sure you don't. It was right when you arrived in Syria. You came up to the monastery one afternoon, looking like you were still in a faraway place. You didn't even notice me. But I saw you sitting alone in the courtyard, and the first thing I thought was, Why didn't I meet her before I was a monk?"

Tears fill my eyes. I turn and look at all of those faces staring down at me, this motley crowd of saints and angels. I don't even know how many times my life has changed in this room by now, losing God and discovering him again, how many mornings I have woken up from my spot sleeping beneath the fresco of hell or paradise to see the light breaking in through the window.

"Frédéric, I think I love you."

The Bread of Angels

He looks down at his hands. "I know. I feel something too."

Before we have a chance to say more, the door to the church opens, and a local peasant woman makes her way inside, a scarf tied over her head, to kneel in front of the altar and pray. I wait for her to leave and she does not leave, and I am superstitious enough to suspect that perhaps she is meant to be here, that she has been sent to slip her body into this moment, to slow us down. Frédéric finally stands up to go. I stay behind, close my eyes, and lean my back against the pillar, and I pray.

Dear God, please tell me that I am doing the right thing here. If I have to walk away, tell me how. I have no idea how to do it on my own.

THAT EVENING, I stand back and look at the way Frédéric's whole face changes when he laughs, the gentle half moon of his arm as he scoops children up from the ground, his hands, where butterflies sometimes come to rest. It is as much a miracle as anything I watched up on the mountain. Life in its essence.

I sleep soundly, and the next morning after the prayer I pack my bags and prepare to descend the steps and return to Damascus. I had planned on saying good-bye to him quickly, but Frédéric stops me and asks me to walk with him into the desert one last time. I leave my bags beside the tiny iron door of the monastery, and we walk until we reach a narrow bridge of earth connecting the opposite sides of the valley. We sit side by side and dangle our feet over the edge.

"Stéphanie, do you remember what we spoke about yesterday?"

I nod, biting my lip. I know this tone of voice, sad and exhausted and vaguely apologetic. I have used it too often myself, fleeing between countries, to be able to escape what it means.

"I was thinking last night. I just want to ask that we remember that this is a spiritual love, a love given by God between two people."

"Like St. Francis and St. Clare?"

He smiles faintly.

I try to keep my composure. "I always liked to think of us as Francis and Clare."

He touches my shoulder, softly, and then removes his hand.

"Otherwise I'll destroy everything. I'll start to question all that I have chosen. My vocation, whether I should be married or should become a monk."

"I'm sorry, Frédéric. We wouldn't want that." I lift myself up from the bridge, with the little dignity that I have left. *Just put one foot in front of the other*, I tell myself. *Walk away.*

Frédéric is still looking out, over the edge of the bridge. "I received an answer in the mountains. I felt it."

I cross the narrow space to the bank on the other side.

"I'll call you," he says, just loudly enough so that I can hear it. I know that he will. I lift my head and take a deep breath.

"I'll be waiting."

7.

FRÉDÉRIC DOES CALL DURING THE FOLLOWING WEEKS, many times, to discuss Arabic grammar, the crowds of tourists flooding the monastery, or just to mention that one of the small kittens in a newborn litter has died. Our conversations remain wholly chaste and almost childishly innocent, completely without mention of our conversation that afternoon in the chapel. Still, I can't ignore the growing sense that we don't want days in our lives to pass without the other being part of them. Often I know exactly when he is going to call, as if I have asked for it silently in my heart and he managed to hear me and respond. Every time I hear his voice, often slightly trembling, I know: we are not Francis and Clare.

I never call Frédéric, and I stop visiting the monastery almost entirely, sensing that I should give him time and space to wrestle with his feelings on his own terms. Still, he increasingly finds reasons to travel to Damascus— once for a photography exhibition at the National Library, another time to visit friends who are leaving the country—and we steal brief glances across rooms, content ourselves with simply sharing time and space. His religious role means that we often find ourselves in improbable situations, him in his monastic robes and me dressed like any other girl, but purposely brushing up against each other. At a reception crowded with priests and sheikhs, nuns in their habits and monks in long robes, he slips a folded piece of paper into my hand:

How does it feel, to know that every time your heart is moving one centimeter, it is moving a thousand centimeters in mine?

I fold the note in my wallet and walk outside to get some air. When he comes to follow me, we stand together silently and watch the lines of traffic passing on the nearby Damascus highway, my dress lifting slightly in the breeze. I feel so intimate in this silence. I am shy and overwhelmed to find myself on the receiving end of the energy emanating from his body. So it is to be loved by a man who has dedicated his life to the practice of learning to love.

I try to continue life as normal, if there can be anything normal about slowly falling in love with a monk in Syria, and in the metric system, no less. For a few weeks I launch a kamikaze mission I privately call OFOL, Operation Fall Out of Love, doing my best to shake myself free of an affair that I am certain can only end in heartbreak for me and at the very least a spiritual crisis if not a scandal for Frédéric. I tell no one about my feelings for him, and instead I try to date—first a young scholar of Islamic studies who translates Persian and Arabic poetry, then a drop-dead gorgeous Palestinian shopkeeper who speaks Italian and calls me *bella*. My attempts at dating end abruptly when the Palestinian shopkeeper asks me why we can't become more serious.

"You're in love with Frédéric, aren't you?" he accuses me.

I look at him in horror. Was I so transparent? I had not realized that I had even mentioned Frédéric's name, except in casual, fully innocent moments when I had spoken of my weekend trips to the monastery. But it seems that I *had* been mentioning him. Repeatedly.

"Don't be silly," I point out defensively. "He's a monk."

He laughs. "I never said that he was in love with *you*."

Well, ouch. Needless to say it is our last date, my last date with anyone in Damascus, for that matter. It takes time for me to dress my wounds, but eventually I resign myself to the fact that I am indeed in love with a French novice monk in the desert, who unfortunately for me is already engaged to a certain higher being named God and so is currently unavailable. Still, I refuse to believe that the creator of the universe works like an amateur postman delivering packages to the wrong apartment by mistake. Frédéric must have been sent into my life like this for a reason, and all I can do is have the courage to take this emotional roller-coaster ride to its conclusion. I just don't understand why. Frédéric, who has been clear about the fact that he can never envision himself leaving his monastic life, has hinted that this must mean that I am supposed to become a nun. Somehow I doubt it. Ever since I made a choice in the desert, I've been plagued with second thoughts. But I've been sure about my feelings for Frédéric ever since that moment in Morocco. Maybe I can't spend my life with him, but at least I know what it is to be certain about something. Surely a true calling must feel like this.

I visit shopkeepers and drink coffee with the Baron, and I study the Quran with the Sheikha every week. I spend my free hours reading and memorizing Quranic texts in my room every day. On mornings when I don't want to be alone, I put on a headscarf and sit in a crowd of women in the mosque, praying, until the hum of their voices lifts my heart from the ground.

Now, it strikes me that I was right when I asked to be a novice in love. I'm not sure even how to begin. I was raised with many stories, but they were war stories and ghost stories, stories of how my father's father was shot down and wounded during the Second World War, or how my grandmother bought a house haunted by suicides in every generation. I was not raised hearing about men and women who fell in love and lived happily ever after, or even men and women who fell in love and struggled to make the best of it. The subject of love is almost entirely absent in my family legends.

I don't know what scares me more, the notion that Frédéric might stay in that monastery forever or that he might leave for *me*. He seems too lovely for the world, too good, and I am worried that I will break him in half, that I will fail him by the simple practice of calling him back to the imperfect earth. Most of all, I feel like I don't deserve him. Not that anyone ever *deserves* another human being—this is perhaps the central mystery of being given a chance to love. It is a force so much greater, so much better than we can ever hope to be. I want to be worthy of it, and at the same time I feel slightly relieved knowing that I can never be worthy of it. Love has been given to me, like a bird that for some miraculous reason has just alighted on my shoulder.

The Bread of Angels

Yesterday morning, Frédéric came to Damascus with some members of the monastic community to visit a mutual friend, and when the visit was over I walked him, Paolo, Dima, and the others back to their car. The streets of Damascus were buzzing with traffic, and I held the space between Paolo and Frédéric as we maneuvered through the cars in the street, trying not to get plowed over. Paolo turned to Frédéric, his beloved novice monk. "What do you think?" he asked. "I think that Stephanie should spend the afternoon with us."

I blushed. Well, what was a girl to do?

We reached the station wagon, and by the time Paolo, Dima, two monks, and another nun found places there was no more room left. Paolo opened up the back hatch. "Stephanie and Frédéric, why don't you sit there? It's good for humility." I looked at Frédéric, shocked. Then we climbed in, too awkwardly, stumbling over ourselves, our knees folded up toward our faces, looking between them at each other. Our sandals moved forward, touching.

We spent the afternoon like that, pausing every now and then to disembark, to visit a monastery, to eat lunch. I was only waiting to be back in the car, the greatest station wagon in the world, which should have poems and national songs composed in its honor. The sun set slowly. I watched the Syrian countryside pass me through the windows, starkly beautiful, all wild hills and desert paths interrupted by minarets and church steeples climbing skyward. We were seven in a crowded, beat-up station wagon, but to me there were only two people in the world.

At sunset the car screeched to a halt on the side of the road, beside an open space strewn with wildflowers and scrub brush, burned out already by the heat, wild. In the distance, the sun had reached its fullest, an enormous brilliant red star on the summit, lowering its head toward us. We climbed out of the car to watch.

The wind was blowing. Frédéric took off his black sweater, came up behind me, and placed it over my shoulders, gently. "You'll be cold," he whispered.

I watched the sun retreat, a flower extinguishing itself, with the scent of him on my shoulders. I wore that sweater for the rest of the evening, until they drove me to the bus station and placed me on the last bus home. I wore it all the way to Damascus. I wore it all the way to the most beautiful house in Bab Touma, where I climbed into bed and removed it, finally, so that I could cradle it in my arms as I tumbled toward sleep.

8.

THE NEXT MORNING I wake up early and change into long pants and a turtleneck and tie my hair at the nape of my neck. Then I make my way across town again, to meet the Sheikha and study the Muslim Jesus.

The Sheikha and I have grown even closer with time, and by now I can recite the verses more fluidly, having prepared them at home before my lessons. While in the beginning she simply told me the meaning of verses, now we debate and discuss them, in the method passed down in every religious tradition, from rabbis with their pupils to Tibetan masters with their monks. The Sheikha no longer views me as a Christian, but as a searcher. *Inti mu'mina*, she tells me with affection each time I notice something in the text. It means, in Arabic, *You're a believer*.

Today the Sheikha and I are reading one of my favorite stories in the Quran: the story when Jesus creates a bird out of clay and then breathes into it, willing it to fly. The Sheikha reads the verses, and I sing them after her, slowly imagining those wings unfurling into the air, the creature flying out of an open window and into the distance.

"SHEIKHA?" I ASK. "Why are there two names for Jesus in Arabic, Yesua for the Christians and `Issa for the Muslims?" I have been too shy to mention this until now. With the Sheikha I only call Jesus by his Muslim name, which makes me sometimes feel that I am discussing a stranger. *The prophet `Issa, peace be upon him.*

"I don't know why the Christians call him Yesua," she says. "We don't have a reason for calling him `Issa—we simply call him by the name God gives him in the Quran."

She seems to consider my question further. "Is he similar to your Jesus?"

Yes, I think. *Yes and no.* Though I can't even answer the question— I have known the Jesus of the Gospels for such a long time and I am just meeting the Muslim Jesus, so it feels like comparing my childhood best friend with someone I just met at a party. Not only that, after a month in the desert, I feel that the Jesus of the Gospels also knows me. When we first began studying the verses on the prophet Jesus a few weeks ago, I banged my head against the wall in frustration over how *different* he is from the Jesus I grew up with. He is human, for one thing, not God, and not the Son of God, and he is scandalized by the very idea of a Trinity. I haven't quite grasped the fact not only that the Muslim Jesus was never crucified, but that he never died, period, that he was taken up by God to be returned before the end of time. When I first began studying his story with the Sheikha, there were so many parts of my Woody Allen Jesus that I missed—the Beatitudes, the scenes with his disciples by the sea, the story of the Garden of Gethsemane. Every few pages I became frustrated. *Who are you?* I would ask. *Who are you?*

Then one day, I stopped fighting it. *Let him be who he is,* I told myself. *Not who you want him to be.*

It took time. The Jesus I watched appearing every day in the mountain was real. I didn't want to let him go. I didn't know how to give this man, with his two contradicting lives, space in my one heart.

So I simply watched him from a distance, and in time he approached me, in all of his *otherness*, and slowly I have grown used to him. He is not my Woody Allen Jesus—he is much more serious, stern even, sometimes. I have followed his life, from the moment he was born out in the wilderness to when he healed the sick, raised the dead. I have watched him ask God to send a table of food down from heaven. I have listened to Muslim neighbors speak to him in the familiar tones they use to speak of family members: `Issa, Jesus, who will appear any day now in a patch of heaven, just on the other side of the street.

Still the Sheikha's question is one I haven't fully answered for myself. What does he have to do with the man I came to know in November? How can a single man have two such different lives?

"Well, some things are the same," I tell the Sheikha. "Of course our Jesus is also born of the Virgin Mary, only we don't have the story from his childhood that you have in the Quran, when he speaks from the cradle to save the reputation of his mother."

"That's a shame." She sounds genuinely saddened by the omission. "You should tell more Christians that story. You would think they would be eager to know the earliest miracle in the life of Jesus, peace be upon him. He is your prophet, after all."

"We also don't have many stories from his childhood. In the Gospels he is born, and then we don't hear much about him until he begins teaching to the disciples."

She nods. "In the Quran, it says that after Jesus was born, Mary sought shelter with him in Rabwa, a mountain with a valley and a stream running through it, just on the outskirts of Damascus." I have heard this from many local Muslims, proud that Jesus came here in his infancy.

"I suppose he's not so different from the Muslim Jesus," I tell the Sheikha finally. "Our Jesus also heals the sick and raises the dead back to life."

I smile, saying that, remembering Jesus in the desert, placing his hands on the blind and restoring their sight. "They kept shouting my name, even when everyone told them to stop," he had told me. I think he would approve of me, sitting across from a female sheikh, chatting about him in the late afternoon. He was never one for conventional companions.

Before I leave, the Sheikha says something for the first time. "Pray for me," she asks.

"Pray for me, too," I ask her, and I mean it.

THAT EVENING, when I am alone in my bedroom, I try to summon forth the Muslim Jesus into the room. Maybe I simply want company, for these last weeks in Damascus waiting for clarity have been terribly lonely. But I suspect that it is something else—that after so much time in the desert with one Jesus, I need to see for myself the truth of his other life. I know that some Muslims might disapprove of my actions—that the ban on images in Islam makes many Muslims hesitant to imagine what the prophets might have looked like. Still, I can't keep holding this Jesus at a distance. I need to see him face-to-face.

So I close my eyes, and in the silence I wait for a long time, before imagining the story. Slowly, I am no longer in my room but outside on Straight Street, and he is passing me, this Muslim Jesus.

Assalamu Aleykum, he calls out, and the shopkeepers respond and place their hands over their hearts. I smile at the utter familiarity of the scene; this could be Mohammed with his carpets, gliding through a busy downtown street. Then they are there again, in front of him, lepers, the blind, and he passes his dark hands over them until their bodies go smooth and calm. He gathers the dead beneath his hands, lifting them back to life. Only this time, when he finishes, and having been entirely humbled, he presses both hands to his face and quietly prays in thanks to God.

He walks down the cobblestone alleys of the Old City, exits through the main gate, ascends Qassioun Mountain on the outskirts of town, and then stops on the side of the path to collect earth from the ground. The earth itself is hard—he has to push his hands deep beneath the surface before he hits upon clay, soft and breaking easily in his hands. He pulls out fistfuls, the red earth smearing his palms, pressing beneath his fingernails. He slowly uses his thumbs and forefingers to mold a body, carefully carves out a set of wings. He presses in the eyes with his thumbnails. Then he lifts the bird up to his mouth and blows softly.

The bird unfurls its wings, but they are too heavy and, after a moment, come to rest.

He takes the bird and holds it against his face for a moment, warming it. Then he slowly cups it between his hands and blows a second time. The two wings tremble, until the weight falls out of them and the bird ascends into the open air, disappearing in the distance.

"Ma'shallah," he says beneath his breath.

"Do it again," I whisper.

He does. I spend the evening watching him breathing into the earth, over and over, unleashing bird after bird from his open hands.

9.

May

TEN DAYS HAVE PASSED since I last heard from Frédéric. I know that he has not disappeared forever, because I can still feel him close by, in the mornings when he awakens, when I am uncharacteristically drawn at five thirty from my bed. I can feel him when he falls asleep at night, laying his head against his pillow. I can feel him fasting on his Monday afternoon, his chest filling up with a space we describe as hunger, but which for him is an empty room, asking to be filled with an answer to what he should do with his life.

I know that he senses me, also. He said as much in the last letter he wrote before disappearing into silence:

Stéphanie,

Yes, we are compagnons in loneliness, loneliness as in my mystery of being a monk, being alone, according to the Greek etymology of the word, being black as death to live in the truth of the Resurrection because for us, death is already defeated.

In the Arabic tradition, the monk is the one who is escaping from the world, only to love it more. That's why I'm able to love you more, the world then revealing its sacred essence. In the French language, compagnon means com, "together," and pagnion, meaning "bread." We share the same bread.

For his thirty-second birthday, I bought Frédéric two small hand-blown blue glasses, keeping a matching set for my windowsill. I wanted to give him that color blue—never found anywhere except in hand-blown glass, in certain Italian Renaissance paintings, and in very rare pockets of the sea. I don't know what to call what I feel for him, but it is that color. That much I know.

We don't speak to each other, but every morning Frédéric and I awaken in our rooms, and we each fill two blue hand-blown glasses with water. His are on his windowsill looking out into the desert, mine on my windowsill looking out into the courtyard of my house. Before we sleep at night, we fill them again. It is our daily ritual to each other. He is my first thought in the morning, my last before I go to sleep at night. I imagine that when I fill the glasses in the evening that I am softly kissing his closed eyelids and sending him off toward sleep.

In these days without him, I wait in silence. The month of May, which is the month of Mary, passes in the streets of Bab Touma, and women appear wearing Alice-blue dresses, proof, so they say, that they have asked the Virgin for a miracle and have received an answer.

The Bread of Angels

Finally, the phone rings.

"Stéphanie?" He says my name slowly, carefully, pronouncing each syllable.

"It's been a long time."

"I know. I'm sorry." He sounds tired. He doesn't provide a reason for his silence, and I don't ask.

"I'm calling because I need a favor from you."

My mind races through all of the possibilities that this favor might be—for me to disappear from his life forever, to become a nun after all, or to carry out some Catholic ritual such as lighting candles for nine consecutive nights in a chapel, asking for answers.

"What is it, Frédéric?"

"I wonder if you might teach me the Quran."

I am stopped in my tracks. It is the last request I was expecting. I can think of so many reasons why I should not teach him the Quran. I am not a religious teacher, and I am not prepared to carry the responsibility of guiding a Christian monk through the texts of another faith. There are far too many questions I won't know the answers to.

But I still say yes. It is the first time in all of the many months that I have known him that Frédéric has really asked me for anything.

10.

THE NEXT MORNING I sit down in my room in Damascus, open the Quran, and begin to read the story of the prophet Joseph out loud in Arabic. Joseph is that incredibly beautiful prophet whose story also appears in the book of Genesis, and in the Quran he is so lovely that the women who saw him were so distracted from their work that they accidentally cut open their hands. Adored by his father, life and fate carry him away to an exile in Egypt, where in his loneliness he survives by reading and interpreting dreams. A mystic, a stranger, he lives a life bound by the memory, both powerful and terrifying, of a night in his youth, when his brothers cast him to the bottom of the well to die. He waited for what felt like forever, alone in the depths, the darkness sinking down on him, but he did not die. In that moment, instead, he received a message telling him the future and giving him the secret meaning of his life. He was then pulled from the darkness, alive.

I can't tell Frédéric that I think that he is beautiful. I can't tell him that I feel his loneliness, his exile in this land far from his family. I can't tell him that the secret of what becomes of our lives belongs to God, who sometimes, in his kindness, gives us a glimpse of its promise in that moment in life when we are stranded at the bottom of the well. I can't tell him that I love him, more than I imagined I could love another human being, and that I miss being with him.

I can't tell him, and so I send him the chapter of Joseph from the Quran. I add a note, mentioning that this is the story of a beautiful young man, exiled in the East far from his family, who dreams great dreams and through his dreams understands the world.

It is the first love letter I have ever sent him.

11.

FOR THE NEXT MONTH, Frédéric and I court each other through Quranic love letters. I wake up every morning and read quietly at my desk, and far away in his room in the desert, Frédéric opens his Quran and reads the same verses. We rarely speak with each other. We cannot see each other. Sometimes, I read a word out loud, feeling it escape into the air, and my only comfort is in knowing that somewhere he might be saying that same word, that he can sense my voice and hold out his hand to grab hold of it.

I know I may never have the chance to sit with him over coffee, for us to fall in love like two people living in ordinary human circumstances, with our day jobs and dates on Saturday evenings. The Quran is the only, small room that we have been given to meet each other in. So I learn to tell him the story of my life by giving him the stories that have moved me. I send him all of the stories of the prophet Abraham, called al-Khalil in the Quran, the intimate friend of God. Early in his life, he sets out to understand God, and yet each time he feels certain, he discovers that he has been misguided. When the night is covered with darkness, and he sees a star, he becomes certain that this star is God. But then it disappears.

When he witnesses the moon rising, he believes again that he has discovered God. But then the moon sets and disappears. When he sees the sun rising, he is sure that he has discovered God at last. But then the sun disappears. Yet he never loses the faith that the majesty of the world holds God's secret, and in the end of his searching, after all of his mistakes, God reveals himself to him.

I hope that he can read behind the text and witness my own journeys, how many times I have been unlucky in love and other matters big and small, how many false starts I have experienced this year in Syria alone, how many times I have felt sure of the truth but then stumbled at the last moment, realizing my error. Yet I always came back to the mystery I discovered in the desert, and that returning brought me, without knowing it, to him.

I write to him about the prophet Moses, who in the desert asks to see God but is told that the vision will destroy him. So God reveals himself to a mountain instead, and the mountain explodes with the presence of him. The mystics say that we are that mountain, that we have to destroy ourselves and abandon everything that we believed was certain before we are able to confront the true mystery of our lives.

I send him the story of the two angels, one sitting on our left and one on our right, recording all of our deeds. And finally, I send the moment when Abraham, who is quietly going about his life, opens his door one day to see angels, asking to enter. He, too, is terrified.

12.

June

MAY TURNS INTO JUNE, two months since Frédéric and I discovered our feelings for each other. It is a secret both of us have carried in silence. I send Frédéric lessons on the Quran at the beginning of every week, with a new lesson for every day, and he looks up the verses, reads them first in French, then a second and third time in Arabic. Every morning he selects a single sentence to memorize, writes it down on a small piece of paper, and carries it in his pocket for the rest of the day.

Seek what God has destined for you, and eat and drink, until the white thread of dawn appears distinct from its black thread . . .

I'm not sure at what moment the lessons become too much for him. But by early June, his responses are confused, jumbled. While the rest of the monastic community rests in the afternoons, he paces back and forth in his room, rereading the verses I send him, moved but scared. The Quran feels real, the music of the language working its way beneath his skin. It touches a part of him that has never been touched before. When I receive his letters, I'm frightened, remembering the stories of men who read mystical texts and become crazy, never able to return to normal life.

Am I dying? he asks me. *I'm afraid of lies. I'm afraid of nothingness. Is it possible for two things to contradict each other, and for them both to be true?*

Yes, I write back to him. *I have no idea how. But I think that it can only be so.*

NOW AFTER SO MANY WEEKS APART, we are once again walking together into the clear, open desert behind the monastery, which after so many months feels like home to me. This time we have taken a different path than those I know, a narrow goatherder's path that climbs steeply behind the woman's monastery, so that we have to lean forward with our hands prepared, should the stones crumble beneath us. Every few moments Frédéric looks back to watch me, to be certain that I have not lost my balance.

"Are you sure that it's not a problem, you disappearing into the desert with a woman?"

He shrugs. "No one will notice. Anyhow, I know that people, especially in Syria, like to talk when they see a monk speaking to a woman alone. But I also have my life, I have my French culture, and there are some parts of myself that I cannot give up, just because the world tells me to. It's natural for me to go for a walk with a friend."

Of course, I think to myself. *Because that is exactly what we are.*

We continue ascending until we reach the top of a desert mountain, overlooking the clouds and the valley below. I recognize the place—it is the same wild mountainside I had scrambled over alone in the rain that morning months ago when I escaped the Exercises to wrestle with God, just before the snow and my first confession.

We sit across from each other on the steep incline, close, tucking our bodies behind two huge stones, to catch us and keep us from falling. He turns to me, taking my hands in his, mine small inside his palms, which are rough from the daily labor of monastic life, from years of working vineyards before he ever came here. He holds my hands, firmly, not like a lover, but as someone who wants to tether another in place, to prevent her from slipping away.

"I told myself, if I just held your hands like this, if I just faced you, sitting like this, then everything would be okay." He looks at me, with that terrible, innocent look of his, of such goodness that it could end civil wars, it could make thieves repent their misdeeds and run home to their mothers.

"Please, just say it. Tell me that you can't leave the monastery. Tell me that you have made your choice."

"My entire life, whenever I needed something, God has sent me a sign." His voice is so low that I can barely hear him. "How many times have I said that—that God would never give a man stones if he asks for bread?"

I pull my hands from his. I am sad and exhausted and not up to the task of begging a man to love me. "What do you want, Frédéric? He sent me. We fell in love. What more of a sign are you waiting for? Are you waiting for it to be written in the clouds? For an airplane to fly by and write GO WITH STEPHANIE in the sky? I'm here, Frédéric. I'm right here in front of you."

He won't look at me. I can scarcely recognize the young monk I met on his way back from Athos, his eyes glowing and a shining coming from his body. Now he looks worn out, uncertain about everything. "I don't think that you understand," he tells me. "You have no idea what my life would be like if I left this place. When I came to the monastery, I came in order to become a stranger, to be nobody, to be invisible. If I leave here I don't exist. I don't even have my French identity card anymore. I gave all of my possessions away. I don't exist in the world, Stéphanie."

"You exist for me."

"Do I?" Finally, he turns to look at me. "You fell in love with a monk, Stéphanie. You fell in love with a man who comes shining out of the mountains."

"That's not fair."

"But it's true. Do you know what happened to me last week? Some guests came up the stairs, and I greeted them with my simple little pot of tea, wearing my normal clothes, my working clothes. I offered them something to drink. They didn't even look at me. They treated me like a servant."

He is quiet. "Then, I returned later, wearing the robes of a monk. And they ran up to me, horrified, and kissed my hands. 'Oh, Abuna! Abuna! Father! Father!' they called out."

"I'm sorry."

"Don't be sorry. But I have a place here, now. I have my life to live here. What are you going to do if I leave this place and I can't become anyone in the world?"

I had never allowed myself to even imagine Frédéric and me together in the world. Now I try to picture him, in his ordinary human clothes, navigating the city streets. Where would we go? How would we live? As it was I had little to offer him—no plans for the future, nothing more than a few thousand dollars left over from my fellowship in the bank. Who knows how we would survive? To be poor, to trust that everything will be given to you, to not think about where your food or shelter or clothing will come from—to offer everything you have to those in need—in the monastic life, these are considered the actions of a saint. In the world, they are the actions of a failure and a fool.

"You were the one who told me about resurrection," I tell him. "You were the one who said that with faith, we can reach the other side of what is difficult. I believed your words."

"Yes, I told you those words as a monk."

"But I didn't receive them as a nun. I received them as a human being. And is that your resurrection then? Does it only work in a monastery? Because I don't want anything to do with it if that is resurrection."

A tear runs down my cheek, and I brush it away, angrily. He can't do this to me now. After everything I have believed, after all of the conversations from this past year that I have taken to heart. If all of this has been rhetoric, for months now, then I am right back at the beginning, I am nothing more than some foolish girl who was in fact born with a curse and who will leave Damascus to fall into depression, get hit by a train, or die in a freak plane crash a few months down the road.

But it *is* true. I no longer need him to tell me that. His hand is on my hand again, differently now. I look up at his face. He also has tears in his eyes.

"If resurrection exists, then you can take it with you," I whisper.

We sit like that, for a long time. He squeezes my hand. "I know."

13.

Two weeks later, I am traveling alone with Frédéric up the coast of Syria, preparing to meet the monastic community in Antakya, or Antioch, the cradle of Christianity, for the feast day of Saints Peter and Paul. This morning he was waiting for me at the monastery, wearing his single ordinary man outfit, loose khaki trousers with big pockets and a long, brown hand-tailored shirt from France. His hair has become absolutely wild, like a lion's mane, and for once his beard is close to full. I think that my heart might just fall through my chest.

"What time do we have to meet the community?" I ask him on the way to the bus station, and he blushes.

"We have all the time that we need, Stéphanie." And because, for the first time ever in the time since I have known him, it is true, I smile as he buys two tickets to Homs, then from Homs to Latakia, from Latakia to Kassab, the longest road possible north, stopping in a hundred places and always pressing us up against the sea.

We spend our day side by side in cheap Arab buses, staring out the windows to the water lapping up against the coast, the sailboats nestled in their ports of azure Mediterranean sea, and I can't believe that I have lived so long nearby without paying it notice. He slides open the window beside me, and we let the wind come through, smelling fresh and full of salt, until we climb into the pine-forested mountains of the north, that land of Crusader castles, where it is more like Italy than any other Arab country that comes to mind.

"Oh, I forgot to tell you"—he smiles, with his wicked smile—"I just found out that I'll be studying Arabic for the entire month of July in Damascus. Which I think means we'll see each other every day."

It is too impossible to be true. Like that moment on a game show when you had hoped to win a washing machine and instead you find out you won fifty thousand dollars and a dream house and a vacation to Europe, and that you get to come back next week for more prizes. Frédéric in Damascus for an entire month. I had been thrilled to be granted an afternoon with him.

But then I remember. The Sheikha has asked me to teach English in her Quranic school for girls this summer, an incredible honor for a Christian. It means that my summer mornings will be all tied up in an Islamic madrassa and my afternoons tied up with a desert monk. I can't quite imagine the two worlds colliding.

"Are you ready to see me in my mosque clothes?"

"I can't wait."

The bus groans to a halt near the Turkish border, at a makeshift bus station that seems to have evolved in a no-man's-land on the side of the road. Frédéric climbs out of the bus and speaks alone to a taxi driver, handing him change through the open window of the front seat. Soon we are driving into the forest on a detour to a tiny Armenian village in the mountains called Kassab, a scattering of quaint old houses in a forest overlooking a rugged, untouched coastline. The wind catches the scent of the sea and pine, compressing them into one.

"I was here five years ago, and I can swear that there is a tiny restaurant owned by two brothers, hidden somewhere in the back of this village," he tells me, grabbing my wrist gently and guiding me forward. He begins asking strangers in the street, and sure enough before long we are cutting through backyards and hidden alleys on the way to the house of so and so Galikian, where two brothers pour us house wine and cover our table with fresh cheese and grape leaves stuffed with rice and lamb, grilled fish and salads, and for once in my life Frédéric is not a novice monk, he is simply the most charming man I have ever known, sitting across from me at a table near the Mediterranean Sea, to the sound of people speaking Armenian in the background. My God, if he only knew, the Baron would be so proud of me.

We laze away our day, drinking red wine and swinging our feet near one another beneath the table, until I don't know if I am drunk from house liquor or just from the look of him. Then, the almost inevitable happens. A young woman sitting at a table nearby begins to eye us curiously.

"Aren't you a monk at Mar Musa?" she asks Frédéric. He smiles, his eyes shining at me, and then answers, "Yes."

By then the waitress, a middle-aged women with a large waistline and a laugh to match, is nearby, fussing over us. "You're from Mar Musa?"

"It's amazing," the first woman insists. "I was there just a few months ago."

Frédéric turns to the waitress and teases her gently in Arabic. "So you know that I'm a novice. Don't give me too much food—we monks have very small stomachs."

Soon we have piles of food we didn't order scattered around the table, extra bottles of wine and house-made *arak*, grilled eggplant and kebabs of ground lamb minced with spices and parsley, an enormous platter of fresh fruit. By three o'clock we have to leave or else we'll never make it to Turkey. So we stumble back to the center of the village and catch a taxi to the border, passing men selling oranges on the side of the road, winding our way through lush rolling hills. Frédéric takes my hand, and I link my fingers in his. We have never touched for more than an instant. But after a few moments, he drops my hand abruptly.

"You'll hate me for this someday," he says sadly.

Then I gently take hold of his hand a second time. "I won't ever hate you for any of this, I promise." His fingers feel warm against mine, and we hold them like that, all the way to passport control, where we stop at the small border crossing and turn over our two passports, stacked on top of each other, and the jolly, cigarette-smoking Syrian guard stamps them: June 27, 2005.

Then we walk. We cross over to that place between countries, a wild landscape full of pine and open sky and the sound of water flowing. We are in no one's country, and for a few moments no one on earth can claim us.

We hold hands, tightly now, until we reach the other side.

IDEALLY, I WOULD HAVE STAYED with Frédéric forever in that coastal town, sitting next to the sea. Yet after two days in Antakya I have to rush back to Damascus early, so that I can become a teacher at an Islamic school.

My first concern about teaching at the Quranic school for girls is not the job itself, but that I might actually throw my entire house off Straight Street into scandal. I can just hear the upstairs neighbors clicking in disapproval. Syria may be a model of religious coexistence, but people tend to keep matters of faith to themselves.

So far I've been discreet about my lessons with the Sheikha and my trips to the mosque, sneaking away my headscarves in my backpack and pinning them on in the backs of taxis, using the rearview mirror for guidance. But I doubt I'll be able to conceal my destination this summer. I am certainly the only Christian in my neighborhood leaving the house in the middle of July covered from head to toe in dark clothing, only my hands and feet revealed. It's a hundred degrees out.

Today I dress carefully for my first day of school, selecting long, loose black pants, a long-sleeved maroon shirt, and slip-on black shoes. I pull my hair back away from my face and hang a scarf loosely around my neck. I stick a few safety pins beneath the corner of the scarf in case I need backup when the time comes for tying it into place, a skill I haven't yet managed to perfect.

As I am crossing the courtyard, the Baron intercepts me. "Where are you going?" he asks suspiciously.

"I'm going to visit a friend," I tell him.

"Wearing that? Isn't it a bit hot to wear long sleeves and pants?"

"I don't mind."

"And black? Black will only absorb the sun."

The Baron knows very well that I am going to the mosque. He has been following my immersion into Islam with a combination of confusion and alarm these past months. More than once, he has come to the window and stared at me reading the Quran.

"The Quran?" he asks. "What's wrong with the Bible?"

Today he is once again trying to torture me, part of his job as my self-appointed mentor. Just as I had to learn the art of Syrian colloquial Arabic from him, the Baron has insisted on teaching me the art of "what should not be said," another exact and very fine science in Syrian life. A girl, for instance, never goes out on a date in Syria—she "goes to a friend's house." One should never decline an invitation outright but should excuse oneself because "aunt so-and-so is in the hospital" or "so-and-so cousin just died, and we have to prepare for the mourning," which is difficult for me, as I have no nearby relatives. Certainly, a girl who is dressed from head to toe in very formal dress should not tell her Christian neighbors that she is on her way to teach in a mosque. She is shopping, or taking a walk, or going to church to pray for forgiveness for her many sins. Even if everyone knows where she is really going, for some reason it isn't very polite to admit it aloud.

This is why I am lying to the Baron quite openly, and he is reacting like a proud parent. "Why don't you ever wear denim?" he presses. "I'll take you to get some nice denim skirts this afternoon if you want."

"I'll let you know, Grandpa."

"Dir balik," he warns me as I finally leave. "Take care of yourself."

Half an hour later, I am standing across from the mosque, using the reflection in a parked car to monitor my progress as I struggle to fasten my headscarf. Pedestrians stare at me, perhaps worried that I have pinned the cloth around my neck too tightly and am suffocating myself.

After several minutes I manage to cross the mosque courtyard with my scarf firmly safety-pinned beneath my chin. Beside me, two women walk with their faces entirely covered with black cloth, not even their eyes visible, leading their young children by the hand. We all enter the mosque together, and I try not to stare as they each lift up their scarves to reveal their faces, both of them pale and lovely and younger than I am. As I turn away from them, I notice the lines and lines of tiny shoes in front of me. Tennis shoes, barely the size of my palm, with lights on the heels that ignite each time a step is taken inside them. Dressy white shoes with buckles, tiny black flats, sneakers with their Velcro straps left hanging to their sides.

Slowly, up the stairs, the shoes climb one beside the other, hundreds of them, steadily increasing in size and weight. Pair by pair, they grow darker in color, more conservative, the second floor a collection of navy and black dress shoes in muted leather, modest and unassuming, barely distinguishable from one another. They stand side by side, like hundreds of mouths open to the sky. And behind them, the buzz of young girls' voices saturate the air:

Qal hu Allah Ahid
Allah al-Sumid
Lum ulid wu lum yolid
Wu lum yukun lahu kufuan ahid.

Say: He is God, the One and Only
God, the Eternal, Absolute
He begets not, nor is he begotten
And there is no other like him.

I close my eyes. Collectively the voices hum like a generator, the sound hanging in the air with its own particular weight, as though I could simply walk forward and part them in half with my own body. One thing is certain—they don't sound at all like ordinary human voices. The throat must give off a special trembling when it believes it carries the word of God.

The Sheikha founded her school when she was only seventeen years old, a brilliant student of Islam who had already memorized the Quran and spent years studying Islamic law. At the time, the idea of an Islamic madrassa under the secular Syrian government was considered revolutionary. Just as revolutionary was the idea that young women should become experts in the study of Islam, a field that was traditionally dominated by men. After all, there were those Muslims who even said that women were not required to pray five times a day, much less memorize and study the holy books. Yet the Sheikha insisted that women had always had a place of learning and teaching in Islam, dating back to the life of the prophet Mohammed. Study, she told her students, is one of the highest forms of prayer.

Today hundreds of girls study every summer at this mosque, beginning to memorize verses when they are just four years old. They learn every single word of the Quran, and only when they have finished do they learn it a second time with *tajwid*, a precise science of reciting each letter of the Quran perfectly. *Tajwid* is familiar to me as the beautiful singsong rhythm the Sheikha had taught me when she recited the verses in her home. Though they do not begin studying the meaning of the texts until they are slightly older, the young girls understand that language—sound—communicates its own meaning.

I stand against the wall and close my eyes, listening to them reciting, until I feel a hand on my shoulder shaking me from my reverie. It is Noor, the Sheikha's precocious sixteen-year-old daughter, bringing me to my senses. I have met her several times at her house, and on more than one occasion we have followed my Quranic lessons with trips into the neighborhood for ice cream. She knows a slightly different Stephanie, one with her hair down.

"I like your scarf," she laughs, teasing me in her almost fluent English.

"Thanks, it's new."

"Wow, you even pinned it? Soon you won't look like a foreigner wearing hijab."

Very funny. I will always look like a foreigner in hijab.

She gestures to a circle of girls chanting in a corner and smiles. "So, what do you think?"

At nine in the morning, the bottom floor of the mosque is already alive with what must be a hundred young girls sitting cross-legged in circles around their teachers, repeating Quranic verses in unison. In a circle of five-year-olds, girls with their heads still uncovered and their hair tumbling bounce anxiously from one leg to the other as they repeat the shortest chapters of the Quran, numbering just a few verses in length. Other circles are scattered throughout the room, the girls six, seven, eight years old, most of them quietly repeating the firm classical Arabic of a teacher in earnest. I can hardly believe the ease with which they are studying one of the hardest Arabic texts in existence.

Noor, having memorized the Quran by the age of twelve, has already been promoted to the role of teacher. Soon she is sitting again with her students in a corner circle, quizzing them one by one, occasionally gently correcting their pronunciation and marking their progress on charts. In other corners of the room, girls are pacing back and forth with pages in their hands, reciting lines quietly over and over to themselves, sometimes placing their hands on the pillars of the mosque and circling around them like ballerinas. I have been so conditioned to imagine a madrassa, or Islamic school, as oppressive that I do not know how to process these images.

I sit down in a circle of six-year-olds as they chant:

Iqraa bi ismi rubika althee huliqa
Huliqa Al-Insan min Aliqin
Iqraa warubuka alikram
Althee alm bi qulum
Alim Al-Insan ma lam yalam

Read! In the name of the Lord who created
Created man out of a clot of blood
Read! That the Lord is bountiful
He who taught the use of the pen
Taught man that which he did not know.

Six years old. When I was their age, I was busy taking gymnastics lessons and riding a bicycle with training wheels. When they finish reciting, I stand up and make my way toward the door leading to the second floor. After a few steps, I am intercepted by some of the young pigtailed girls, only one of them old enough to wear the headscarf.

"What's your name?" they ask me, shyly.

"Stephanie."

"Are you here to memorize the Quran?"

"No," I answer. "I'm the new English teacher."

One of the girls pulls a package of potato chips from her bag, opens it, and offers them to me. I take one.

"How many chapters of the Quran have you memorized?" she asks.

"None." I am a little ashamed to admit this, for I already sense that there is status attached to how many Quranic chapters you know, and in some childish way I want in on it.

In the youngest circles, there are a few small boys, the sons of teachers, allowed in the women's mosque only because they are much too small to worry themselves with the presence of girls in the room. Noor motions for me to wait for a moment. She walks across the room toward me, and on the way plucks one of the boys from his circle and leads him to stand in front of me.

He is small and very shy, his hair in a bowl cut, his dark eyes staring down at the floor.

"Ahmed is our best student," Noor says, patting him on the shoulder. "He memorized the Quran when he was only six. Now he is learning the entire book over again, with *tajwid*."

It strikes me that many Muslims do not learn *tajwid* in their entire lifetimes. "How old is he now?"

"Eight."

I nod my head to him, signaling him to begin, and stand and listen as he recites verses from the story of the Virgin Mary. He closes his eyes, and the words begin flowing out in a torrent, too quickly for me to understand all of them, rising and falling, his voice holding the last note in each line. He is chanting, singing the verses.

When he finishes, he looks up at me, with that face of his as young and clear and innocent as the moon. I think, *How will I ever read this book in the same way again, knowing it is held within the body of this singular child?*

15.

THE SHEIKHA IS WAITING FOR ME in her office upstairs, with teachers swarming around her as she answers the phone, balances trays of coffee on her arm, and engages in several conversations at once. I love that the Sheikha is at every moment both a teacher and a mother, caught up in being a spiritual guide while simultaneously lamenting, "Eat! Eat! You haven't touched your cake!" This is one of the most endearing elements of the women's mosque. It feels like such a holy place, and at the same time vaguely like an Arab woman's kitchen.

When she sees me she manages to keep everything in her hands and still lean over to kiss me on both of my cheeks. She introduces me to the others. "This is Istifanee, and she will be the new English teacher." They all put their hands on their hearts in a gesture of respect or lean forward to take my hand.

The Sheikha gives me the flimsy green textbooks I will use to teach my class: *The Book of Islam in English*.

"I can't read it," she says, apologizing for the fact that she can't read English. "But can you tell me if the textbook is appropriate?"

I sit down among the dozen other women crowded into her office and flip through the book. My class is designed to help Muslim students already proficient in English talk about their faith. But even for them this text will be a challenge. It is a difficult intermediate text designed to explain Islam in English to non-Muslims considering conversion. The book has clearly been written after September 11 and with feminist critics in mind. Chapters clarify the role of women in Islam, the difference between jihad and terrorism, the role of the family. Over all, it seems a rather liberal text.

It is only then, in flipping through the first chapter again, that I notice a detail I had overlooked. In a section on the most commonly asked questions about Islam, the author of the book poses the hypothetical question, "My friends and family tell me that I can be saved outside of Islam. Is that true?"

The answer given is uncompromising: though our friends and family may balk at a conversion to Islam, on the Day of Judgment, non-Muslims will certainly be sentenced to hellfire.

I become nervous. I know her stance on non-Muslims, but I have experienced that only privately. I take a deep breath. At her desk, the Sheikha is busy writing down the names of the dozens of girls interested in studying English. I stand in front of her hesitantly.

"How is the book?" she asks, still writing down names.

"It's not bad. The topics look interesting: women in Islam, the family, jihad . . ."

"*Ma'shallah,*" she says approvingly.

"There's only one problem . . ."

She raises an eyebrow.

"In the first chapter, it teaches that all non-Muslims will go to hell on the Day of Judgment," I begin, shifting from foot to foot. "I don't think I'll be able to teach that."

She looks at me for a moment, trying to register what I have just told her. I know that she has placed an enormous trust in me by allowing me to be here, that in mosques in many places, non-Muslims are not even permitted inside, much less asked to become teachers. Then, slowly, her lips turn upward. She begins to laugh, softly at first, and then louder and louder, until the women around her can scarcely suppress their giggles.

She stands up with a majestic air and announces to the room, "Listen to this! Stephanie looked at the book on Islam in English, and in the first lesson, it says that non-Muslims are going to hell. And she said she can't teach that, because . . . she's a Christian!"

The room erupts into laughter at her punch line. "Oh, you poor girl!" someone calls out. I manage a shy and awkward smile.

When it quiets down again, the Sheikha turns to me and says softly, "You know I believe that others can go to heaven provided that they follow what is in their own holy books. God is *Rabb al-Alameen*, the Lord of the Worlds, not *Rabb al-Muslimeen*, the God of Muslims."

Cool water is what her voice sometimes sounds like to me. I walk to the other side of the mosque, breathing again, the pile of books in my hands.

At eleven o'clock my students begin filing into the back of my classroom, one after another, each of them approaching me individually and shyly introducing themselves. "*As-Salamu Aleykum*, Peace be upon you, Teacher," they say, half in Arabic, half in English.

"*Wu Aleykum Salaam*, Please don't call me Teacher," I respond. "Call me by my name."

The classroom for Islam in English is not a classroom at all but an empty corner of the women's section on the second floor of the mosque, with windows overlooking the main hall where the men gather to pray. At the beginning of class, the muezzin recites the call to prayer, and the sound empties from the speakers above our heads into the room and onto the streets around the mosque. Some of the students excuse themselves and prostrate in the corner in prayer.

Most of my students are between twelve and twenty years old, and unlike the children with vibrant clothes I saw downstairs, they all wear the exact same white headscarves tucked firmly beneath their chins, the same long tan-colored coats, and skirts that reach down to their ankles. Only their faces are all distinctly different, almost all without makeup, glowing.

From the color of their eyes, I can imagine what they might look like in the privacy of their homes, with their hair unfastened.

We do not have tables or chairs. I sit on a cushion on the floor, my legs crossed, in front of a small wooden table with a Quran placed on the side of it. In front of me, twenty girls sit on the floor in a semicircle, staring at me intently. I ask the girls their names, and then ask them how many of them have memorized the entire Quran. About two-thirds raise their hands. It is incredible, the patience it must take to memorize some five hundred pages of Arabic. I can't even remember my own phone number.

I reach into my bag and hand out sheets entitled "The Five Pillars of Islam," on which I have neatly written the basic principles of the faith in English: the Profession of Faith, prayer five times a day, fasting during Ramadan, paying charity, and the pilgrimage to Mecca for all those who can afford it. We review the material, beginning with the first pillar and moving down the page.

Noor taps on my shoulder. "Teacher? What is the Profession of Faith in English?"

I respond hesitantly, realizing that, technically speaking, to say the words of the *shahadeh* out loud is enough to officially make me a Muslim. "I witness that there is no God but God, and that Mohammed is the messenger of God."

All of the girls begin copying the sentence obediently.

"So *Rasul* means 'messenger' in English?" Noor persists.

"Yes," I say, carefully. "But it is a little more complicated than that. In Arabic, a *Rasul* is a prophet who receives a holy book from God, like Moses and Mohammed. But in English, a messenger can be anyone. The mailman is a messenger. When you're on your computer corresponding with and sending e-mails to your friends, you might use Instant Messenger. And a message can also be anything. It can be a book sent by God, or it can be a note written down by your sister reminding you to return a phone call."

The girls seem uncomfortable, particularly that the mailman carries the same title as the prophet Mohammed in English. I make a mental note not to tell them that New York City can be called a "shopping Mecca."

It is the first of many difficult questions, and I soon realize that I am not as prepared as I had anticipated. I stumble over whether Muslims fast from dawn to dusk or sunrise to sunset and whether they are required to pay a charity or a tax. I can't remember if the Profession of Faith is the name Muslims give to their statement of beliefs or the name Catholics give when they recite the Nicene Creed during Mass. I can't fathom the English names for the prayer positions in Islam, and after one of the students demonstrates all of them we finally settle on *bowing, kneeling,* and *prostrating.* I have spent years studying what Muslims believe, but I have not even grasped the basics of what they *do.*

We arrive at the final pillar, the hajj to Mecca, and Noor asks again what *hajj* means in English.

"It means 'pilgrimage,' " I say, sighing at the gap between the word and its translation. "But again, a pilgrimage can be a journey to any special place, to Rome, to the village where you were born, to visit the grave of a poet you love. To make a pilgrimage is simply to travel with a special purpose in mind." The mystics say that the greatest pilgrimage is into our own heart.

"So there's no special word for the pilgrimage to Mecca?"

"*Hajj,*" I answer. "We just say *hajj.*"

I am tempted to tell them that there is a certain tragedy in translation: the sense of diluting what was once a powerful drink, of tearing a small plant from its roots and trying to place it in a soil and climate where it does not belong. Arabic is so exact, the vocabulary so vast and specific, that each thing takes on its own world of associations, nuances, *suchness.* In English, the concepts of the holy merge so quickly with those of the mundane, the prophets with the postmen, the pilgrims making a journey to Mecca with the passengers on the *Mayflower.* There is a sacred space in the Arabic language where only the holy can live.

Wa'fa, a shy, soft-spoken girl in her early twenties with a quiet round face and pale green eyes, asks me, "What does it mean, *to have faith*?"

It takes me aback. "I suppose," I say, "it means to believe in something that you don't see." Then I reconsider for a moment. To have faith is not the same as believing in ghosts.

"Why don't you make some sentences, beginning with 'I have faith'?" I suggest to them.

The girls nod.

"I have faith that God created the sky."

"I have faith that the Quran is the word of God."

"I have faith that on the last day, God will ask what I have done right and what I have done wrong and will judge me with justice."

"I have faith that beside me there are two angels, one on my left shoulder and one on my right shoulder."

I look at them, answering me so earnestly. I have no business, really, knowing these intimacies. I will not tell them mine. That this question— What is faith?—is the raft I have spent my whole year clinging to in the midst of rough waters.

I look up again. Some of my students are taking notes, others glancing at the clock. The hour has passed without my noticing it. I fold up my notebook, and as the girls prepare to leave, I have a thought and hold the class for a minute longer.

"In English, we often use the expression 'have faith.' If ever any situation seems hopeless, without a way to escape, you might hear someone say to another, 'Have faith. Things will only get better.' "

There is a look of recognition on their faces, and we smile at one another. *Have faith*, they all say softly. I watch them as they leave the class, repeating the phrase over and over to themselves: *Have faith. Have faith.*

16.

July

A WEEK LATER, Frédéric knocks on my front door, and my summer balanced between a monk and a mosque begins. He has slung a battered green backpack full of notebooks over his shoulder and tucked his cross into his shirt, so that I sense immediately that he is a monk incognito, that for the next thirty days he wants simply to live like everyone else. He waves from the window and I grin at his loose hair and normal clothes and the funny, laid-back, and unmonastic way he is suddenly carrying himself, so much less transcendent that he could almost be wearing beach sandals. I have been waiting for this knock on the window for days, for the morning when I would open my door to him as though it were the most ordinary gesture in the world.

"Do you want to grab something to eat?" I ask casually after he kisses my cheeks hello, celebrating in my heart as I utter those words. They are so normal. They are the kinds of things ordinary people in love ask each other.

He grins. Then we set off to grab a sandwich at the Armenian restaurant around the corner, because they give me a discount after all, and the food is clean.

"You're the Baron's girl, aren't you?" the man behind the counter asks.

"That's right."

"That's what I thought. You give him my greetings." Then he hands me a substantial wad of change for being a member of his clan, and I wink at Frédéric as we walk away.

Despite the fact that Frédéric knows Damascus, I am determined to be his guide through *my* version of the city, the life I discovered after my post-Ignatius descent into despair. I lead him to the stall where Ahmed sells his famous sweets, informing Frédéric that he is partaking in the famous *knafeh Nablusi*, the finest *knafeh* in the world, and that this shop is hallowed ground. I introduce him to the neighborhood coffee shops, the florist who descends from a family of florists and insists that he has "flowers in his blood," the Kurdish juice vendors and Shiite pizza vendors and furniture seller who speaks Aramaic, the language of Jesus. As I walk up and down the streets, I narrate to him the gossip of everyone's lives, and we duck into all of the churches and chapels dotting the streets to light candles, while just nearby is the house of a famous neighborhood saint who has oil flowing from her hands.

"I thought I was coming to Damascus to study Arabic," he teases me. "I wasn't expecting an intensive English course."

When the day is over, we say good-bye in the crowded streets, and he tells me the second sentence I have been dreaming of hearing: "I'll see you tomorrow," he says.

It takes a while for Frédéric to get used to life in the city. He wakes up in his room across town with the Little Brothers of Jesus, fills his blue glasses, and reads for an hour from the Quran. Then he catches a bus to the French Institute, to sit through several hours of lessons in Arabic. The first day, he arrives to meet me almost in tears.

"It's so violent," he says softly. "They just talk at you, and you don't have a chance to speak."

I hadn't considered the shock of classes after the silence of his life in the desert, this sudden immersion into noise and rote learning. The first time I took an Arabic immersion course, I woke up in the middle of the night from a nightmare of Arabic letters raining down on my face, penetrating it like bullets from a machine gun. It must be even more difficult for Frédéric, who has become truly otherworldly in his monastic life. He doesn't know how much cabs should cost or whom to ask for directions. He is scandalized when merchants try to cheat him—he hasn't been in a world of bargaining for three years, and as a monk he doesn't even handle his own money. I can see him reacting to car horns and arguments, he who has spent the last years in a world where people tend to be on their best behavior.

"Just be patient," I promise him. "It will be easier in a few days."

Sure enough, by the end of the week we are sitting in a café where he is smoking cigarettes and drinking coffee, and he is beaming, having just devised a new system for memorizing Arabic words. He calls it "mapping Arabic," and it is the most complicated form of memorization I have ever seen. He writes each Arabic word on the center of a card in black ink, and then he sketches a map of all of the places it has ever traveled, the words it has been in its past lives, all of its roots and relatives.

He shows me a note card covered with islands of green translations floating around a single black Arabic word. "Look. Here is the word *gaib*, which means 'hidden,' concealed. But it is also related to the words for absence, invisibility, and mystery." He points to the word *gaibi*, another cousin, showing me how he has written the word *secret* in French beneath it in green ink, anchoring it. He'll be okay in the world. In whatever bizarre and unique way he has to chart his travels, he'll learn to make sense of this place.

"Stéphanie?" he says suddenly. "I forgot to tell you. This morning when I was on the bus, I finally understood what everyone was saying when they want to get off. *Al-yamin!* To the right!" He chuckles. Really, it doesn't make any sense, this phrase. "It was so great. When I wanted to get off I just stood there with everyone else and I called, *Al-yamin!*"

"Did it work?"

"Of course it worked. And then when I was walking to class, I saw a boy on his bike, and instead of calling out and asking people to move in the street, he rang his bell and called, *Habibi! Habibi! Habibi!* My love! My love! My love!"

I can't help smiling. Then we pay our bill and I take him to the mosque for the evening, so that he can watch the children glowing like angels.

17.

MY STUDENTS AT THE QURANIC SCHOOL keep me from going completely insane, my classes an unexpected dose of normality in the midst of an otherwise confusing summer. My students have become almost like girlfriends, and our classes in the mosque are, to some extent, simply an exalted form of girl talk. There is Noor, the wisecracking, exuberant daughter of the Sheikha, and Ahlam, a twenty-year-old and one of thirteen children, who often defiantly wears tight long-sleeved T-shirts to the mosque and attends both English school and classes at the Department of Islamic Law at the university. Last week, she took me to eat ice cream after class and asked, "You know that my father has two wives, don't you? That's weird, isn't it?" When I asked her why she wasn't married yet, she mentioned that her mother and aunts had been parading a steady stream of suitors through her house, but that she had rejected them all out of hand.

"I'm just waiting for the right man to come along," she said, shrugging, before digging into her second scoop of pistachio ice cream.

There is Khadija, an extremely traditional Muslim in her thirties with severe eyebrows and dark features who has also never married, and who made a decision to devote the rest of her life almost exclusively to the study of Islam. While the girls all wear identical white headscarves, she always wears a navy headscarf and a matching coat to class, the habitual black sheep.

I thought nothing of Khadija's conservative streak until she invited me to her house one day, and she greeted me without a headscarf, her long, glossy hair falling down her back, wearing a floral shirt and blush on her cheeks. I was shocked.

"You're beautiful, Khadija," I told her. "Why don't you wear a lighter headscarf when you come to the mosque?"

She just laughed. "You have no idea! I used to wear a black headscarf and a cloth that covered my entire face. Now I wear a navy blue headscarf. *Shwayy, shwayy*, Slowly, slowly, Stephanie! Can you imagine if I just moved from having my face covered to wearing a white headscarf? It would be a scandal!"

There are Hiba and Ismaa, teenagers and members of a prominent Syrian family of Muslim reformers, anxious to learn English so they can become doctors and engineers. There is Zeineb, a young girl from the Emirates with exotic good looks who speaks English with a perfect American accent. Finally there is Wa'fa, my lovely newlywed with her round cheeks, who admitted to me that she sneaks off to the American Cultural Center whenever she can to watch Hollywood movies.

Together, they have put to rest every image I ever had of life in an Islamic madrassa. They eat chocolate bars between classes, want to be astronauts when they grow up, and know more about Islam than almost any man I have ever met. I thought that I was sent to the mosque to teach them English, but I've found myself learning far more from them than I could ever teach them in the few English phrases that I manage to impart.

For example, last week we had a class discussing the headscarf. Now I must admit that in the last several months I have grown rather attached to the headscarf. I've bought dozens, pink scarves and blue scarves, striped scarves and silk scarves. I am a sight to behold during our classes, with all of my students lined up in their perfectly tied white headscarves while I alone have one in very bright pink. I have discovered the headscarf as a fashion statement.

So much of life in the Middle East consists of reading between the lines, and I'm learning that you can tell a great deal about a girl by how she wears her headscarf. There are traditional, conservative girls (or in some cases, those with very conservative husbands) who completely cover their faces with a black cloth, not even leaving room for their eyes. There are women who wear the *niqab*, a veil worn over the face but with a space left open for the eyes, so that sometimes a pair of stunning blue or green pools will stare out hauntingly in the streets. There is the traditional white or navy blue scarf, worn often by my students, tied firmly under the chin so that every inch of the neck is covered. But then there are pinks and blues, scarves with glittering threads or even sequins, scarves wrapped around the top of the head instead of tied on the bottom, pinned or unpinned. There are sheer scarves that show the hair beneath.

I have always been curious about this matter of the headscarf, the perpetual symbol of "Islamic repression" in the American media, and so last week I sat with my girls in a circle on the floor and asked them why it is so important to them.

Nisreen, a lovely, shy woman with a narrow face and almond-shaped eyes, announced quietly, "People think that we don't like wearing the headscarf, but we like it. It makes us feel safe. For example, it keeps us from being assassinated."

I had to stop myself from laughing. "Are you sure that you mean 'assassinated'?" I pictured a Muslim superhero sporting a magical, bullet-proof hijab.

"No, no, no, she means being kidnapped," Ismaa corrected.

"How does wearing a hijab possibly protect you from being kidnapped?"

"Well, if there is someone and he wants to do something bad, and he sees that you are wearing a headscarf, then he knows that you are on the straight path and he won't harm you."

This time I couldn't help but smile. "If some crazy person wants to harm you, I don't think a headscarf will stop him. I don't think that's a very good reason to wear the hijab." I thought for a moment that this was a very Syrian answer—for in America wearing a headscarf after September 11 was probably more likely to put a girl at risk for ridicule and harm.

Then Ahlam suggested, "It's hot here and it protects your head from the X-rays of the sun."

Hmm. Another reason I hadn't considered.

Ismaa said, "I think my religion is beautiful, and I'm proud to be a Muslim. I want people to know that I'm a Muslim when they see me."

I was relieved to finally receive a coherent answer. "Now that seems like a logical reason to wear the hijab." The others nodded.

Noor added, "The Quran tells me to wear the hijab, and I want to obey God. All of these other reasons, such as protection from the sun and feeling safe, these are extras. But we don't need any reason other than doing what God requires." She paused for a moment before explaining, "Women are very expensive, very precious in Islam. A woman is not something simply to be seen by everyone. She should be protected and seen only by very special individuals."

I remember the story of Mary in the Quran, which said that when she removed herself to a place in the East, she had placed a screen, a *hijab*, between herself and the rest of the world. I am slowly getting used to this extended, intimate world of Muslim women in Syria, so that each time I slip past the curtain of the front door of the mosque, I have the sense that I am entering somewhere precious.

My girls don't ask me to change. They watch me cross over from being someone who wears the headscarf in the mosque to the person I am out there in the world. Every day after class, some of the girls walk with me from the mosque out into the street, and they are there beside me as I shyly pull down the scarf from around my head to reveal my long brown hair tumbling from beneath.

18.

SPEAKING OF FASHION, yesterday morning, when I was walking down the streets of the Islamic Quarter, a woman passed me wearing a floral skirt that stopped just above her knees, the hemline lifting slightly in the breeze. The sleeves of her lime green shirt ended just after the shoulders, and her two small feet were balancing in open-toed sandals with heels. I just stood there watching her, a tropical bird alighting on the sidewalk, amazed that a woman in a short skirt in Damascus was not bringing about the Second Coming. I looked at her and I decided, *I want to be myself again.*

It has been such a long time since I woke up in the morning and asked, *What do I want to wear today?* My wardrobe doesn't include what I want to wear. My closet is stuffed with turtlenecks and long skirts, polyester mosque pants and dozens of scarves, every outfit intended to hide my body. I think that Frédéric has probably seen my elbows a handful of times, and frankly I'm tired of it. I want Frédéric to know someone other than the girl who prays in the monastery and teaches in the mosque. It is perhaps time to stop dressing like a pre–Vatican II nun and to try my hand at looking beautiful.

I spent yesterday afternoon completely overhauling my Damascus wardrobe, pulling the light, airy dress I had brought from Boston from the back of my closet up to the front. I went shopping at a handful of boutique stores for short, filmy skirts and dresses and slid a sheer layer of lipstick over my mouth. I made an appointment at the hair salon for the first time all year, allowing the *coiffeur*, as their sign proclaims, to layer my hair to rest on my shoulders. So that today, when I approach Frédéric in the conservative, mostly male coffee shop where we often meet, I am wearing a bright pink tank top, a midlength skirt covered with flowers, and a pair of pink open-toed sandals, and the whole room is watching me.

His cheeks flush red. "Well, look at you. You're my pink American."

"I do believe you're blushing," I tease him.

"Me?" He keeps looking at me, blushing, then glancing nervously at his cup of coffee. "Umm, could you please sit down?"

The fact is, this *also* isn't me. I have never worn pink in my life. Academics don't wear pink. Yet I want to wear it now, for the fact that I love pink is like the fact that I love bad romantic comedies—a dark secret I have kept hidden in my scholarly life. Now when we walk the streets together, my arms bare and hair loose on my shoulders, he is no longer a novice monk and I am no longer trying to be invisible. We are two lovers, navigating the narrow streets together, our hands briefly touching as he guides me through traffic or passes me his blue glass prayer beads, our steps easily falling in line with one another, until my heart filters out all of the noise and car horns and I can only hear birds and church bells and the wind blowing.

"Will you sing to me?" I ask him. "Something nonmonastic for a change?"

He nods and then sings softly:

Quand il me prend dans ses bras
Il me parle tout bas
Je vois la vie en rose

Il me dit des mots d'amour
De mots de tous les jours
Et ça me fait quelque chose . . .

"One day I'll teach you to speak French," he promises, "entirely
through the songs of Edith Piaf." We walk the streets, my skirt blowing in
the wind and Frédéric still singing beside me, and I am falling in love with
him and Damascus all at once, with this crumbling city with its old men
smoking *nargileh* and laughing shopkeepers, with its Virgin Mary statues
and hands of Fatima hanging from windshields, its carts of roasted nuts,
its pigeons released at night, its tea vendors carrying trays and taxi drivers
calling out, *Amman! Amman! Amman! Homs! Homs! Homs! Beirut! Beirut!*
Beirut! Beirut! I am falling in love with the Military Museum, displaying
jets and cannons outside that hardly look like they could harm a dog, the
booksellers with their Islamic books and the cookbook of the Prophet,
the music vendors blasting Egyptian pop into the streets. I even love the
posters of the president.

I love the way the edge of Frédéric's mouth turns up when he smiles.

We walk together, brushing against each other until the sun begins
to set, and we find ourselves facing each other at the curbside on Nasser
Road. I also love this curbside, seemingly no different from any other
curbside, with its crowds of pedestrians and single policeman stationed,
motionless, in his perch. We call it *the place where we kiss*, because like old
French friends Frédéric kisses my two cheeks good-bye before he enters
the crowded white minibus that ferries him home each evening. Every
night we hold that kiss on the cheek slightly longer, until one of us
blushes and pulls away.

"Did you ever manage to get the buckle on my belt fixed?" he asks.

I laugh. "Of course not." Just now giving his belt back is the last thing
on my mind.

"I see. So you plan on just taking away my chastity, I mean my monastic belt?"

I cough. "It's not my fault you were allergic to it, is it?"

I lean toward him, and he kisses my cheek good-bye on the curb of
the place where we kiss, and I find the courage to put my arms just barely
around him, on what might be the single most beautiful day of my life.

The Bread of Angels

19.

I RETURN HOME TO THE HOUSE off Straight Street beaming with that peculiar, utterly transparent glow of a woman in love, still adorned in my pink clothes. The Baron, who had seen me come home from the mosque and change from an entirely black outfit to a pink floral one, is now keeping vigil in his torn-up plastic lawn chair, waiting for me at the door to his room. A cigarette is dangling from his mouth, and he has the stern, somewhat tired look of a father who is waiting up for a daughter who has stayed out past curfew. He motions me over to join him.

The Baron has never been one to mince words. "So, Stefanito, did you see the padre today?" he asks.

"Yes." I look guiltily at the floor, and he gets up and gestures to the sofa, where I take my traditional seat on a cushion with half of the stuffing falling out. He pours himself a glass of whiskey.

"You know, he's in love with you," he tells me. "Why else would he see you every single day?"

I shake my head. "It's not true. He's a novice in a monastery."

"*Shoo*, Grandfather, are you blind? Where is he from again, Spain?"

"No, he's from France."

"All right then. So he must have had his heart broken by a French-woman and so gone to live in a monastery in the desert. Why isn't he in a monastery in France?"

"He likes Syria. He's touched by the monasticism of the desert."

He snorts. "Don't kid yourself. Have you tasted French wine? And the cheese! A monk in France can eat like a king. Like a king, do you understand me?" He shakes his head again. "Like *un roi*."

He rises from his chair, in full force now. "*Yalla*, Stefanito. Talk to him. Promise me. He's dressed up like a monk but he's just a man. Do you think he can resist a beautiful woman?"

I stare down at the ground. "I'm not going to talk to him."

"Listen, suit yourself. But these are the best years of your life. If I was forty years younger, I would marry you myself."

Who knows? At this point it might just come to that. I throw up my hands in frustration. "What do you expect me to do, Grandpa?"

"It's easy." He puts his two arms out, pretending to hold an imaginary partner. "You hold him like this." He squeezes his arms tightly against himself, embracing his own chest and rocking back and forth. "Then kiss him." He smacks kisses in the air. "Say, *Ya* Padre, I love you!"

I groan. He is still kissing the air when I duck out of that room as fast as I can. If only life were as easy as the Baron's imaginary, soap-opera-conditioned life. Frédéric has made it fairly clear that I don't have a say in the matter. He is waiting for a sign from God that will tell him which path he is meant to take. Though personally I am of the opinion that the magical concept called free will means we can't lay the burden on God entirely, I cannot choose for Frédéric, and in my heart I don't want to guide him away from the life he already lives. The world needs those who have the courage to speak on our behalf, to carry us when we do not have the strength to carry ourselves. My world is so much lighter knowing that monks and nuns exist, that they are praying for us, that in some unknown way they are participating in holding the world in place.

Then there is the other, more ordinary reason I can't choose. I want Frédéric to choose me all on his own. I want to believe that love is like any other calling. You receive it, and if you have to, you leave everything and go.

The end of july approaches, and still Frédéric shows no sign of making a choice. Instead he prepares to return to the monastery and resume his life as a novice in the desert. I can't comprehend that a man who has lived beside me for a month can suddenly be gone, that I will be exiled from a country that until recently I had not even known existed. I have forgotten, even, that he is a monk. I can't imagine him simply slipping back into that life, awakening in the morning and sliding on his gray monk's robes, bowing three times to lead prayer in the chapel.

At the beginning of Frédéric's last week in Damascus, I sit down to write the last set of Quranic readings I will ever give him:

Dear Frédéric,

According to Muslim scholars, the hoopoe bird had the special ability to discover water beneath the sands of the desert for Solomon and his army to drink.

It was this water in the desert that he was flying in search of when he went beyond the borders of knowledge and instead discovered a woman. And he returned to Solomon, waiting and thirsty in the desert, and said, I have crossed territory you have not crossed.

Maybe the story is not only about love, but about the answer to a thirst. And about what we really need to stay alive.

These next Quran readings are, I think, about being at the border between two realities, between night and day. Or perhaps they are more like those moments when the sun has not gone down and yet the moon is already visible, and we seem to be alive in two worlds at once.

Carry them with you this last week in Damascus, in this time you live in two worlds at once, the desert monastery of the heart and the green monastery of the world, and you feel so small in their midst.

Maybe the soul is a bird in the Quran because he is not limited by the earth, he doesn't have to choose between worlds. He can keep traveling between them. And so instead of sacrificing one world for the other, he learns to contain them both.

Love,
Stephanie

We spend our last five days walking the streets, drinking lemonade with mint and eating handmade ice cream covered with pistachios, visiting our favorite alleys. The night before he leaves Damascus, I close the windows and the door to my room, a scandalous act for a girl with a man alone, much less with a novice monk. I don't care. There is something I need to say to him.

"Frédéric, I was thinking—maybe we could just get married."

He stares at me. Even I am surprised that I have uttered the words aloud.

"I mean, I just thought that I could say it."

He doesn't answer. He just quietly takes my hand.

He takes my hand, and for a few moments we are alone in the world. We are somewhere above it, even. I rest my head against his chest.

Then I walk him one last time to the place where we kiss, and we say good-bye. By the time I look back through the swelling crowds of people, he is gone.

20.

August

I TRY THROWING MYSELF back into my daily life, resuming my visits with Mohammed and my coffee with the Baron, spending extra time each day planning my English lessons for the mosque. Yet everything that was easy when Frédéric was here now feels like an effort. Today I walked alone in the empty, hidden streets, searching for the Damascus I had known at his side, the alleys with their wooden awnings and tumbling vines in bloom, the boys with their bicycle bells, and the canaries, singing in their cages. I couldn't see anything on my own. Instead I found a city of heat and noise and political turmoil.

I miss the city that I lived in when he was here.

Yet once again, the girls at the mosque call me back to earth. Today in the middle of a vocabulary lesson, Ahlam leaned over and handed me a small folded-up piece up paper.

What happened to you? she had written in her childish, awkward English scrawl. *Are you okay?* Then Hiba sat beside me and gently unfastened my crooked headscarf and tied it again, winding it around my face, taking in every loose hair, and then fastening it neatly at my chin, as if this one gesture could hold the world in place.

For the rest of the lesson, we discussed a single question: What is jihad? The girls sat around me with their lovely round faces and gave me sample sentences for this word we so often misunderstand, which can mean "holy war" but which more often means "to struggle," "to wrestle," in the world or within ourselves.

"It's a jihad to come and study English," Ismaa said. "Being at home and sleeping, watching television, just about anything is easier than coming to the mosque to study."

I tried to appreciate the comment.

"Coming to the mosque at all is a jihad," Hiba said. "It's hot, and there's traffic, and we have to wear the headscarf when we leave the house."

Ahlam, in her typical teenage way, added, "Not taking what we desire is a jihad. For example, I often want to buy tight pants, and then I have to remind myself that this isn't allowed and so I shouldn't do it." All of the girls nodded in agreement.

Noor added, "For me, being kind to people is the greatest jihad. Sometimes I'm tired and it's hot and I don't really like that person and I don't have the patience to be kind, but I have to. I really struggle with this."

I thought about Frédéric, waiting in the mountain for God to speak to him, to tell him what his life, and mine, might become. That morning I had received a letter:

> Last night, I dreamed that I was in France and my life had two possibilities. The first was to go to the city of Nantes, and the other to Marseilles. Nantes is the big harbor on the Atlantic, where I was dreaming of America when I was young. Marseilles is the harbor on the Mediterranean Sea, facing the Arabic world. And I was saying, I need to choose soon, not in one year, but soon . . .

"Sometimes," I said, "the greatest jihad is just to wait."

21.

I LET MORE THAN A WEEK pass before I visited Frédéric at the monastery, and even then I could only allow myself to stay for a day. It was a shock. I climbed the long flight of steps, expecting him to be standing at the summit with a glass of tea in his hands. But he wasn't waiting. I saw him in the courtyard later, greeting guests in his gray cassock, and in the chapel, prostrating to the floor, his head touching the ground. I couldn't recognize him anymore.

Christ put on the body, they say of the Incarnation. Now I understood. How it was possible to slip, so quickly, into another and completely different life.

I arrived on Friday evening for Mass and dinner, and in that time we barely spoke at all. When he went to bed he waved to the visitors and disappeared without even looking at me, without so much as saying good night. What had become of the man I loved who leaned toward me on the curbside of the place where we kiss?

The next morning, we took a walk together through the desert, Frédéric leading the way to Madeleine, and we sat side by side in his quiet hermitage in the desert. I sat far away from him, afraid and also ashamed at myself for having been so naïve.

"Who are you?" I asked. "I don't even know you anymore."

"I'm still a monk, Stéphanie. Until I make a choice about my life, you have to let me assume this one."

"You didn't even look at me when you said good night last night."

He brushed my hand. "You know that I wasn't looking at you with my eyes. But that entire good-bye was for you. There's not a single moment when I'm not thinking of you."

I wanted to believe him, and at the same time I could only believe what I saw.

"I love you." Despite all of our time together, these were words we had almost never said aloud, as if expressing them was betraying a contract of silence made between us both. But I no longer had the energy to stay silent.

"I love you too, Stéphanie," he said. "But I love my monastic life also. I'm not rejecting one life I don't care about so that I can choose a life that I love. Now I have to choose between love and love."

"Choose quickly, Frédéric. In three weeks, I'm leaving Syria."

We sat together, holding hands, Frédéric in his monastic robes and me in my ordinary clothes.

"I've run out of Quran readings," he said finally, as I was getting up to leave. "I wonder if you could send me some more."

"I can't, Frédéric," I told him. "You have to find your own way now."

22.

THE NEXT NIGHT Frédéric traveled with Paolo to the nearby village of Nebek to visit local families, and they finally made their way back to the monastery in the dark. They walked side by side up the steps from the valley beneath the enormous and deep black sky. As they climbed, Frédéric confessed that he had fallen in love, as he had never loved another woman in his life. He said my name. I can only imagine what happened in Paolo's heart, to hear our two names mentioned together, I, who he still thought might one day become a nun, and Frédéric, his beloved novice monk.

I had been dreading that moment for months, for the last thing Frédéric or I wanted was to wound the man who had given us both so much. For an abbot, losing a novice can feel much like losing a child. An abbot spends his life passing on all that he knows to his monks, watching over them, teaching them and learning from them in what becomes a monastic family. It is an intimate life, the life of a few people living together in a home in the desert. Yet the vow of poverty rules, even in this. One can only love by allowing those he loves to be free.

Frédéric told him that we had fallen in love while reading the Quran together. "You will become a Muslim then?" Paolo asked.

"No, Abuna, I will remain a Christian."

"Take your time with this decision," he said. "Don't hurry. Take a journey to India and make your decision there."

So it was decided that Frédéric would wait and make the decision about what path his life would take during two months' traveling in India and Nepal in September and October, far away from any pulls and pressures of Syria. Then they walked the remaining two hundred stairs in silence.

23.

IT IS MY LAST DAY teaching in the Quranic school for girls. This morning as I fastened my headscarf outside the mosque, I surprised myself by how effortlessly I managed it, winding the blue striped scarf around my head and wrapping it tightly beneath my chin, my face framed inside it. I smiled at that final, veiled reflection staring back at me from the car window. I'll miss this version of myself.

I'll also miss my students, more than they will ever understand. I have loved the privilege of giving them words, in the same way I have received so many this year from neighbors and teachers, each new word giving me a sense of power, of belonging. *Only say the word and I shall be healed*, the prayer says. I taught my students the names of things and collected the looks of radiant surprise that sometimes crossed their faces when they learned how a word translates into my language. I taught them *sacred*, *spiritual*, *existence*. It felt like holding clear pieces of glass up to the light.

I also taught them terrible words, words I never wanted to teach anyone, because that is what is required in telling the truth. I taught them *terror*. I listened to them forming sample sentences using the word *suffering*. I taught them *extremism*. Still, I also loved the quiet miracle of receiving my own words back from them, washed clean and made new. Such as the day when I taught them the word *incarnation*, so that they could explain, if anyone asked them, that Muslims do not believe in the Incarnation. Yet when I asked for sample sentences, Wa'fa, with her shy, chubby face, blushed and said to the class, "The magnificence of God is *incarnate* in all of his creatures." She looked at me with a face full of hope. "Is that right?" she asked.

I nearly cried. "Yes, that's right," I told her. "That's just perfect."

TODAY, MY STUDENTS HAVE ASKED ME to teach them something about Christianity. I have always been rather private about the subject of my own faith, and it was Noor, the Sheikha's daughter, who initiated the discussion. "You've spent two months learning from us about Islam," she said. "It's only fair that we should be able to learn something about what you believe."

So here we are, me with my new, handwritten worksheets, after receiving permission from the Sheikha herself to give a few words about Christianity in this mosque in the Islamic Quarter of Damascus. There is a light coming in through the windows of the upper story, and a wind. We can't get the windows to close, so the breeze keeps blowing in on our faces. We all sit close to one another on the floor, and I teach them the words I have known since childhood, but which most of them have never heard before in any language: *Old Testament*, *New Testament*, *parable*, *baptism*, *manger*, *Mass*, *Eucharist*.

Then I tell them the story of the birth of Jesus as I had known it all of my life, of the angel Gabriel appearing to Mary alone, telling her that she will conceive a child. I detail the long and arduous journey of Mary and Joseph to Bethlehem.

"Joseph?" Ismaa calls out, astonished. "You mean that Mary is *married*?"

I laugh, recalling my own astonishment at discovering the lonely, contemplative Mary of the Quran. "Yes, Mary is married. But we still call her the Virgin Mary, just like you do."

"But that doesn't make sense," Noor pushes. "So you're telling me that no one knew that Mary was giving birth to a miracle except for her husband?"

That had never occurred to me. "In the beginning no one knows, but then I suppose the angels begin telling people." This explanation sounds flimsy to me, but they all accept it as perfectly reasonable. Angels do funny things sometimes.

I teach them about John the Baptist, whom they believe in as the prophet Yahya in the Quran, and about some of the more touching moments of Jesus' ministry, such as when a frail and impossibly kind Christ commands us in the Gospel of Luke, "Love your enemies, do good to those who hate you, bless those who curse you, pray for those who mistreat you. If someone strikes you on one cheek, turn to him the other also. If someone takes your cloak, do not stop him from taking your tunic. Give to everyone who asks you, and if anyone takes what belongs to you, do not demand it back. Do to others as you would have them do to you."

It's lovely, they tell me.

Then I lean forward, and I teach them the parable of the lost sheep. They gather around me like children listening to a bedtime story. I begin to read aloud:

"The Son of Man came to save what was lost. What do you think? If a man owns a hundred sheep, and one of them wanders away, will he not leave the ninety-nine on the hills and go to look for the one that wandered off?"

"Of course not!" they all call out in unison.

I burst into laughter. "The answer is yes! Of course he will go and find the lost sheep."

"Well that doesn't seem very fair to the other ninety-nine sheep," Noor comments. "What's going to happen to them while he's going to look for that one sheep? Then they'll all wander off and get lost also. And then he'll really be in trouble."

"Maybe he'll take all the other sheep with him while he goes searching," Khadija suggests, and everyone considers this for a moment before nodding. This seems a clever solution to the problem of leaving all of one's sheep behind.

I am at a loss, so I simply continue reading.

"And if he finds it, I tell you the truth, he is happier about that one sheep than the ninety-nine that did not wander off. In the same way, your father in heaven is not willing that any of these little ones should be lost."

"*Ma'shallah*, it's beautiful!" they all exclaim. Some of them start clapping.

Wa'fa looks perplexed for a moment. Then gradually her face lights up: "We have this! We have this same story in Islam! The prophet Mohammed, peace be upon him, said, 'Allah is more pleased with the repentance of His servant than a person who has his camel in a waterless desert carrying his provision of food and drink and it is lost. He, having lost all hopes of getting it back, lies down in the shade and is disappointed about his camel, when all of a sudden he finds that camel standing before him.' "

"It's the same!" I say, laughing. Though I must admit that I might even prefer the Muslim parable, for on first hearing, losing a single sheep sounds minimal compared to losing a camel carrying everything that you need to survive. All I know for certain is that they are both stories about what it means to be lost and to be found again for no good reason that we can understand. I suppose that it doesn't matter if our camel has abandoned us, or if we are the one who has walked away. We are found in the end.

I say good-bye to my students, one by one. They write down their addresses and ask me to keep in touch, kissing me on my cheeks. Khadija hands me a set of prayer beads from Mecca that she had blessed on the Kaaba stone, the holiest place in the world for Muslims.

"I can't accept these," I tell her.

"Please," she says. "You'll remember me whenever you use them to pray."

On the way out, I say good-bye to the Sheikha. During our last lesson in her house, she had given me a gold ring, adorned with precious stones, as a parting present. Now I shyly hold my hand out to her to show her that I'm wearing it. It looks like a wedding ring. "Don't stay away from us too long," she insists and folds me in her arms to hug me good-bye.

Then I walk down the staircase of the mosque. Most of the shoes have been removed, slipped back onto the feet of their owners, so that now I pass only a few scattered pairs—dark black flats on the highest level, pink slip-on shoes in the center, and then the tiny white tennis shoes of children scattered on the bottom floor. Noor walks me to the front door.

"Stephanie?" she says. I smile down at her, already a woman at sixteen, and still so innocent. "You know, it is not important to me what you believe. To me, it is important how you live."

I stand at the doorway to the mosque for a moment, part of me wanting to go back again and keep my girls in that room forever, to protect them from whatever might be coming to them, to their country, to hold them back from all of the frustrations of growing up. I want to protect them, but at the same time I want them to go. They are going already. I have only caught them for a moment, between places.

Have faith, I whisper to them silently. Then I leave the mosque, remove my headscarf one last time, and disappear into the busy streets of Damascus, on my way home.

24.

Dear Frédéric,

Today you asked me again if I really want to marry you, if I dream of this.

I thought then that maybe it was time to tell you what I dream of.

I dream that I could steal you away for a while, so that you could see me as I truly am. Not someone deep in prayer, or walking in the mountains, or meditating in a mosque. But messy, imperfect me.

I love bad, bad romantic movies, and playing basketball, and drinking Guinness, and climbing mountains, and dancing. I love being in love. I love short skirts, and good cheese, and the symphony, and Chagall, and Rodin, and the way Cézanne makes fruit look more real in a painting than in real life.

I love hearing jazz music live, I love the smell of old books, I love the wings of angels in churches, and the scent of bread in the morning, and strawberries, and Roman cities, and the sea. I love hearing poetry out loud, and the sound of rivers, and the color of leaves changing, and the hands of children. And I love you, but not in the way that you imagine. I love you playing "Blackbird" in meditation, and your swollen, bee-stung hands, your breath, your laughter, your deep and salty tears, the way you fall in love with alleys and read the hearts of those you barely know.

Sometimes I wonder what would happen if you could touch me, if you could hold me, and then you would see that your hands don't go through me, that I am just a girl. And that I'm not ashamed of this—this is really who I am.

Do you know what I dream of? I dream that one day we might wake up and not read the Quran together, but read poetry together. Go to the symphony instead of the church. I dream of sitting by the sea and drinking wine and eating chocolate and laughing.

I know that this is too much for you. But I don't want you to think that I'm a lie. You see part of me that no one else sees. But there is a part of me that you've never been able to see. I wonder if you'll be able to love all of me. I guess that is my dream—that you'll love all of me, the me that doesn't always go to church and who struggles with Jesus, who eats too much sugar and never washes the dishes. Because I don't want to have to change in order to be good enough for you. I want to know that if I no longer studied theology and instead became a poet, that you would still love me. I guess I am asking you to see my mystery, because I don't feel that anyone has ever seen it before, no one has ever had the eyes to understand all of me.

Do you know what I dream of? I dream of being with you in a room, far away, in the dark, where no one can reach us. And I dream of holding you and being held by you—not to make love, but to hold on to your being, not the dream of you. To hold on to the reality of you. Every day I dream of this, of feeling your bone and skin and hair and eyes and breath, of touching your humanity.

I dream of reading the newspaper and eating cereal and making mistakes with you. I want to simply be human with you. And for that to be enough.

Love,
Stephanie

The Bread of Angels

25.

September

MY BAGS ARE PACKED, zipped shut and waiting next to the double
doors of my room, vacant as I found it almost exactly one year ago, those
two arched windows opened to the sky and the high spearmint wooden
beams crossing the ceiling in the most beautiful room in Bab Touma.
Soon it will be six thirty, and the two lovebirds will appear from somewhere over the rooftop and settle in the ancient citrus tree, just above our
rooms, to rest.

It is my last day in Damascus. Is it wrong that I have said good-bye to
almost no one in my neighborhood? I traveled to the monastery to thank
Paolo and Dima, but when the time came to say farewell to Straight Street
I couldn't find the courage. I considered it. I planned on spending an
entire afternoon walking from shopkeeper to shopkeeper with my
camera, snapping photographs and taking my formal leave of
Mohammed the carpet seller, eating my last slices of *knaffeh* from Nablus,
sitting down to endless cups of coffee and gifts. I know that I may never
be back here again, and that war might come at any time. Still, I would
rather just disappear, keeping everything exactly as it has always been.
I need to believe that I can return here, in three years or thirty years, and
somehow slide effortlessly into the rhythm of life. The Tin Man will call
out, "How is your *sikkine*?" The Hezbollah pizza vendor will exclaim,
"Where have you been? We've had the tea on, waiting for you all day!" The
rest of the shopkeepers will simply lean out of their front doors and wave,
calling out one after another, *Al-hamdulillah al-salaami*, Thank God that
you returned in peace! And the Baron will be waiting in his green track
shorts at the door, glancing at his watch and asking just what took me
so long.

Last night, I dreamed that the monastery descended and became part
of the world. It unfastened itself slowly from its perch up in heaven and
then lightly, lightly fell down, blending into the cars lined up in traffic
on Straight Street, the unfinished buildings, the men shining shoes and
hawking cantaloupe from rusty carts. For a moment, everything took on
a quality of the ethereal, two worlds collapsed into one. When I awakened

in the morning, I could not shake myself from the dream, so that I still saw a gleaming beneath my crumbling walls and dust-stained curtains, and for a few moments I lived in two worlds at once.

Then the Baron was knocking at my door. "*Yalla, yalla,* Stefanito. It's time for coffee!" I climbed out of bed and quickly threw on my clothes.

He was waiting in his room, still wearing a red and blue striped bathrobe, in front of the television, our two cups of coffee prepared.

"So you're leaving tonight, Grandfather?"

"That's right, Grandfather."

"Do you already have a taxi?"

"I'm leaving from the other side of town."

"Because I have an Armenian friend . . ."

"No, no, you shouldn't bother."

"Well, well, watch over yourself, do you hear me? You really shouldn't take such a long taxi ride with a stranger."

"Don't worry, Grandpa. I'll be fine."

"Did you double-check your ticket?"

"Yes."

"You're sure it's leaving tonight?"

"Yes."

"Because people can make mistakes."

"I checked three times."

He searched the table nervously until he secured his hands around a blue box of Gauloises cigarettes, then pulled one out, lit it, and inhaled deeply.

"Grandfather?" I asked him.

"*Nam . . .*"

"Why have you been so nice to me here?"

"It's nothing, *habibti.*"

"It's not nothing." The man had taught me a language, stuffed me with Arabic pastries, and fostered an addiction to caffeine and nicotine for an entire year. Had we lived in America, I would have encouraged him to list me as a dependent on his tax returns.

"Stefanito, in all of my years here, so many people have lived in that room. Boys and girls, old men, young men, you name it. I never had any business with them. Nothing more than *sabah al-kheir,* good morning, *sabah al-noor*, good night. But then you came to that room one morning, and I saw that you were different. You couldn't speak. You were alone. I looked at you, and I thought, *We're the same, you and me.*"

I felt tears rising in my eyes. "How will I know if something happens to you?"

"Nothing will happen to me."

We stared at the television for a long time, a Lebanese pop star singing a love song on silent.

"Grandfather?" he asked me.

"Yes."

"Did you see the padre at the monastery this weekend?"

"Yes, I saw him," I said quietly.

"Did you tell him that you love him?"

"No," I said.

"Did you take him in your arms?"

"No, of course not, Grandfather."

Then he turned and looked me in the face. "Listen, Stefanito," he pleaded with me. "Look at what my life has become. You turn on the news, and all you see is war, war, war. War in Iraq. War in Palestine. War in Somalia or whatever it is called. Who knows what will happen in Lebanon."

I tried to interrupt him, but he wouldn't let me. "I'm an old man, my life is over," he said. "I can't go back to what it was. But you're still young. You still have time to live."

"*Yalla, habibti*, Hurry up, my love," he told me. "Live."

26.

THE NEXT MORNING I left Damascus.

On my last night, I borrowed a friend's apartment across town, and Frédéric arrived late, released from the monastery for a single evening, wearing his normal pants and button-down shirt and an unfamiliar glassy look in his eyes. We slept in our clothes, on two mattresses, near each other, and he had never been so close to me.

All night, there was a wind coming through the window, breathing beneath the curtains, lifting them and setting them down again. My last memory, before drifting back to sleep, is of looking over at him and thinking, *This is what life could be like.*

I slept deeply, through the night, and in my dreams I saw that open window, with the wind coming in, as if the dream and the world were the same. I woke up early in the morning to the wind touching my face. Frédéric was sitting beside my bed, looking at me.

"Who are you?" he whispered. "Where did you come from?"

He lifted me up and held me in his arms. We were trembling, clinging to each other, like two people who had not been held in such a long time, in perhaps our entire lives.

I LEFT DAMASCUS on September 1, 2005, almost exactly one year after I arrived. Frédéric rode with me to the airport and sat beside me while I waited for my flight to appear in flashing letters on the large black screen above us. And then he let me go.

It is hard to know what to say about the days in which I traveled between two worlds. My last day in Damascus, nearly one thousand Iraqis were trampled to death on a bridge in Baghdad, frightened by the warning of a suicide bomber. It was the single highest death toll of any day in the war.

By the time I landed in America two days later, New Orleans had already begun its long descent under water, the floods consuming the galleries and cobblestone streets, the jazz bars and cafés, the homes with their cars parked out front, and the lives of nearly fifteen hundred people, in what would become another painful chapter in my country's turbulent entry into the twenty-first century.

Hassan once wrote that between two successive tragedies, there is always just enough space for "the appearance of a star and a lilac and a forest of mirrors, and words." Even as I watched those images on television, I tried to remember that we all live in two worlds: the world we physically inhabit, and the world we carry within us. Surely, if those I loved in Damascus had taught me anything, it was that the only way to break free of a story of one death after another is to liberate our own heart. It is the only country that is ever truly ours, after all.

That September, Frédéric journeyed to India, and I waited for his answer. I waited in a house in New England, where maple trees ripened to yellow and auburn, and the vast open sky changed from blue to rose in the evening. Every afternoon, I walked through the neighboring fields and gathered the leaves scattered into the pasture, pressing them between the pages of books, as if that would allow me to preserve each day entirely, as an offering to him.

In the evenings, I whispered to him in my room, hoping he might hear me.

Frédéric traveled to India with only a change of clothes, a small icon, my letters, and an empty book that he wrote in every day. He carried that book with him for two long months, on his journey through the crowded, monsoon-saturated streets of Bombay and on to New Delhi, scribbling on the thin, cream-colored pages his questions about his choice. He wrote in it as he looked at the countryside passing by the windows of the train as he traveled to Varanasi, where he watched dead bodies burned and then set adrift upon the waters of the Ganges. Then, after four long weeks in India, he carried that notebook on to Nepal, where it was pressed against his chest as he climbed five thousand meters into the Himalayas, the warmth of his skin shielding the pages from the snow.

In my room across the world, I folded and unfolded a last slip of paper he had given to me before I left.

Maybe God finally spoke, he wrote. *I met you.*

He had been hiking with a group for a week in the mountains when they were hit by an unseasonable snowstorm. It fell all morning in thick, heavy sheets, until no one could see farther than the space in front of them. They could only walk through the blinding whiteness, one step at a time. Several people died that day.

But Frédéric did not die. He kept walking, putting one foot in front of the other, until he finally arrived at the other side of the pass and made his way slowly, slowly back down to earth. Until I woke up one morning in Vermont, packed my bags, and boarded a plane to fly one last time to an airport in Damascus to meet him, following his exhausted voice on the telephone:

Stéphanie? It's Frédéric.
Come soon.

Acknowledgments

This book would not have been possible without the love and support of a great many people. First and foremost, I am indebted to all of my teachers in Syria, both personal and spiritual: Paolo Dall'Oglio, the Sheikha, the Baron, and Hassan. I will always be in awe of your kindness, wisdom, and bravery.

Julia Meltzer, David Thorne, and David Bender were wonderful friends who helped me maintain my sanity during an intense and often stressful year. Hillary Kalambach is the most generous scholar I have ever met. She shared all of her Syrian contacts with me, introduced me to the world of women and Islam, and often joined me for Quranic lessons. I owe much of what I learned about Islam to her.

I want to thank my family for their patience, compassion, and good humor throughout my year in Syria and the writing of this book: Thank you Dad, Toni, Lisa, Rob, and Steve, for always pulling me back to the earth. Thanks to the Cantu family for their inspiration, and to my mom, for allowing me to share her story with the world. Many thanks to Barbara Ganley and Larry Yarbrough for their constant support over many years. Thank you to Bernard Masson, who lent me the use of his house in the Alps for much of the planning of this book, and to Suleiman Mourad for his help in my research on Jesus in Islam. And I only wish that Russell Bennett, who was such a strong supporter of my writing and an inspiration to so many, could have lived to see this book in print.

Judy Heiblum is my agent, but most of all my friend. She gave me the courage to write this book, coached and supported me when it was just an idea, and saw it through every stage of writing. I can honestly say that this book would never have existed without her.

I was incredibly fortunate to have an exceptional editor, Kris Puopolo, who never lost faith in me and in the story I wanted to tell. Stephanie Bowen was invaluable both as a reader and in ushering the book through its final stages. Amy Ryan was copyeditor extraordinaire, who not only fixed all of my grammar but also taught me that stallions don't gallop in city streets and that most plants survive in the wild. And Jennifer Jackson did a wonderful job of cheering me on and helping this book find a new audience in paperback.

It was only because of a generous grant from the Fulbright foundation that I was able to travel to Syria in the first place. I must also thank the Syrian government, who, in the midst of very tense times between our two countries, still decided to grant visas to a group of young Americans. I could have written this book no other way.

Finally, I would like to thank every single person I met in Syria, all of those who welcomed me into their homes, their shops, and their lives. A special thanks to all of my students at the Quranic school for girls, to the entire community of Deir Mar Musa, and to my neighbors in Bab Touma.

Joseph, I hope that this book helps you to understand how your mom and dad fell in love. Thank you for being you, the fruit of that love.

This book is dedicated to Frédéric, forever my partner in loneliness. Thank you for saying yes.

The Bread of Angels